Dedicated

With love to my family and their forbears,
for whom this book was written

At the feet of the Master

Waiting the feet of the Master
Watching the hidden light;
Listening to catch His orders
In the very midst of the fight;

Seeing His slightest signal
Across the heads of the throng;
Hearing His slightest whisper
Above earth's loudest song.

Annie Besant 1910 The Theosophical Society

Acknowledgements

I should like to thank the following:

Bernard Hare of HIRE-A-GHOST EDITORIAL (UK) for his professional help

Ronald Hyde for his photographic expertise

My family in general for their constant encouragement and belief

My daughter Hazel in particular for editing and typing the first part

My late husband for his undying love through all my faults

The Smell On The Landing

by
Gladys Shaw

The Smell On The Landing

by
Gladys Shaw

The Smell On The Landing

by
Gladys Shaw

First published in 2004 by:

Gladys L Shaw
40A High Street
Kingsthorpe
Northhampton
NN2 6QE

ISBN 0-9547184-0-2

Edited by:
Hire-A-Ghost Editorial (UK)
PO Box 642 NORWICH NR3 1WL

Printed by Barnwell's Print Ltd.
Aylsham, Norfolk NR11 6ET
Tel: 01263 732767

The Smell On The Landing

CHAPTER ONE

Leonard James Cleminson returned from the First World War in 1919, aged 27. Serving with the Royal Engineers in France and Egypt, he was wounded like so many of his compatriots but counted himself lucky. He was to be reunited with the woman he loved, Ada Adeline Soar, who had waited with what patience she could manage throughout the long months of alternating hope and despair, never sure that the day she so wanted would come. Now that it was upon them, there was no time to waste. The banns went up in the Wesleyan Church in Stratford, east London, and a few days later they were wed.

It was soon clear that the years apart had changed their expectations. Adeline had assumed that her new husband on rejoining his family's building, plumbing, painting and decorating business would be quite well off. Instead he was re-employed at exactly the wages he earned before the war – seventeen shillings per week, or 85p in today's currency. Adeline's £4 weekly from the jewellery shop in the Strand where her exceptional abilities as a sales assistant were recognised must have seemed a fortune beside Len's pittance. She had even bought her own engagement and wedding rings from it. Yet by the conventions of the times he was supposed to be the sole breadwinner and she to give up her job. Trouble was brewing already!

The newly-weds rented two rooms at 83 Chobham Rd, almost opposite Len's father's business, for 3/6d a week. That left barely enough from Len's wages for food, let alone other household items. Adeline did her best to manage, but one day her patience snapped and she confronted her father-in-law. They couldn't possibly manage on what he was paying Len, she told him. If he wouldn't agree to pay more she would go back to work.

Len's father refused in no uncertain terms. She was a brazen hussy who had no business interfering. There would be no more money.

To call a woman a brazen hussy in those days was deeply insulting, but a few days later Adeline had something more serious to think about. She was pregnant.

The manner of my arrival on July 1st 1920 was not auspicious. Cross-breach births, even today, are fraught with danger, and the doctor summoned by my father had to work hard for his fee. In later years I often heard my mother laughingly relate how he braced his legs under the bed for the necessary leverage to deliver me. Exhausted at the end, he craved a cigarette and asked my father, who replied that he was a pipe-smoker so couldn't oblige. When he had gone, my mother was furious. Len could easily have walked the few yards to the shop to buy some cigarettes, she said. It was the least he could have done to show gratitude. They argued about it, and on looking back the incident seems to me to sum up the rejection I've felt all through my life. Father had wanted a boy. Was it a case of 'no boy, no cigarettes?' True or not, his disappointment coloured my life from the very beginning.

When I was about 15 months old we moved across the road to a house next door to the builder's yard. With grandfather retiring from the business he and his brothers had set up, my father was next in line of succession as the remaining heir after his brother Albert was killed in the First World War (the Great

The Smell On The Landing

War as it was known then) at only twenty-one. I didn't know until much later that taking over the business was the last thing my father wanted. Just to complicate things, mother was pregnant again, and now she was expected to help run the business, taking telephone messages, checking supplies at the yard, receipting customers' bills at the door. All this while looking after her young family and without offer of payment.

A few months after we had moved, I was taken at the age of two to stay with my mother's sister Aunt Dolly, who lived in nearby Forest Gate and was married to my father's cousin Stanley. Aunt Dolly had thoughtfully borrowed a doll's pram for me to push about. No doubt it came complete with doll, but what made it special was the sound it made when running over the paving-slabs – clickety-click, clickety-click, clickety-click…such a wonderful noise. What with that and the way I was fussed over I felt ten feet tall.

Aunt Dolly had the habit of going to bed every afternoon in the belief that the resting would prolong her life. When I went up with her she gave me a wrist-watch to play with. Listening to its tick and examining the strap was great fun until I fell asleep with it beneath me, and woke up to find it broken. Luckily Aunt Dolly took it well and I really enjoyed my several weeks there.

I arrived home to a big surprise. I now had a baby sister, Joyce, whom mother had placed asleep in a cot on the table out of my reach. Somehow I found myself alone with her. I really wanted to see her but she was too high up. I pulled up a chair to the table and climbed on to it. Still I couldn't see her properly. There was only one thing to do. I clambered on to the table. That was better. Now I could see her tiny, soft pink face with little hollows where the closed eyes were. I was fascinated. On the table was the pepper-pot. Picking it up I began shaking it to fill in the little hollows in her face.

At that moment my mother came in. Quickly she picked up the baby and turned her over to brush the pepper from her face. The next thing I knew was the awful sting of my mother's hand on my buttocks and her voice screaming *"You stupid girl. You could have blinded her!"*

At two years old I could not have been expected to realise the consequences of my action, and the memory of this event is still fresh eighty years on.

There were other instances when I was punished for what seemed to me inconsequential actions that hardly deserved it. On one occasion, at three, I decided that enough was enough. Defiantly I held the back door open and said to my mother, "we can manage quite well without you, so you can go." I pointed the way out. Her response was to give me a good spanking.

Alone, my juvenile logic suggested that if she would not go, it would have to be me. Thinking ahead I put on my coat and three hats, as I would need alternative clothing as I grew up. I then left the house by a route we never took, which led into Hackney Marshes, believing that nobody would think to look for me there. As it happened I was soon missed and my uncles at the builders yard organised a search-party. I was brought back by Uncle Stan, to further punishment. Mother would boast that I was so naughty she had to cane me at least once a day.

Her chastisements left tell-tale marks behind my knees that my school-teacher was so concerned about that she sent an inspector to speak to my mother. Because I dared not disclose that she caned me I may have tried to draw attention to myself in other ways – pretending I could play the piano and dance, kicking my legs about in an unco-ordinated fashion and generally showing off. I never did know what effect, if any, the inspector's visit made, but later my mother did send me to piano and singing lessons. Coincidence? To this day I cannot be sure.

Great Uncle Ted used to call most days to play crib with my mother. The cribbage board would lay across the table to the accompaniment of strange phrases like "fifteen-two, fifteen-four and one for his knob…" Of course, I was too young to understand, and used to hope that mother would be too busy with other things to entertain him. On such occasions this gentle, white-bearded man in his seventies would sit me on his knee and read to me aloud, his soft white beard brushing against my face as he did so. I feel now that he knew of my torment, and reading to me was one way of protecting me from my mother's frustrated rage. To this day I have a fondness for bearded men.

On the twenty-third of May 1924 my father's wish was granted at last with the birth of my brother Kenneth, in anticipation of which I had been sent away, this time to my grandfather's house in Wanstead. Nan, his second wife, was a gem who would peel grapes for me while I perched on a large carver chair, feeling quite important. I would have enjoyed my time there, but grandfather was a teaser and I soon asked to return home.

The arrival of a boy may have gladdened my father's heart, but for mother it was one more burden heaped on to an already dispirited and overworked woman. I well remember her holding up the baby in one hand and declaring pointedly to my father, "this is the last baby that will ever come into this house!"

At the time I was standing by the kitchen window overlooking the street. The window had a piece of lace across the lower panes for privacy. I decided to improve its appearance, so when nobody was looking I fetched a pair of scissors. The lace was ruched along the stretched wire that held it. Suppose I just nicked those little tucks…here, and here…now, wasn't that better? I stood back to admire my work, but mother's reaction was far from approving when, inevitably, she spotted it. "Stupid girl! How could you do such a malicious thing?" She had saved for ages to buy that precious piece of lace, and now it was ruined. My bottom was sore for days.

No matter what I did in those early years, nothing seemed to go right for me. Take the caterpillars. They fascinated me; some hairy, others bald and green – my favourite colour. They lived among the dahlias father grew in the back garden and were his sworn enemy. Every morning on his way to the office at the bottom of the yard he would stop to collect as many as he could and squash them on the concrete path. He must have missed quite a few, because I was able to fill my hands with them, so full that some of the poor things were squashed anyway. The survivors were put in a child's shoe-box and hidden in my room. Knowing that mother would throw them out if she found them, I took them to bed with me. Alas, the lid would come off and I would wake up to a horrible mess on the sheets. Secretly I took to keeping some downstairs but had not allowed for the fact that they could get themselves into unexpected places. Nobody was prepared one teatime for the horde of boiled caterpillars that issued from the spout of the kettle!

Then there were the spiders, living among the forest of tall weeds that sprouted among the cisterns, broken slates, ball-cocks and other debris piled high and strewn across the builder's yard. I scooped them up from their lovely, dewy webs and installed them in father's greenhouse, hoping they would thrive. Some did, but in decreasing numbers, until only one very fat one was left, having managed to eat or kill all his (or her) competitors. Snails were brought back from the occasional trip to Epping Forest. With their coloured spiral shells, and twice the size of those in our garden, I set two of

The Smell On The Landing

them on a leaf in the builder's yard. Some time later, the neighbours began to complain about the rash of huge snails that had invaded their gardens. Amid all the speculation as to where they had come from I never let on. How my prodigies had prospered!

The year in which I turned five stands out for several reasons, notably the first day at Water Lane School in the Infants class. We assembled in the hall for prayers, our class being the newest and placed at the very front. Behind us were the big girls, seven years old and familiar with how things were done. I watched them put their hands together and begin to recite the Lord's Prayer, though I couldn't make head or tail of what they were whispering. On returning home, mother asked me what had happened at school. "We shut our eyes, then put our hands together and said 'as it tizzy, as it tizzy.'" That was all I could remember, and my mother couldn't help laughing at my interpretation of …"as it is in Heaven." Even now, the occasion is referred to as "as it izzy" day.

Mixing with other children at school was a welcome break from mother's constant presence, though some of the habits and expressions I picked up were less than welcome to my parents. I was playing in the road one day when I saw my father coming towards me, wearing his first pair of spectacles rather self-consciously. I called out as he passed "look at old four-eyes," just as we called children at school who wore glasses. Father was very upset, which I found hard to understand.

A potentially more serious incident about this time was when I spotted Aunt Dolly on the other side of the road. There were so few cars in the neighbourhood that without thinking or looking I dashed across to greet her. A moment later I was startled to feel a bump and then, somehow, I was sitting on the running-board of a car as it braked to a stop. My mother, who had witnessed it all, maintained that she was more shaken up than I was.

As though she did not have enough to bear, mother suffered with gynaecological problems following the birth of Kenneth and could not cope with three children and her other duties. We were to be mostly looked after by a young girl called Ivy, whose left arm was missing from the elbow down. Despite the handicap, Ivy proved a wonderful help to us and our mother. There was hardly a job she could not do. I remember her sewing by laying the garment on the stump and holding it firm against her body, stitching away like anyone else as she ran up dresses for Joyce and me. She would take us for walks, especially in the recreation ground which had a children's play area and where I ran into a swing one day which knocked me cold, to wake up in the park-keepers's hut wondering how I had got there and why my head hurt so much.

Sunday was considered a rest day and I was expected to make tea for my parents and take it up to their bedroom – no small task to entrust to a five-year-old. When I forgot to put sugar in father's cup he would call me up to collect the cup, rectify my mistake and take it up again. One Sunday I was so upset when the tea spilt and burnt me that I threw cup and saucer down the stairs. Father's cup was a large, breakfast-sized one, so I was in trouble again for breaking it.

The fact that mother was always the one to punish me rankled. It seemed that from the outset they had an agreement. Dad would earn the money and mother would bring up and discipline the children. This was all very well for them, but to us he was a remote figure, unreachable like a demigod who seemed to inhabit a different world. He hardly ever stayed in of an evening. Much time was spent playing billiards in the church hall where he won many a contest, which meant that mother spent a lot of time alone. For such a gregarious and

The Smell On The Landing

active person this must have been quite awful. Year after year it went on, having no social life, knitting and crocheting for her own children and Queen Mary's Hospital in Stratford E15. for whom she made such things as long white stockings for post-operative patients and vests for premature babies in the maternity unit. Her efforts were rewarded by a life membership of the Hospital, which in pre-NHS Britain meant free medical treatment for the rest of her natural life. She was very proud of the Certificate, presented to her by a dignitary of Royal descent, that was framed and hung in the house until 1940.

A similar certificate hung alongside, awarded to my father for services to the Aid Committee of the same hospital, though he came to it by a different route. It seemed to me as I grew older that he had by far the best of things. While I'm sure he loved my mother dearly, he was either unaware of her frustration with her lot or was unwilling to change his habits. A man was the acknowledged master in his own household, and it took two World Wars to change a view now considered chauvinistic. No wonder my frequent punishments for small misdeeds often looked unduly harsh. Mother's unhappiness needed an outlet!

Looking after a house and family in the early twenties was sheer hard work, with few of the modern facilities we take for granted. The water supply to the house was via a cold tap in the scullery. Water had to be heated either by a kettle or saucepan stood on the iron coal-fired range in the kitchen, or at bath-times and washing-day once a week by filling a slate-lined, brick-built enclosure known as a "copper" and lighting the fire underneath. A zinc bath was placed in front of the kitchen range and heated water ladled from the copper into the bath until it was ready to use. When brother Kenneth was very little, he used to be washed on the wooden scrub-top kitchen table. He stood on a towel with a bowl of water beside him and scrubbing down would commence. He was very curious about his "chimney-pot", asking why the girls hadn't got one!

Away from the kitchen and warm hearths the house was very cold in winter. Standard floor-covering in the bedrooms was a square of linoleum, icy to the feet once you'd stepped off the bedside rug. Terraced house like ours had no bathrooms or internal lavatories. Basic functions were performed in a toilet integral with the rear of the house with an outside entrance, where you sat on a plain wooden seat with a lid. Spiders lurked here, and I had to force myself to use the place, so was often constipated.

In our front room, known as the parlour, was a brass gas-lamp that could be pulled up or down by counterweighted pulleys, according to whether you wanted maximum light for letter-writing, say, or general light for the room. The parlour was used only on special occasions, as when a huge coal fire would be lit in the grate, the room rearranged and our parents would hold family "dancing parties", for which the slippery lino floor was ideal. Joyce and I had the unwelcome job of washing endless sticks of celery under the cold tap, which when cleaned would be set on the table with a bowl of salt. On one visit Aunt Flossie, mistaking it for sugar, spooned a large helping into her tea, to general merriment. What a face she pulled! A treat for us children on these occasions was jelly, left overnight in a green meat safe with a zinc mesh door and sides for ventilation that lived in the cool greenhouse at the back. Meat safes were common then in an age without refrigeration.

Houses could be bought for as little as £250, which even at that low price very few could afford. A shilling and sixpence (1/6d) was a typical rent and 3/6d could secure an extra bedroom or a house in a better neighbourhood. Working conditions reflected the rather primitive standard of life. Men in manual jobs, especially in the building trades, started work at 6am in the summer, 7 in the winter and left off when it got dark. The bulk of building work came from various types of emergencies – leaking roofs, burst pipes in winter, windows falling out from neglect, blown-down chimneys and the like. Workers had to walk to the yard in the mornings to load the barrows with tools and materials and return to base at day's end or after completion of a job, pulling the two-wheeled tip-up cart. When not in use its handles rested on an iron stand to make it easy to raise the barrow to waist height for pulling, or pushing, to the next job. Along the sides and on the ladders it carried was emblazoned the name and address of the firm and its trading style.

Although times were hard and unemployment high in the aftermath of the First World War, there were compensations. People were much closer in their communities than today, and door-to-door deliveries by tradespeople was the norm. Milk arrived twice daily by horse and cart, at 6am and 11am from the nearby dairy. The horse that pulled the two-wheeled jig knew the route by heart and would stop without prompting at every call along the way. The jig was purpose-built, low at the back and with two central steps. You mounted the steps and ladled the milk into a jug or other container from a churn on either side at 1d per ladle. So you could buy as much or as little as you needed and knew that the milk was as fresh as could be.

Muffin men plied the streets too. They carried their wares on a square tray balanced on the head and rang a hand-bell to let you know they were in the street. The Rag and Bone man rode on a cart pulled by a tired-looking horse, and shouted, 'rag and bone, rag and bone.' If you took him something he would usually produce a goldfish by way of a thank-you. These traders could move about freely in streets that were often completely free from parked cars and the rubbish that litters our cities today. Yet modern Ministry of Health inspectors would have been appalled to see butchers outside their shops in their blue-and-white striped aprons, calling "come buy, come buy," beneath meat hanging on hooks all open to the air, and the white-coated fishmongers standing by open windows of their shops to display fish upon the slab.

A particular treat at this time was the Saturday meal of fish and chips. 1d bought a good-sized portion of chips. Add 3d and you'd get a large fillet of fried fish with it. When mother first sent us to the shop we were too small to see the top of the counter where the gherkins, salt and vinegar were kept, and quite often we were not noticed until another customer drew attention to us. Then the assistant would smilingly lean over and see that we had all we needed.

Other prices of the period look ridiculously low now; eggs five for a penny; whole leg of pork 2/11d; ladies rayon stockings 9d, or if you could run to fully-fashioned silk, 1/11d. It was all geared to what people could afford, and my mother must often have cursed the day she had to give up her £4 weekly wage to live on a quarter of that.

We lived opposite a public house which was at the corner of two streets and very lively from the buskers, mostly unemployed men desperate to earn a few pence, who entertained the customers of the Chobham Arms by the simple expedient of placing a foot inside the door in the hope that those inside would appreciate their efforts. Sometimes the trumpeter came, when our yard dog would howl throughout his repertoire. Then there were monkeys on barrel organs, violinists, mouth-organ players and Salvation Army girls who would shake their tins and exhort the drinkers to repent while collecting their money. This was a thankless job as drunks used to lay in the gutters, to return home penniless to their unhappy wives and families. Tuberculosis was rife, said to be spread by spitting, and when the pub doors were open we could see the spittoons on the sawdust-covered floor by the bar. Spitting was taken seriously by the authorities. The penalty for being caught at it on public transport was a fine of £5. Sanatoria were being built, especially on the coast, where it was believed in that pre-penicillin era that sunshine and good clean air would itself effect a cure.

The cars of the day were black and square, with running-boards along the sides. I had already survived an encounter with one, but as they were infrequent it was thought safe for us children to play in the road, within sight and earshot of our ever-vigilant mother. The delivery square in front of the pub opposite was our favourite spot. Here we could fully extend our skipping ropes, and the space was sufficient to play a game we called "Queenie." For ball games we usually played against the wall of our own house, since neighbours objected to the knock, knock of the ball on their walls, and who as an adult could blame them?

Horses were an integral part of the street scene. They were used in pairs for drawing heavy loads, and brewer's drays as they were known came with a team of four to deliver beer to the many pubs. These great horses were a beautiful sight in harness of gleaming brass, plaited hair along their necks, their fetlocks like white socks that flowed and rippled with each majestic step.

These dray horses were the aristocrats, decked out to show off the brewery and well looked after. Others were less fortunate, made to wait long hours for their owner's command and becoming frustrated with much pawing of the ground and not above taking a bite at a passer-by's shoulder. In winter they often slipped and fell on the wet cobblestones, when someone would have to sit on the horse's head until it calmed down. When ordered to stand by the owner, sparks would fly from the hooves as it struggled for grip. Sometimes the terrified horse would bolt, scattering onlookers in its quest for freedom.

Before going into the pub at dinnertime the tradesman would fix a nosebag of corn and bran on the horse's head so that its nose was in the bag, and the procedure was repeated in the evening. By then he would likely be the worse for drink, stagger on to the cart, release the reins and call "home, boy." Horses knew where to find water along the way, provided for them in long, concrete troughs at just the right height on the pavement and fed by fresh mains water. The trough incorporated below it a smaller one for cats and dogs to use. In some places, separate facilities invited people to drink too, from iron cups on heavy chain attached to an elaborate plinth decorated with gargoyles, etc.

Once a horse knew the round, he could make his way back, duly fed and watered, without the aid of his driver, who was often asleep by the time the horse halted at the depot to await the removal of his harness and stabling for the night.

Having a sister to play with was fun, except when we quarrelled over toys, especially the doll's pram we'd been given to share. Mother's solution to that was simple and dramatic – knock our heads together and throw the upholstered pram down the cellar steps! Toys generally were kept in a cupboard secured by a fastener known as a "dolly-peg," fixed at a height supposed to be beyond our reach. We soon learned that if we pushed against the door the fastener would drop level and then bingo!…we could play without asking mother's permission. Some old lace curtains kept inside gave us the idea of playing "brides", which required a wooden form to be placed alongside the kitchen table. Then we would parade for hours dressed in lace.

The kitchen was a warm and homely place. On the built-in wooden dresser that occupied most of one wall were kept such basic items as the crockery, a large flat fruit dish usually full of expensive Cox's Orange Pippins (the only apples I would eat) and a hook for holding a hand of bananas. On the wall above, just below the frieze that traditionally joined the top of the wallpaper to the ceiling edge, were rows of black *Robinson's Golliwogs*, taken from jars of jam, that extended right round the room. When you had collected enough of these stick-on figures you sent them to Robertson's and received an enamel brooch – something for nothing! Somehow we never got enough to claim our reward. They were needed to complete the frieze.

The adjoining scullery, by contrast, was a rather grim place of work which, like the outdoor lavatory, became flooded in heavy rain due to inadequate drainage in the yard. As the water could not run away it was difficult to mop dry. It only dried out when the copper fire was alight, when the mice had to leave their cosy warm home inside and we would hit them with sticks as they scurried away. Once I caught a mouse in my hand, and when it bit through my finger I drowned it in a bowl of water – something I regret now, as it had a lingering death.

Of course, father saw little of this as he was rarely in, but I do recall him at the sitting-room table fiddling with a mysterious device known as a crystal set, which involved getting a "whisker" (piece of wire) connected to a broadcast waveband. When successful he could listen to music through his headphones introduced by Christopher Stone the radio announcer. But it was a hit-and-miss affair, and it only needed the vibration from one of us children jumping about on the floor to move the whisker from the crystal and create crackling noises that drowned reception. Then began the laborious business of finding the waveband again and we would not be popular at all.

Our brother Kenneth caused a panic one day by disappearing. He would have been about three, and his bed was found empty. Anxiously we searched the house, top to bottom, growing more worried by the minute. Then we started again, and this time spotted him on the bedroom floor, between the bed and the wall, wrapped in a sheet. I can't describe the relief at finding him – my parents imagining the loss of their only son and Joyce and I wondering how we would manage without him.

He gave us another shock about a year later, holidaying at Westgate, when he wandered off alone by the water's edge and had no idea where he was. We learned later that he had asked someone to take him to the Police Station as mother had often told him to trust policemen as they were his friends. Dressed only in swimming trunks our four-year-old brother found himself swathed in a policeman's cape and plied with questions, though he could not give them the one thing they needed – his holiday address. When mother and father found him, they were laughingly told that they had no secrets left – Ken had "spilt the beans." The policemen thought he was wonderful. Kenneth also had a mysterious gift. While still small he would talk about the house as it was before he was born, almost as though he had been waiting for conception. It was weird. When he told mother, who had known the house before we moved in and knew the layout as it was then, she clearly remembered one room just as he had described it. Nobody could offer an explanation.

At the age of seven I was still getting into trouble for doing things that only I could justify. On the greenhouse floor stood a magnificent *Aloe* plant my father had brought home, which reminded him of the cactus gardens he'd visited in Egypt, where he'd served in the war, and often said he had felt at peace there among the tall plants with their exotic blooms. The plant had thrived under his care and recalled happy times. Unfortunately while playing near it I brushed against one of

The Smell On The Landing

the fleshy leaves. The long needles at the end punctured my skin painfully, so to avoid a recurrence I got a pair of scissors and carefully cut off all the "finger-nails" as I called them. If only I had known better! The plant gradually wilted, and nothing could save it from dying.

Not long after, I tripped while running and flattened my face against the wall, breaking my nose. It happened just at the spot where the *Aloe* used to stand. Retribution? Not really. My act of vandalism was etched into father's memory, and I was never allowed to forget it throughout his life. That hurt much more.

For a while, when money was very short, my parents decided to let two rooms to a Mr and Mrs Jones, who became great friends. In due course, baby Granville arrived and they had to find other accommodation. But they continued to visit, bringing the baby in his pram. On one such occasion Granville, by now sitting up and taking notice, had been left in the garden in his pram. I had been told not to touch the baby, so I decided to move the pram as the hood did not seem right to me. I thought the sun ought to be on his face. I lowered the hood, at which Granville let out a terrible scream. I had managed to trap his little fingers in the wire that held up the hood.

Out rushed his mother to console him. When she had calmed him down she took him for a walk in the pram with me alongside, being given a good lecture. She told me what a problem I was and how I made my mother cry. Oh, what joy these words gave me as I remembered how many times I had been made to cry by *her!* I burst out laughing, much to the disgust of Mrs Jones, who decided I was a hopeless case, and mother was right in the severe way she dealt with me.

Shortage of money didn't mean that we were dressed in rags, though I had on occasions seen the tattered underwear my mother was at times reduced to. At least she always saw to it that if anyone had to go short it wouldn't be any of her children. She couldn't bear to be inactive, and in the long evenings she had to spend alone we benefitted from the crocheted dresses she made from pure silk thread. The bodices were quite plain, but the skirts in a shell pattern hung beautifully, swinging from side to side as we walked. We soon stopped wearing them at school, though, where nobody else had such dresses and were very jealous and cruel.

Another source of unusual clothes was a friend of my mother's in the East End, who used to call about twice a year with a selection of secondhand garments. The clothes were more gaily coloured than was common at the time, and were thought to have come from ballet students a little older than we were, and Joyce and I felt very grand wearing them. We always had new shoes, over which fleece-lined leather gaiters were worn in the winter. These came up over the knees and buttoned down the outside of the leg with a buttonhook. We had to wear liberty bodices over our vests and fleecy black or navy knickers, washed once a week. Sometimes "spencers" were worn – woollen garments like a fitted jumper, which could have long or short sleeves. Made from very fine yarn, they went under 'normal' clothes for warmth. We also had long black woollen stockings held up with black elastic garters half an inch wide. Yet all these measures were in vain for me. I suffered so much from the cold that in severe weather I had to strip off gaiters, shoes and stockings to have my legs and feet massaged with oil that was kept warm on the top of the kitchen range for my return from school. I suffered from chilblains too, which would sometimes crack open and bleed. Brother Kenneth also needed the warm oil treatment for chilblains, which affected the outer edges of his ears. When very cold and dry the skin would erupt with a little 'ping' and fly off, which greatly amused Joyce and me but must have been quite painful for him. Boys caps left their ears cruelly exposed in winter. I feel sure that winters then were much colder than is common today, when most people seem to accept that we live in an age of 'global warming'.

Added to my other difficulties was the fact that I was a poor traveller, even on the trams. The main road that joined ours had four tram lines running along the camber of the road, two in each direction. These clanking trams had a long pole on the roof to connect to the overhead power cables. When the pole became dislodged, which was quite frequent, everything stopped until it could be repositioned. For the minimum fare of a halfpenny you could ride quite a distance, but for me the motion of the moving tram set up a kind of sea-sickness and I would vomit all over the slatted wooden seats. The floor was also slatted, so my mess was very hard to clear up. I had the same problem on the Underground. When we attended the dental hospital in Leicester Square, it was a matter of riding one station, getting off and walking to the next. The treatment at the hospital was free, as the students were allowed to practise on us, and it was sometimes painful as they had to work with slow, foot-operated drills – very different from the high-speed modern ones where you rarely feel a thing. Altogether I must have been a very disturbed child. I began sleep-walking, making my way downstairs at dead of night – to knit! Mother soon devised a way of stopping it – or so she thought. When I was safely abed she would tie the door with string to leave it slightly ajar, but even in my sleep I was able to undo the knots and continue downstairs. Perhaps this activity was brought on by my mental anguish. Not being as clever academically as my siblings, and being told so, was hard to bear, and my aspirations of entering the veterinary profession were scorned. I was fit only to be a shop assistant.

When the weather allowed we played outdoors – hopscotch, hide-and-seek, bowling a hoop, cricket with a chalked wicket on the wall, football with two jumpers or coats as goalposts. The street was our playground – unthinkable today. 'Piggyback' or 'donkey'required the first child to face the wall supported by their hands. The next would line up behind, and so on. Those left would run and try to ease themselves along to the first donkey before we all fell off laughing.

One day father decided we would have a holiday. We found him poring over brochures until he came across a boarding house in Canterbury Road, Westgate, Kent. The family's name was Cleminson, the same as ours, and there was much speculation as to whether we could be related (as it turned out we were not) but we booked up with them. They made us so welcome it was almost a home from home. The problem for me was the four-hour journey from London on the pleasure steamer *The Golden Eagle*. At first I was happy watching the dolphins swimming in front of the boat, then my stomach would start churning and I'd have to lie down in the centre of the boat. If I could sleep, all would be well, but if as often happened our travelling companions were noisy I couldn't, and it would take the rest of the week's holiday to recover. We went back year after year as it was the cheapest way for us all to travel, and I had to make the best of my condition.

On Bank Holidays the family would take the train from Leytonstone or Stratford station to Chalkwell or maybe Southend, for which the adult return fare was a reasonable 1/11d. A very different trip was to Kew Gardens, by river-boat along the Thames. Often the weather would be hot and humid enough for a thunderstorm, which one occasion was welcome. The river level was so low that the boat grounded just outside the quay at Kew, and it took the downpour of rain and possibly some help from the tide to refloat it. It was a huge adventure for us children.

As we grew older the pressure eased on our parents, who began going out together to play cards or badminton at Len's sister's house at Wanstead. My interest in the world about me was stimulated by the cigarette cards collected by my uncles. One set illustrated creatures living at the bottom of the sea in perpetual darkness, and one in particular that had a light source at the end of a stalk. How I wished I had something like that when I forgot my torch at night.

Another set of cards that intrigued me showed the beauty of the heavens, and this was something I could see for myself outside. The gas-lamps were well-spaced out, each casting a ring of light that left extensive dark areas between the lamp-posts. It was wonderful to look up and marvel at how brightly the stars shone, watch the halo round the moon, and think that its movement round the earth actually moved the tides along our shores.

One night, sister Joyce and I were confronted with a "flasher" under the light of a gas-lamp. After exposing himself he ran away down a poorly-lit street. As we were very close to home I got Joyce to run and get father, but in the few minutes it took him to arrive, the man had disappeared. Father decided to report it to the policeman in the box at the top of the road. Asked to describe the experience, I was confused. How does an eight-year-old girl put this into words that grown-ups would understand? All I knew about what I had seen was that it was called a 'chimney-pot', because my brother had always referred to his penis as such and nobody had corrected him.

Having told what I could to the police, the incident was never mentioned again at home, but I continued to puzzle. Why was it so hairy and such a funny shape, like nothing else? Counselling was not available in those days, but I've often wondered about its possible effects on me in later life. Certainly I began to fear walking out at night. The tall uncut hedges in front gardens seemed to hold untold dangers, and I would walk on the edge of the kerb and hurry home with my music case when returning from lessons in the dark.

Summing up my feelings of those early years from an adult perspective, I can begin to see why I was so unhappy. While my mother looked after our physical needs as best she could on a very limited income, she failed to understand the psychology of bringing up children. She herself was raised in the strict Victorian manner, with its severe disciplines, and practised it on us. She was not at all tactile. Cuddling us was out of the question, and I never remember having praise or encouragement from either parent. It is now known how important these are in the development of a well-balanced child, and it was hardly surprising that some of my problems were carried over into later life. Mother had named her daughters Gladys (after Gladys Cooper the actress) and Joyce; Glad and Joy for short. I'm afraid I didn't bring her much gladness at that period of my life…

Adeline in 1918

Adeline in Torquay 1929

Grandfather James Cleminson.

Leonard in Torquay 1929

*Leonard and Adeline's Wedding
1919*

Adeline with Gladys, Joyce, Ken

*Ken, with Gladys and Joyce in
crocheted dresses, 1927*

Gladys and Joyce

Gladys, Joyce, Ken

Ken aged 4

Ken, older

Kenneth - Doctorate and Wedding

Ken with wife Elaine (Elsie) before emigrating 1957

Ken's last day in Surgery (Australia) before retirement

Joyce with children Christine, Duncan and Quentin

CHAPTER TWO

From about the age of seven my sister Joyce suffered from 'noisy bones'. While we laughed at the clunking and clicking she made as she moved about, it was no laughing matter for her. The condition developed into arthritis as she grew older, necessitating operations on thumbs and knee joints. Of a heavier build than myself, she was not as lissom or accomplished at field sports, but she took up cycling and later toured Ireland with a cycling club. She also became a very good swimmer, without the tendency to pass out without warning that dogged me, and was much stronger in the water. So when we swam together, mother insisted that she 'kept an eye' on me.

Being so agile, I enjoyed standing on my hands and would head down the street with my feet in the air – quite a sight for any onlookers! I could walk upside down for ages before dropping my feet backwards, tummy facing up, to make what we called a 'crabwalk'. I could even fold my body backwards until my feet were tucked under my chin! This suppleness was almost fatal for me one day at the swimming- baths. When I dived from the springboard, the spring of the board was so powerful it folded my body so that I hit the water belly-first. When I came to, I was receiving first aid on the side of the baths, having been saved from drowning by the attendant. Earlier on a seaside holiday I had got out of my depth in a hole not far from the shoreline and was brought out by a boatman's hook in the shoulder-strap of my bathing costume, feeling very much the worse for wear. Perhaps I was accident-prone.

It was another seaside holiday that exposed my limitations in the water. We three had ventured out on to a sandbank some distance from the shore. Suddenly we saw the tide racing in behind us, and mother, watching from the beach, waving her arms frantically to warn us. But the water had become too deep to allow us to retrace our steps. We were completely cut off. Looking back on it, I can only wonder how we could have got ourselves into that situation. I was an acknowledged weak swimmer and Ken had not even learned. Everything depended on Joyce. There was only one decision to make, so with deep breaths we set off to swim for the shore. While Joyce managed to keep Ken's head above water, I held on to her costume using what strength I had to propel us. Slowly we made progress and finally reached the beach, no little shaken by the experience and forever indebted to Joyce, who has continued to mother me ever since. Thank you, dear sister, for all your support over the years.

Although today's Stratford, with its tower blocks and grid-locked traffic, is a far cry from the place I knew as a child, it is still a major rail junction. The railway yard at Angel Lane, a few streets away from where we lived at Chobham Rd, employed hundreds of men. They worked hard for little money – upholsterers, wheelwrights, wheel- tappers, locomotive engineers; all the trades associated with the railway industry. From miles away they converged on the depot, on foot and bicycle, sometimes encountering as did we children herds of cattle or sheep being driven to the nearby abattoir. The poor animals, unwatered and hungry from the journey in the cattle trucks, were herded along our road. I sensed they knew their fate as the bullocks would charge at you if you stood between them and their escape into any garden where a gate had been carelessly left open. It was frightening. When they had passed, the road was slippery and dirty and stank with the smell of their dung.

We were always walking, and not only because I was such a bad traveller. Most Sundays Joyce and I would visit relatives in nearby Forest Gate or go to a park that had a stream. I once fell into it in a vain attempt to jump across, though luckily the hot sun dried my clothes before we got home. A regular trip was to the one wet fish-shop open on Sundays, for father's tea. The winkles we had come for were simply dumped in a brown paper bag that rapidly disintegrated in a soggy mess. For some reason nobody had thought to provide us with a container before we set off, so that very soon on the return journey through the streets and alleyways we had to knock on someone's door to beg a fresh bag! We should have done better on our visits to Wanstead to see our step-Nan, who was thoughtful enough to put money on the table 'for the children'. This was to save us the walk home and pay our fare, which she knew we could not afford. Mother soon cottoned on to this perk and demanded it on our return, claiming that her purse was empty. It was no good complaining, so we continued to walk back.

As we grew older, the weekly bathtime ritual moved upstairs to the bathroom, where a gas 'geyser' had been installed. This was a dangerous thing to light, as it tended to blow back unless the window was opened, and it was not uncommon to hear of geysers exploding, or the inhaled fumes making families ill. So despite the bitter winter wind blowing in while the bath was filling with hot water, we had to endure it. Father would go first, every Sunday morning, as he liked the water really hot, followed by mother, and we were supposed to share the same water. Joyce and I preferred to take our bath alone whenever possible.

Beneath the bathroom window ran the long glass roof of the greenhouse, a nightly meeting place for the neighbourhood's 20-odd cats. If we didn't keep the bathroom door closed, the cats would get in through the open window, slink into our room and snuggle down into bed with us. Many a time we would wake up to find a cat clawing and purring with pleasure. Sometimes a cat became the subject of nightmares, when the animal would take on a lion-like stature, sitting astride my chest and roaring into my face. Perhaps it was after one such experience that I began sleep-walking – trying to escape what appeared to be a frightening reality.

It was hardly surprising that getting up on a winter's morning for school required a huge effort of will. When that failed, father had a solution. He would take me from my lovely warm bed and lay me full stretch on the icy linoleum. What a start to the day! Thinking back, it may be that he disliked getting up as much as we did. On a really cold morning the first thing he had to do was break the ice on the glass of water in which he had immersed his teeth overnight on the washstand in the bedroom. I can see those dentures now – an unnaturally red vulcanite in which the inset sheer white teeth looked strangely out of place.

Although coal at the time was only £2 per ton – enough to last a family several weeks if they were careful – the only fire kept in overnight was in the kitchen range. Father managed to keep it in on wintry nights by heaping the live coals with slack – mostly dust – from the coal-cellar and shutting down the ventilation. In the morning a good rake to clear the ash would soon get a blaze going. Chimney-breasts were known to retain warmth, and it became the custom to set bedroom wardrobes in the recess alongside to help keep clothes aired – no small task in the days before central heating revolutionised living conditions.

In the evenings those of the family staying in would huddle around whichever fires were lit. The man of the house took pride of place with his chair while we vied for the next warmest position. We lost out badly when uncles descended on us. They would stand with their feet apart, backs to the grate, "warming the hole of their body," as we used to snigger while they absorbed all the warmth.

When I was about eleven-and-a-half, round about the time Joyce and I joined the local Girl's Life Brigade at the Wesleyan Methodist Church in Stratford, an incident at school brought my general health problems to the point where they could no longer be ignored. Because I excelled at the high jump, the Life Brigade instructor and my Sports teacher were always urging me to go 'just another notch' on the high-jump pole. This was before the Fosberry Flop technique was developed, and I jumped scissors-style. Perhaps I damaged my heart by too much exertion, which left me very tired. At any rate my condition was thought serious enough to merit a visit to the Great Ormond Street Hospital For Sick Children. A thorough examination revealed that I had a heart defect that would require me to rest more. I also had rising bile into the stomach, aggravating my queasiness and travel sickness, but it was the discovery of the heart malfunction that made the biggest impact on my life. From then onwards I was granted absence from school in the afternoons so as to rest for two hours after lunch, which made it less likely that I would faint.

For a child as active as I was, the news came hard. However, there was a positive side that I soon discovered. The BBC Schools programmes on radio were interesting and informative, and I became a regular listener. It was like being taught on a one-to-one basis by a private tutor, without any of the interruptions of the classroom. The knowledge I acquired went a long way towards recompensing me for being deprived of a large part of school life.

Somewhere around this time, when our parents were out and we three children had put ourselves to bed, we had an unwelcome visitor. Through the landing window shone the light from a large electric lamp that hung outside the public house across the road. It shone directly on the wardrobe door in our bedroom, and suddenly there was the shadow of a man on that door! Someone was in the house. I was frozen with fright. Then whoever it was must have realised his image could be seen, and disappeared into my parent's bedroom. I lay listening to my own thumping heart-beats, but heard no further sound of the intruder. I managed to drop off to sleep, and in the morning the burglary was discovered and the police called. I was never able to tell my parents what I had seen, I'd been so frightened. It remains one of the worst moments in my life.

Unhappily we were to be burgled three times more – once in the house and twice in the builder's yard. One night when were left alone again our dog would not stop barking. Wondering what best to do, we finally shone the beam from a powerful torch into the area from a back bedroom window. To our horror we could tell he'd been seriously injured. Close inspection showed that the poor thing had been slashed with a razor from the top of his back to under his belly. Luckily the vet was able to stitch him up, and being nursed back to full health inside the house, he was then returned to the yard and a kennel stuffed with fresh straw.

We were all jittery after this. Once mother tried to open the bathroom door and found it pushed back towards her. She tried again with a good heave, and once more the door was pushed back. Alarmed now, she fetched the dog and took him upstairs to help catch the burglar she had trapped in the bathroom. Renewed efforts finally forced the door open, and our burglar was revealed as a strip of old lino that had been stood upright against the wall. Softened by steam from the hot water, it had simply fallen down, giving us a real fright.

Joining the Girl's Life Brigade opened the way to other activities. On Friday evenings we were taught useful skills – first aid, cane-work, Greek dancing, drills and sports rallies. It was here that I won a medal for the high jump which I wore proudly on my uniform. I also met Rose, a girl of my own age, who became my inseparable friend, much to the annoyance of my mother. She perceived Rose, from the slums of Stratford, to be of 'lower class' than us, but it made little difference to our friendship.We did everything together, even signing the Temperance Pledge and keeping to it. On the first Sunday of each month we had Church Parade, a formal occasion that saw us marching through the local streets to music from the band of the Boy's Brigade. We wore a sailor-type uniform of navy blue serge with a wide collar spread over the back and shoulders and edged with red braid. The Girl's Life Brigade logo was displayed on a white bib, put on before the blue serge, but almost every time church parade came round Joyce and I could not find our white bibs, and we would have to get one of father's white handkerchieves and pin it to our vest. This was against the rules, and the officers would want to know where the logo was. Mostly it languished in the laundry basket as mother had not washed it, so we had to put up with these ritual tellings-off on parade.

For the all-important rally at the Royal Albert Hall we were required to make flimsy dresses and shoes to match, then perform a balloon dance that had been diligently practised for the big day, followed by a drill display in competition with other companies.

I really enjoyed our Fiday evenings in the church hall, especially the First Aid classes, which brother Ken had cause to thank us for when he almost severed his thumb while splicing a piece of wood. Joyce and I were with him at the time, and using the knowledge we'd acquired were able to make a tourniqet for the thumb while help was summoned. The Life Brigade training was to prove most valuable a few years later, when I served with the ATS in the Second World War.

Life at home was as hard as ever. In 1929 the newspapers had been full of the Wall Street Crash, in which the New York Stock Market collapsed. There were pictures of financiers facing ruin throwing themselves from skyscraper windows; American loans to Europe ceased; British banks closed, and when they reopened, people found their accounts depreciated. Business confidence slumped to an all-time low, many customers drawing cash whenever they could to stuff into chairs and mattresses. The effects of the Crash and the Great Depression that followed may be seen today in the habit of elderly people who refuse to trust their money to any institution and keep it hidden in their homes. Alas, today their 'safe' hiding places are all too often violated.

With unemployment rising, my father could only cope with the loss of trade by laying off workers. It was as much as he could do to keep the firm going during the worst years with the help of uncles Will, Stan and Tom, who despite the poor turnover gave us half-a-crown each at Xmas. Uncle Will, much better off than us with a flourishing catering business, sometimes gave us rides in his Rolls-Royce car. But any pleasure for me was quickly replaced by nausea, as the smell of petrol fumes turned my stomach, calling for a rapid stop and exit.

The builder's yard, at the bottom of our garden, seems to have played a big part in our lives, so perhaps it's time for some reminiscences of it. Among all the debris described earlier was the lime-pit, used when making mortar. Sometimes the workmen would forget to cover it, and a thin crust would form on top. When one of the neighbourhood cats walked across, the skin would crack like thin ice and the cat was in trouble. When mother and any of us children, alerted to its plight, rescued it and tried to wash the lime off under the cold tap, the fun would begin. The cat did not want to be washed, and struggled and scratched like a mad thing until it was released.

Then there were the day-old chicks that father bought to rear, housed in a wire rabbit cage. I can remember their little legs running along the ground as the cage was re-located to the yard where they would grow into laying hens and eventually become our dinner. Father told us once that he'd seen a chicken run about 100 yards after having its head chopped off, stopping only when it crashed into the yard gates. It was believed that the flesh would only mature properly if hung upside down in the cellar for three weeks, as game would have been, before being plucked, drawn and cooked. The yard dog did well from us. Each day after dinner the scraps from our meal would be piled on a plate, together with any left-over custard from the 'afters' and taken up the garden path to be pushed under the gate. When all was gone, the dog would nose the plate back under the gate as if to say "thank you." I can still hear the grating sound of that plate passing under the gate.

In the yard immediately to the right was situated the office. This held a sloping eight-foot desk, fixed to the wall at both ends. It was placed beneath a window of the same length, so that the window-sill could be used as a shelf holding ink-well, rulers, files and other documents. All bills were written by hand on headed paper, then entered into a ledger with a nibbed pen and ink. The speed at which letters were carried across the country makes today's deliveries look snail-like. The Royal Mail was delivered three times daily in our part of London. My father might receive a letter posted that morning from Brighton, say, answer it straight away, and his reply could reach the correspondent that same evening – all for the price of a 2d stamp! This same denomination stamp also had to be affixed to a receipt for any value exceeding £2, with a signature across the stamp to authenticate it.

In winter father would often take red-hot coals on a shovel from the house-fire to the office grate to get his own fire off to a flying start. No-one ever bothered to clean the place up. They raked the dead ash away from the fire-basket, and the ash would fly around the office to leave a gritty deposit on everything. The workshop and carpenter's room was equally neglected, with a cellar beneath that I explored to find a workbench that had not been used for some time, many rusty tools and a floor covered with about two inches of soft grey ash, the accumulation of several years of neglect. Among the clutter was a pair of dumb-bells that I managed to lift above my head but could not support. As I let my hands drop I trapped my fingers between them – a bruising lesson to remember!

We children were well drilled to respond to emergency calls. Sometimes the customer would report a water leak – always a matter of urgency. We'd advise them how to find the stop-cock and turn off the water, then take their particulars and pass them on to father, who would get a plumber to call.

Due to my mother's ideas on schooling, we did not attend the school nearest our house. This meant that we rarely played with our classmates, who lived too far away, and the local children viewed us with suspicion as we didn't attend their school. We felt like outcasts, and poor Joyce had to cope additionally with my school reputation as a rebel, though in fact she was much quieter and better behaved. She was not so good at sports but rather studious and keen to learn, but was automatically "tarred with the same brush" in the eyes of the teachers until they got to know her.

I had developed a flair for needlework, and was soon pressed into service by the teachers to make petticoats and cami-knickers for their personal use. I enjoyed producing such hand-stitched items, but Joyce, who had excellent command of a sewing-machine, could only manage 'elephant stitches.' For some strange reason mother had stipulated that Joyce was not to have sewing lessons. Instead, she would knit father's socks! These were produced on four needles, surprising the teacher with her facility to 'turn the heel,' a skilled operation that she achieved without supervision. Joyce went on to pass her 'eleven plus', but as she was told there was no money even for the uniform, she missed out on High School and attended evening classes instead to learn shorthand and typing. By that time I was already in work.

In 1934, at fourteen, I was cycling to Epping town. On reaching Woodford Green I encountered traffic lights for the first time. I couldn't remember anyone telling me about such things, as road safety training was in its infancy, so when I saw the red light facing me I thought nothing of it and carried on across the junction. Imagine my surprise when a man shouted at me "do you want to get yourself killed?"

After that I was much more careful. Just as well it wasn't foggy. In autumn and winter we suffered from a succession of "pea-soupers," when the fog was so dense it was difficult to move around even on foot, and traffic came to a standstill. These fogs were yellow in the dim street lights and tasted horrible, as they were the result of smoke from houses and factory chimneys being unable to escape into the atmosphere. The only way to get home from school or wherever you were was to feel your way along hedges and walls in the hope of recognising some familiar feature. Sometimes you might bump into somebody who could tell you where you were. But this didn't always happen, and on one particularly foggy day I walked into a stationary horse and found my face flat against its stomach!

Brother Ken was growing up rapidly and discovering an interest in the physical world. The present of a chemistry set encouraged him to stage a 'proper experiment,' as he termed it. The focus of his attention became the chicken coop, empty since father's chickens had developed the red mite disease in their feathers. When Ken decided to blow it up the explosion was bigger than he'd expected and he was lucky to escape injury. Following that his interest turned to wireless and he besieged the library for books on the subject. Night after night he studied until he had assembled a working wireless receiver in his bedroom, along with all the wires and apparatus that entailed. Sometimes mother would creep in, and finding him asleep would gently remove the headphones and switch off the power. He was about twelve then.

At fourteen came the first big change in my life. My school record was nothing to boast about, and now I had to leave and find work. But what? Nobody had given me any advice on how to go about this, or what my particular abilities – whatever they were – might be suited to. Mother was typically unsympathetic. "You've got a good tongue in your head, Gladys. Use it." I construed this terse instruction to mean that I should begin by finding out about possible vacancies. Accordingly I set off on the day with the *Daily Telegraph* in my hand, my return train fare to Liverpool Street and mother's parting words ringing in my ears – "Don't come home without a job!" It happened that Waterlow's, the printers, had a vacancy. I arrived at the building to see a commissionaire on duty outside. He looked a forbidding figure in his immaculate uniform, peaked hat and white gloves. My courage failed me.

I simply could not cross the street to ask him about the vacancy. Eventually, two hours later, I managed it. "I've been watching you," he said in a deep, official voice. "You're too late. The job went long ago."

That was a hard lesson learnt, but the next day I set off telling myself "go for it, even if you're scared," which I certainly was. I had much to learn, and made a few false starts. There was the Jewish lady who ran a coat and dress shop. She wanted me to approach anybody I saw lingering at her window display and entice them into the shop, which I learned later was called 'touting.' I found it very embarrassing and didn't go back the next day.

Nearby was a shop selling eel pies. It was customary to choose one or more live eels, which the vendor would then slice up, beginning with the tail. They squirmed until the very last second, and my stomach squirmed with them! Seeing them killed in such a cruel way put me off eels for life.

Eventually I found work as a warehouse assistant with a firm named Sandle Brothers in Paternoster Row, nominally filling shelves. Here I was taught how to carry boxes of games so that the lids didn't get damaged, and to price items with a special code. The first time I answered the telephone I shouted into the mouthpiece to make my voice travel to another department, which the staff standing nearby thought hilarious. Of the 7/6d weekly that I earned, mother took 3/- and what was left went on fares. Financially there was no point in going out to work at all.

Next was a factory workshop, where we wound elastic on to cards for retail sale. Picking up the empty card, the elastic would be turned so many times, then cut and tucked – a yard of elastic on each. Perhaps to dispel the boredom of such a repetitive job, the senior staff got amusement from sending newcomers on silly errands. I was once asked to go to the basement for some sky-hooks. They might have been real items for all I knew, and I only lasted there a few days. I'd become bored, my quota was down and I was sacked anyway. It was an ugly world at the tender age of 14.

Much more interesting was work in a warehouse supplying fancy goods, which I had to lift and carry to the shelves for the retail trade. The goods were sold in dozens and prices not marked. We had to learn the codes for each item and the corresponding price, which customers would be told only if they asked. I dreamed of owning some of the lovely things I saw here and could certainly not afford, so I decided to pretend that some of them belonged to me. Accordingly I choose a powder compact and a lovely handbag. I put the compact into the bag and hid it behind a stack of goods so as to enjoy handling them when I got a spare moment.

When I went back to my secret cache a few days later, my probing hand fell on something painfully sharp. When I withdrew it, blood was streaming from my fingers, which needed first aid treatment. Unbeknown to me, my secret had been discovered, and pieces of broken glass put there to catch the culprit. Nobody believed my story, and I was given the sack like a common thief. The worst part was yet to come – explaining to my parents how I'd lost a perfectly good job by my foolishness. And my hand still bears the scars.

So it was back to the *Daily Telegraph* and job-hunting. Then something happened that I have never been able to explain satisfactorily. Walking alone one Sunday afternoon, I found myself in Keogh Rd, Stratford, where my grandparents had lived. When I was passing the actual house, I became aware of a strange sensation, as though I was being pushed gently along the street. In this manner I was gradually guided to a nearby Spiritualist Church, where I found a service about to begin. I'd no idea what I was supposed to do. People were disappearing into a room, one by one, and then came my turn. Oh dear! A kindly lady invited me to sit down and asked what I had got for her to hold. I knew nothing about psychometry at that time. She indicated that I should find something in my handbag, so I rummaged through and gave her a powder compact, something cheap and cheerful that was a present from my brother Ken. She took it and concentrated a while before assuming a serious expression. She patted my arm reassuringly. "You must go home and tell your mother that your brother is going to be very ill. He will be taken into hospital, and things will look bleak for a while, but he will recover, and the stay in hospital will influence his whole life."

I was amazed, worried and curious all at the same time. She couldn't tell me exactly when it would happen, but apparently it was all there for her to see, and it could be quite soon.

Of course, I was quizzed when I got home to remember exactly what the medium had said. How could she possibly have seen, for example, that Ken would become a "very important person?" Those were her very words. Amazingly, not long after that, Ken developed acute peritonitis with complications and was taken to Queen Mary's Hospital. Had he not responded to treatment his life expectancy was no more than two hours, they told us. While in hospital recovering he decided to study for a medical career, and in later life became a famous orthopaedic surgeon. It was hardly surprising that spiritualism was to play a major part in my life from then on. I found that I could raise my level of consciousness by meditation, and even 'travel' on the astral plane. Wonderful as the experience was, I dared not tell anyone for fear of ridicule. I tried to keep silent, but at times words came from me unbidden, without my conscious thought, and were usually predictions for friends who were worried and needed advice. This led in later years to my becoming a medium, but for the present, here I was, full of impossible thoughts and ideas, but no work. It was back to the *Daily Telegraph* and job vacancies.

The Lancashire and Cheshire Rubber Company gave me a junior's job cleaning the floor of the shop using a mop and galvanised pail – work that gave me callouses on my hands. I also had to cook the Manager's dinner in the cellar, which was infested with rats. It was my job to keep their droppings swept up, and I remember cornering one of these rats, which flew at my thoat to escape my beatings. Luck was with me as it didn't bite. The firm also used me to run errands, sometimes as far as the West End to pick up something that a customer wanted urgently. Regularly I would have to fetch the Manager's tobacco from a kiosk tucked away in a nearby alley. There being no toilet in the tiny place, there were times when I caught the proprietor sitting on a bucket with his trousers round his ankles, and had an unpleasant wait for him to finish and serve me.

While travelling to and from work by train I caught head lice, probably from the moquette head-rest. It took mother ages to comb them out, killing each one between her thumbnails as they became dislodged. She killed so many that her thumbnails split. At work I had to confess the embarrassing condition to the shop manager. I was kept away from the other staff and then sent to the Cheapside branch. This was an upgrade for me, as I was allowed to serve customers except for those who specifically asked for the manager – some because they wanted little packets for the weekend. Beside those intimate items for male use the shop stocked almost everything you could think of in rubber – ends for walking-sticks, hot water bottles, raincoats, Wellington boots etc. Another line stocked was lady's bathing-costumes, which had the unfortunate habit of splitting when being used. I sometimes wonder whether there was difficulty importing raw materials, for suddenly the shops were closed down. Nobody knew why. The move had gone well for me, I enjoyed being allowed to dress the windows, and although I still had the cleaning chores to do, the manager was very human and understanding – not a bit stiff-necked like others I'd known. The closure was very disappointing, and my search for work began again.

Luck was with me this time. I quickly found a job in Regent Street, working in the stockroom of Jays Limited, a very up-market store classed as haute couture and with a clientele to match. Our customers were mostly debutantes and their parents, there were mannequin parades to show the latest fashions, and an 'on appro' service to Her Majesty and her Ladies-in-Waiting. The machinist would then take notes about any necessary alterations for 'madam'. All clothes were made to measure. The Pages - young lads in red-braided uniform and white gloves – took messages round the store, and staff had to learn to recognise customers of high rank. I would be asking myself, "is this Lady So-and-So, or could it the Countess of Blank…?" Getting it wrong could cause offence and the loss of the valuable account. Outside, the commissionaire would open the doors of taxis for our rich clientele, carry parcels or sometimes a lap-dog on a cushion to the department of madam's choice. In Europe the threat of war moved ever closer while we lived and worked in an atmosphere of artificial gaiety, lulled by Prime Minister Chamberlain's return from Munich brandishing his 'no war' message from Adolf Hitler. Many were struck down by another enemy - a nasty bout of 'flu which claimed several lives in the country. My friends at work were all recuperating at the same time, and we decided to enjoy an outing in Epping Forest. This was daring, as we were drawing sick pay from the insurance company, in my case the Prudential, who employed inspectors to check on claimants. The strict rules meant that we had to be back by 6pm, and if we were found to be out gallivanting during the evenings our benefit could be withdrawn. We got away with it.

In my time with Jays I attracted the attention of a man we would now term a stalker. He used to wait outside our house, accompany me to Maryland Point station and then on to Oxford Circus. No matter where I went, he was there with a present of fruit or some other small gift. At first he seemed a nice companion, but his constant presence began to irritate me. He wanted me to marry him and accompany him to Australia. "Come to the bush with me. Please come with me to the bush, Gladys," was his constant plea. I tried to humiliate him on one occasion by smacking his face in front of other passengers, but that didn't work, so I asked the Store Detective to accompany me to Oxford Circus. That failed too as he simply caught up with me at Liverpool Street. The nightmare – for that was what it had become for me – continued until the outbreak of war. Shortly after, he failed to turn up one day, and I assumed with great relief that he'd been called up.

A potentially more dangerous encounter began on the bus that ran from the Thatched House along Cann Hall Rd to the open area of land known as Wanstead Flats, a stretch of parkland with trees and a pond. I used to take this route as a short cut to Forest Gate. As it was such a beautiful day I travelled on top of the bus, paying little attention to another top-deck passenger, a young man who followed me off. I began walking across the Flats and eventually he caught me up. His approach and manner was gentle at first, but it soon became clear that he wanted sex, there and then. In an attempt to put him off, I told him I was sorry but it was impossible. I was indisposed. But this was not someone to be easily diverted. He put his hand up my skirt to find out for himself if I was telling the truth, and it was only when he felt my sanitary towel that he left me alone. I just wonder how many other girls he had approached in the same way.

The war ended my mother's dream of my becoming a music teacher – a sedentary occupation that she thought would not overstrain my defective heart. But there was more to it than that. I sometimes find it hard to believe that she came from a musical background. She played no instrument and could not sing. Yet her father was First Violinist for (Sir) Henry Wood, and her brothers also played the violin. My father played piano and the harmonium, and I'm told that to soothe me to sleep as a baby I was left in a room where Granddad Soar and father were playing a duet. What cruel fate had decreed that my mother, surrounded by all that musical talent, should be born tone-deaf?

To her credit she was constant in her desire that Joyce and I should have at least a grounding in musical practice and theory. Joyce and I progressed to Grade 5 before the war came, but although I thoroughly enjoyed the piano, the theory caught me out, and it was an added pressure when the examiner was none other than that musical genius Sir William Walton. During my early teens I took singing lessons from a Miss Newton and was taught violin by her husband whose name was Drake, who took a rather dim view of my prospects on that instrument. But it was a handy arrangement, as mother looked after the Drake children when both parents needed to teach. Mrs Drake, whose daughter Sheila died tragically young, kept in touch for some years after the war and loved talking about 'old times.'

Classical music seemed to enjoy a higher status than today. Where now will you find live performances between films in the cinema, where sometimes a full orchestra would play light classics? It was a real occasion to go to the 'pictures,' being directed to your seat by the light of the usherette's torch and often enjoying a Mickey Mouse film between features. The sound quality was often poor and scratchy, and if you wanted the real thing you went to a concert or the opera, of which my first experience was at Bow, for *Carmen*. Carmen was very buxom in the tradition of the day, with a wonderful, rich carrying voice. The whole event was so involving I became hooked on opera from then on.

There are many reminiscences of this pre-war period still unmentioned. Perhaps I should summarise the most vivid before moving on. Cod-liver oil and malt – a spoonful each night before bedtime of this delicious, toffee-tasting vitamin supplement like thick treacle; in summer, buying ice-cream from the bell-ringing boy on his tricycle with a large ice-box on the front; having my hair cut shingle-style when small, sitting on a wooden board placed across the arms of a barber's chair, watching the hot towels around the faces of the men being shaved. There were dandies to be seen too – men dressed in checked waistcoats and soft leather spats with leather fastenings over feet and ankles. They affected coloured cravats, sometimes an eye-glass or monocle, and looked unnaturally clean beside working men. Those workers we witnessed in 1936 – the Jarrow Marchers – were dirty, dishevelled and desperate, with blistered feet from ill-fitting shoes, on their way to central London to put their case to Parliament. But nothing could be done until the outbreak of war, when they were either called-up or were needed to resume work in the shipyards as a reserved occupation.

The following year, 1937, my father stood as Conservative candidate in the local council elections. All the family pitched in to help, especially by pushing leaflets showing his photo and outlining his manifesto through letter-boxes in the surrounding streets. My boyfriend at the time was a Labour supporter. When I foolishly asked him to help with my leaflet campaign, he refused. In my idealistic way I'd thought that love would conquer any problems. We stayed together for a while and then I asked him to come ballroom dancing with me. His reply, that it was a "degrading" pastime, finally ended the relationship. On the night of the election, we stood outside the Town Hall awaiting the results of the count. Father had not qualified. All that work for nothing. Ah, well!…

My first bicycle, a Raleigh, was bought with money borrowed from a money-lender who ran her unlicenced business from a house a few doors away. She was kept busy calling around the houses to pick up instalments and chase debts. Borrowing and repaying small amounts on a weekly basis was the only way most people could buy goods, and she had a thriving business. Insurance was also sold house to house, and for many years I held a policy from the Prudential at a penny per week that mother had paid from my birth. Much later I had to redeem this policy at a loss, but that's a story that belongs elsewhere.

Let me end this part with mention of money, the currency. The lowest denomination coin was the farthing, whose value had shown a steady decline since Victorian times. Even so, you could buy a large sweet, called a gob-stopper, for a farthing in the 'thirties (four for a penny) It would last for ages, changing colour and flavour, but it was all too easy to swallow, and then you could be in serious trouble. Two farthings made a halfpenny, or 'ha'penny.' Next came the penny, the last of the copper coins. The range of 'silver' coins began with the threepenny piece, known as a 'Joey.' Slightly larger was the sixpence, and in gradually increasing size and weight the shilling (12 pence), florin (2 shillings), half-crown (2/6d) and the crown (5 shillings) that was rarely used. Gold sovereigns were worth £1 and recall a family tradition whereby the one given me by my grandfather at birth is to be passed on to the first grandchild of succeeding generations. It is with me still, locked inside its heavy safe, the property of grandson John who is happy for it to remain *in situ.* Paper money began with what was commonly called the 'ten-bob' note (10/-) which had a reddish colour; the £1 note (green) and the £5 note (white), which when father first showed us we hardly dare touch, as it represented more than a week's wages for the average working man. Strangely, prices for such as paintings, racehorses, men's suits, ladies costumes and lawyers' fees etc, were expressed in guineas, worth 21 shillings each, and not in general circulation, like notes of higher denomination that we never saw. How much more exciting money was then, in those far-off days!

CHAPTER THREE

On that terrible day in early September 1939 we all sat listening to the radio. I well remember the feeling of utter helplessness as Prime Minister Chamberlain told the nation that we were at war with Nazi Germany. Immediately afterwards the sirens sounded, and it was as though the pit of my stomach had dropped out. Fear and disbelief that we could be bombed so early in the war made us all edgy, but on this occasion it was a false alarm.

One of the first tasks Joyce and I set ourselves was to visit people in our street who owned pets. My ambition to become a vet having been frustrated, I felt I had to do something to alleviate the inevitable suffering of animals in wartime. So we went round offering people identity discs to attach to the collars of their dogs and cats so that they could be registered. The plan was in response to our concern that if bomb blast blew out windows or doors, terrified animals could escape and be scattered who knew where. Our scheme would offer at least a chance of their recovery. But not enough people took us seriously. "It can't happen," they scoffed, but this is exactly what transpired later in our part of the East End. The Co-op's delivery horses escaped when their stables were bombed, racing past our house with eyes flashing and hooves pounding, the fires from the burning buildings lighting up the neighbourhood.

Following the declaration of war, I went to work as usual in Oxford Circus to be greeted by our Director, Mr Lines. He was sure that London would be reduced to a heap of rubble within a matter of weeks, and had convinced himself it was no good keeping us in employment. He retained only one buyer from each department and one other member of staff. It was an uncomplicated matter in those days for an employer to give his workers the sack, and we were given our cards to return home to begin job-hunting all over again. Fortunately, the local shops in the East End kept going. I applied to Bearmans in Leytonstone Road and was hired to work on their hosiery counter, with the advantage of being able to travel to work by bicycle. But what a change of atmosphere! I was used to hosiery being made to order, with the family monogram set in pure silk at five guineas a pair. Now it was rayon at 1/11d a pair - not even fully fashioned. The children's socks were sold at about fourpence a pair. The staff comprised local girls, and our First Hand was a lady who had lost her sweetheart in the First World War. Touchingly true to his memory, she had remained a spinster. She always took the first customer and the resulting commission from any sales. We were then lucky if we attended to the second or third hand of sales, so the prospect of earning extra money was not good. As a consequence we only made any money from comission during the sale. Most of my time was taken up sewing tags on second-rate stock for reduced sale. I often had to fetch stockings from the stock-room and in doing so passed the Upholstery Department where some fresh-faced young men worked. I was particularly interested in one of them, a lad called Ronald, and after working long hours we would walk to his house in Leyton. On arrival, if his mother and brothers Raymond and Terry were out it was necessary to prise open the front room window in order to get in, as he had not been given a key. During the war this house was damaged by flying debris which crashed through the roof. Ronald's grandmother, Mrs Herring, had recently been evacuated to King's Lynn in Norfolk, and might well have been seriously injured by the metal that landed on her bed.

Ronald and I became engaged, much to my mother's disgust. She'd made it clear she didn't think he was good enough for me. Before he was called up, we had our photographs taken together – an augury of bad luck, we'd been told – and he was soon posted to the Rifle Brigade and sent to France as a Despatch Rider. It wasn't long before he was captured by the Germans and kept at Stalag 8B near Dusseldorf. I received one letter with a photograph, sewn in with grey sock wool, showing him with a violin. It brought back happy memories of the musical evenings we'd enjoyed before he left. With his being allowed only one letter monthly, routed via Sweden as a neutral country and taking three months to arrive, it was difficult enough without my mother destroying some of his correspondence on the grounds that it might have upset me. Although I wrote to him from the ATS camp where I was then stationed, all letters were censored for sensitive content. I also sent many parcels of vitamin tablets and clothing to the POW camp, but didn't know until I met him again after his release by the liberating forces that he received no gifts there. By that time, we had each changed too much for the magic to survive.

Many years later my husband found some mementos of the romance and destroyed them. The very precious photographs in my album survived, however, and I tried to locate him in the year 2000, thinking Ronald might welcome their return. But not remembering his regimental number has proved a drawback, and to date my search has not been fruitful. If he has a family, I feel they should have these things.

In the early stages of the war the government felt that young people should have a choice about which branch of the Armed Forces they joined. The alternative was to go into munitions factories, making shells and torpedoes to aid the war effort. I applied to join the Auxiliary Territorial Army for Women, known as the ATS. As I had suffered from a heart condition I was doubtful that I'd be accepted. But at my medical I was told, untruthfully, that my feet were not flat, and my heart was pronounced good! While awaiting my call-up papers I was travelling to and fro on the Underground, amazed at first to find whole families encamped on the station platforms. They kept well back from the edge and were thought to be safer underground than anywhere else. For the most part they were, although tragically a direct hit by a bomb on the Bank station caused many deaths. There were later rumours that the site had been sealed without recovery of the bodies, and it was not until years later that we learned this was true. It would have been too damaging to public morale to have admitted this at the time.

My call-up papers arrived. I was elated. At last I could leave home and live beyond the reach of mother's strict discipline. She, however, was devastated. She had just been told that my sister was to be evacuated to Banbury, and brother Ken accepted as a medical student. The outcome was that all three of us left home within a ten-day period. It must have been dreadful for her.

I travelled to Northampton via Euston on a specially designated train. We were met at the station by army trucks with open backs and no seating. I expected the soldiers to handle my luggage, as a gentleman would have done on civvy street, but I came down to earth with a bump, realising that I was just one of a mass of raw recruits, and had to carry my own case. We were dropped off into very unfamiliar surroundings known as the Talavera Camp.

We were instructed to call at different buildings to collect our uniforms and equipment, and then shown to our wooden huts, known as sleeping quarters. These looked like a hospital ward, with 20 beds lined along each side of the wall. Others of our intake were allocated to Nissen Huts, which were temporary buildings with curved roofs of corrugated iron that were icy cold in winter. A person with one stripe on her uniform instructed us. Her rank was Lance-Corporal and she was the one we should go to if we needed help with anything. We were escorted about the camp for various lectures and drill parade, and it soon became familiar. After three weeks training some recruits were posted away to other camps while a few, including me, remained attached to HQ Company as privates.

We learned that several women in Northampton had volunteered to join the army prior to the outbreak of war. They kept the title of 'volunteers' throughout their service and had special privileges such as being allowed to live at home and report for duty each day. Some were billeted in large houses in Kingsthorpe Hollow, but when a large influx of conscripts was called up the accommodation on the Racecourse – housing militia men – was made available to women. Talavera camp covered approximately half of the Racecourse area in a fenced enclosure. The remainder was left to provide a recreation area for local people. Unfortunately for us, the people of Northampton did not take to the girls in uniform, and often showed resentment. The reason was that they felt we had commandeered their Racecourse, and there was no telling when, if ever, they'd get it back.

Men from the Fifth Battalion, who were housed in the barracks in Barrack Road, remained to help the ladies become soldiers. Several Sergeants showed them how to drill on the barrack square, although in time a lot of service-man's jargon had to be forgotten - the language was not suitable for women!

As more time passed and ATS personnel took over drill, the more complicated manoevres such as those still seen today on Horseguard's Parade were discontinued, as they were not necessary. A contingent of Privates was detailed for heavy duties, such as moving coke, grass- cutting, painting, carpentry and plumbing. The Pioneer Corps was in charge of the guard-room which was situated at the Bailiff Street end of the Racecourse.

Captains Downes and Lovesy, RSM Johnson (a male) and Colour Sergeant Pond were detailed to make sure that we learnt how to run a military camp. They certainly achieved their objective, and when they left us to 'carry on' the camp was a very happy and efficient concern. Our officers and staff were very professional, so that the "rookies" who came to us left after their three weeks induction knowing how to conduct themselves with pride in His Majesty's uniform.

Attached to the top barrack square was a large NAAFI where the band of the Fifth Battalion would play once a week for the ATS girls to dance with soldiers invited from near and far. Sometimes troops from the American base at Molesworth would come, or the ATS would be transported in trucks to their camp, which I remember as a sea of mud. At the top end of the camp was the Sergeants Mess, built in a spider shape in brick. Nearby was a large gymnasium, beautifully equipped, where concerts would be held and the Entertainment National Service Association (ENSA) would sometimes entertain us. Then came the Passive Air Defence or PAD Centre, which housed the decontamination instructors and their equipment etc. We had to wear gas-masks at times and attend lessons on how to decontaminate ourselves should such a raid occur.

About halfway down the camp a cookhouse was situated on either side. In front of these there were always bowls of water for the recruits to wash their knives, forks and spoons after a

The Smell On The Landing

meal, and a pig-swill bin for uneaten food. Dotted about were the Nissen and wooden huts used as dormitories. These housed nineteen girl Privates and one Lance-Corporal who was in charge. In the centre of each dormitory was a combustion stove. It was a devil to light, as we had mostly coke to burn, so everyone would search for paper and sticks to make the task easier. Orders were "no heating until 4 pm", though by the time the stove was going well it was often time for lights-out at 10 pm!

The huts were grouped into companies, around ablutions and latrines. There were four companies, all at different stages of training, on a rota system. Coal and coke was used to heat the water, which was a job done by men. At about 5 am one would hear them stoking up ready for the rush at 6 am, which was announced by a bugle call known as 'Reveille'. The Pioneer Bugler, who had manned the guard-room all night, would wake the camp in this manner every morning. Other bugle calls told the whole camp what was expected according to what call was made. Post-call was the favourite one. Each company had a number and a colour, so it was easy to find a Private in about two thousand girls. A letter would be addressed thus; No.4 Coy, Hut 5D. On hearing the call the post clerk would go and collect the mail for that company. Overall it was an extremely well-run camp.

Next on the camp came Headquarters Offices, situated close to the guard-room. Further down came the Officers' Mess at the Barrack Road end of the Racecourse, along with a small hospital, dentistry and Medical Officer's Surgery. The hospital was staffed by VAD nurses who had officer status and had to be saluted if met on the camp. Dotted around this end of the camp were food stores and the Catering Company. The office of the Clerk of Works was manned by civilians, responsible for keeping all buildings in working order.

When I first entered the service we had to shower in a row without any cubicle curtains. Because this was the way men showered, it was expected that women should do likewise. It was typical Army thinking. We girls found it very embarrasing, so most opted for a bath instead. The hot water soon ran out, and the bath-plug disappeared, requiring me to buy my own and keep it safe.

Our laundry was sent to Hinkley. Most of the time they seemed to boil everything, so that clothes came back shrunken and unwearable. So I did my own in the ablution room, where we had a drying room heated by hot pipes. Unfortunately items were often stolen, and one could begin to see one of the reasons for the regular kit inspections. All clothing had to carry a name-tag, and there would have to be some explaining to do by anyone found in possession of an unmarked garment. My aptitude for craft work was soon discovered and found myself showing those who could not darn how to use a needle to repair items rather than order a replacement.

I took to life in the ATS and was quickly promoted to Corporal. One of my first tasks was to inspect new recruits for lice on 'Nit Parade.' About ten on an intake of 150 were infested on average, mostly those we knew as peroxide blondes, who had to be separated from the others until declared clean. Besides this were body inspections and jabs, during which some at the back of the queue would faint. Perhaps they knew that needles used in these injections were refilled and used repeatedly, and when their turn came they might face a painful encounter with a blunt needle!

Once conscription made joining up compulsory, there were always some recruits who went absent without leave (AWOL) as soon as possible. Some stayed and cried for several days until they got used to their fellow rookies, made friends or decided that the military life was not so bad after all. I was surprised that out of the whole weekly intake most actually enjoyed it, although it was hard going for them. Many discomforts had to be overcome, such as the uncomfortable iron beds with three stuffed straw mattresses, hard and uncomfortable. These would separate during the night, so one learned to wrap a blanket round them to hold them together. The physical discomfort, together with being in a room of 20 girls, meant that a good night's sleep was difficult. Some snored, some talked in their sleep. Others groaned, or moved noisily from their beds to visit the toilet. Being a light sleeper I found it particularly hard. The huts were damp and cold, and there was often a shortage of hot water.

The food was certainly not to everyone's taste. On one occasion, some very tough meat, dressed in onions that repeated on me, turned out to be horsemeat. To get fed we stood in a line, knife fork and spoon in hand, pushing a plate along the counter until the food was dumped on to it without ceremony. We then sat on forms at well-scrubbed tables to eat it and gossip and joke, until the Orderly Sergeant stopped us for being too rowdy. An Orderly Officer strolled about, asking if there were any complaints. It took a brave girl to speak up, and very few did!

Shoes were Oxford style, which we spat on and polished for hours, but one's feet took time to shape them for comfort. In the mornings, it was sitting on the bed polishing brass buttons and cap badges. If they weren't clean enough on parade, the offender faced a reprimand or possibly a charge, which involved the punishment of having to carry out menial or unpleasant duties. So strongly was this discipline instilled that years later I would have nightmares about being on parade with dirty badge or buttons.

When I was made up to Staff Sergeant I would be detailed to inspect the huts and the personnel's clothing for Kit

Inspection. This required all items to be laid out on the bed, when the condition of the garments would sometimes reveal who had scabies or VD. Another inspection, carried out by the Medical Officer, looked in particular for pubic lice and pregnancy. When lice were detected, all clothing was stoved.

A red sash was issued to me to indicate that I had been appointed Orderly Sergeant. This meant I had extra duties to perform, such as patrolling the camp at night to see that all was well. I had to ensure that no-one was ill, and the girls were tucked up in bed as they should be. It was necessary to man the 'phone on a 24 hour basis, as messages could arrive at any time and require urgent attention. Sometimes a convoy of drivers would have to stop for the night, and accommodation, bedding and food would have to be found for them. I had to attend also to late-comers in the guard-room, and if they were drunk and disorderly, put them on a charge. I had to liaise with the Military Police for those who had gone AWOL, and finally call the cooks from their beds to prepare breakfast for all.

One night I got a real fright. A message came in that an invasion attempt had been made and the sea on the south coast was on fire. Our Officer Commanding had sealed instructions for such an occasion and ordered that trenches be dug and the camp made ready for evacuation. Some time later we received a futher message to say that the emergency had been a false alarm. It was all rather puzzling to say the least, and it was many years before I learned the truth. At Slapton Sands, near Torcross in Devon, is a memorial to the American troops lost when the sea caught fire. Like so much else in wartime, details were kept secret for years. But the night of 14th November 1940 really brought home the dangers we faced. I stood with others on the top barrack square, watching the northern sky alight. In the morning our fears were fully realised. There had been a heavy raid on Coventry, and we had witnessed the city burning.

My promotion to Quartermaster Sergeant included a remit to see that buildings and barrack equipment generally were in good order. This often involved organising the repair of items like broken door hinges, cracked windows, dripping taps etc. I remember on one winter's day going to investigate a blocked toilet. As the weather was cold I wondered whether the cistern had frozen over, and removed the cast iron cover. I was fascinated by what I saw. Clinging under the lid were hundreds of greyish-white blow-flies hibernating until the warm weather came again. I realised that the sun must give them the beautiful greeny-blue colour when they emerge once more in the Spring. It was also part of my job to read the water- meters, in order to record the volume of water consumed on the camp. The stop cock was in the ground not far from HQ Company offices. The huge tap located there had leaked and formed a small pond of fresh water which had been colonised by lots of little frogs. Fortunately I am fond of all creatures and it didn't bother me to do this duty, but I can imagine what a scare it would be to some women.

The Racecourse was also a rich source of insects. On one occasion when the weather was very hot several members of the Sergeants Mess decided to sleep outside. We brought out the bedding, and after a lot of giggling settled down to what we thought would be a romantic night under the stars. It didn't last. A storm blew up and when we abandoned the idea and decided to take cover we found we found the sheets, blankets and pillows had been invaded by loads of earwigs.

We had a tailoress workroom for altering uniforms to fit. You can imagine how busy they were when an intake of raw recruits came in every week. Sometimes it was necessary to contract the surplus work out of the camp and a shop in Bailiff Street, called Rigging Tailors, was used.

The Officer Commanding, a Mrs Raynsford, operated from the Adjutant's Office, near to St Georges Avenue. The garage repair sheds were opposite the guard –room, and for recreation we had some grass tennis courts. A lady gardener tended flax, grown in the centre of the camp. In a dip in the ground an incinerator worked overtime, sometimes burning louse-filled clothing but more usually a constant supply of soiled sanitary towels, an unpleasant job done by men.

When I was on duty my pockets bulged with keys. Just above my waist a pocket would sag with the amount of keys held on the lanyard that adorned my uniform. For example I kept keys for my office, a warehouse full of clothing, the utensil store, another store for bedding and yet another for shoes.

During the time I served at the Talavera Camp we acquired a lady Regimental Sergeant Major, known then as RSM Barley. She decided to make use of the talents to be found on the camp to stage a concert, and I found myself picked to sing Jerusalem. The Regimental Band was asked to perform, but no-one had any rehearsal. I was announced and went on stage. The pianist struck up and I started to sing, but then the Regimental Band cut in unexpectedly. I was so surprised I stopped singing. I apologised to the audience and we had to start again, but we still couldn't get it together. It was all most embarrassing, and afterwards I had my leg pulled mercilessly by all.

RSM Barley used heavy make-up and hated to be seen without it. If emergencies arose during the night it was sometimes necessary to rouse her. This was the time, naturally, when she had removed all 'war paint,' and the Orderly Sergeant would take great pleasure in shining a torch full on to her face to cause her maximum discomfort.

Dealing with people from different backgrounds often caused surprises. I was asked to take a class for drill and cross-country running. This posed no problem as I had learnt basic

Drill in the Girls' Life Brigade long before joining the army, had enjoyed improving on this as a recruit, and was happy to pass on my knowledge. I soon developed the knack of shouting orders to the platoon and got good results until we received a group of bargee recruits, who were unable to tell left from right. I tried "you're going to turn left, that's the hand in which you hold a fork." No good. They came from backgrounds where cutlery was not used! Eventually, I resorted to "port" or "starboard," as they were familiar with boating jargon. That worked nicely. The object of the training centre was to turn raw recruits into trained soldiers – a tall order in just three weeks. After training the girls were posted away to smaller specialist units to be trained again to do what was then thought of as 'a man's job.' Before they left us, however, they had to be able to obey orders instantly, look smart on parade and perform drill correctly. We had ensured that their uniforms fitted properly and they recognised the insignia on the sleeves of officers and non-commissioned ranks. They were told what standards of cleanliness were expected and how to achieve it, both bodily and in the barrackroom.

For the first three months in service they were allowed only a short 48-hour leave, by which time we hoped they would have developed a little *esprit de corps*. It was evident on church parades, when the regimental march applicable to a particular unit was played, that the transformation of 'belonging' had indeed taken place, as the girls would stand with particular pride. The regimental march tune of the unit to which I was attached was *The Lincolnshire Poacher*. It was a magnificent sight to see some 1500 girls marching to St Sepulchre's Church, led by the regimental band of the 5th Battalion. Someone from each company, usually a lance-corporal known as a 'marker,' would leave the church just before the end of the service and take up position. They would be drilled to stand evenly spaced to signal the spot on which each company must assemble for the return journey. The whole parade would stretch from Church lane on to the Mounts. As Senior NCO of Headquarter Company it would then be my job to shout the order to set them all marching back to camp. My voice was inadequate for such an occasion, and they sometimes came to attention in a very ragged fashion that I found acutely embarrassing. Once back at camp we would be served tea and go into the NAAFI or over to Nelson Hall (now demolished) in Nelson St. This was manned by volunteers - often by the Salvation Army who were a godsend to the ATS

At Christmas we would take a few girls and a lamp round the camp singing carols (a moving rendering of *Silent Night* in the small hospital comes to mind as I write) Christmas Day was the only day in the year when the roles of officers and other ranks were reversed. It was certainly a novel experience to watch the officers serving Christmas Dinner. But one year something went wrong in the kitchen, and the Christmas puddings unaccountably sank into the water in which they were being heated! A salvage operation was quickly mounted, and the failed puddings were put into the ovens to dry them out. Luckily no-one complained when they were served with loads of custard to cover our mistake. Worst of all, when it came to do the washing-up, not a drop of liquid soap could be found, and cleaning the greasy dishes without it turned out to be a long and messy business.

After America entered the war on the side of the Allies, some of their GIs, as the soldiers were known, were billeted at a nearby camp. It was a big event when they were invited to attend our camp dances. Sometimes they'd bring ice-cream with them – a rare luxury for us, commonplace to them. Then there were the hot dogs they provided, which would be sent to the cookhouse for heating up ready for the interval.

I remember the morning after one such event finding the taps in the cookhouse adorned with water-filled condoms – *French letters* as they were more commonly known. Each man was issued with more than he could reasonably use for sex, and they often served a more light-hearted purpose in practical jokes. I feared for the safety of our girls. An ample supply of these prophylactics implied that sex was expected. From time to time we were invited to the American base, and on one occasion when I felt that things were about to get out of hand I ordered everyone home early. Needless to say, I was more than a little unpopular. The men were furious, especially the driver detailed to return us to camp. He drove like a madman, careering around the bends, throwing us from side to side in the back. He could have killed us all. The girls were so frightened that some began to pray for safe delivery. What a night!

As Company Quartermaster Sergeant I was responsible for pay and equipment. We had stores for every conceivable object that might be needed on the camp, and girls from lower ranks were detailed to manage the equipment and report to me accordingly. Payment of wages was fortnightly. Those whose surnames fell between the letters A-M were paid in one week; N-Z the following one, the payroll being made up only of personnel attending early parade. Initially I paid not only the 250 girls of HQ Company but also the men attached to us for heavy duties from Gibralter Barracks and the VADs who operated our little hospital.

After a while the Catering Corps also came on to my payroll, boosting the numbers to 600 or so. On pay-days someone would need to go into town to collect the money – either an officer in a car or me on my bike. I would set off with a cheque in one hand, unaccompanied, to the Bank. The possibility of my being robbed on the return journey, laden with cash in bags whose handles I slid over the handlebars, never seems to have occurred to anyone. It was a heavy load too, mostly made up of small change since the average wage was between 2/6d and 12/6d. (or even less if your pay had been 'docked' for some misdemeanor!) Back at camp, my precious cargo would be checked by an officer, and only then could everybody's favourite ceremony begin.

Talavera camp played a vital role in preparing female military personnel for training in specialist fields, often in the occupations they had been employed in as civilians – cooks, clerks, telephonists, drivers if they had previously held a licence. Otherwise they would learn a new skill. Some became armourers, some motor mechanics, electricians, aircraft spotters. We knew of women trained at Talavera who operated artillery along the coasts, or manned searchlights – a particularly dangerous activity, as the Germans found it all too easy to fire down the beam of a searchlight and kill the crew. Likewise when operating anti-aircraft (ack-ack) guns, the flash of the weapon discharging gave away the position. These guns were often located on a desolate, lonely piece of land where the elements of wind and rain were as relentless as the enemy.

Women who had not joined up could be as much at risk as those on active service. It is often forgotten that the enemy maintained, at least early in the war, aerial reconnaissance that provided photographs of munitions factories that became prime targets. Factory employees making bullets and shells for the Army or torpedoes for the Navy risked their lives every day they went to work, and the nature of their work, inevitably with toxic chemicals, posed its own dangers. Tales of women whose hair had turned green often did the rounds. In Northampton itself, parts for the war effort were made at the Express Lifts site in St James. The role played by women in wartime has never been properly publicised. It was a major contribution that should never be underestimated.

It was at the Talavera camp that I first met the man who was to become my husband, serving in the Northamptonshire Regiment and attached to us for heavy duties. It was a 'compassionate' posting, as his wife who lived at their home in Aldwincle a few miles away was dying from tuberculosis. His marriage had not been a success, and we were mutually attracted. As he was on my payroll I knew quite a lot about his circumstances. For instance, his real name wasn't Jack, as he'd told me. His initials were 'G H' for George Henry. 'Jack' originated in 'Jakes,' a term of endearment between an affectionate father and son. Moreover there was another George Shaw in his barrackrom, so he volunteered to be known as Jack, a name he kept throughout his life. That other George Shaw, we learned later, was killed in action.

We were drawn together partly by our love of sport. He played tennis, cricket and football, could have played for Northants had he not been part of the 1938 call-up, but was allowed to join the Northampton Police side during the war as they were short of players. When I was asked to make up a foursome at tennis with another couple, I was delighted at the chance to know this handsome, kind, considerate man better. We went on to play many a tournament together, winning some, losing others. All the time our relationship was deepening.

We soon fell foul of Army regulations. It was fine for me as a Staff Sergeant to play tennis for the regiment with those of other ranks, but 'walking out' with someone of lower rank was strictly taboo, and when RSM Barley got to hear of it, I was on the carpet. Jack at that time was merely a Private. I was not alone, however. I knew a Subaltern who was going out with a Private, and their answer was to attend swimming lessons at the same time. With neither wearing a uniform, who was to know?

One of the opportunities to meet those of other ranks off-duty was at the Salon-de-Dance at weekends. It was a good walk back from St James to the camp, and we were supposed to be in by 10.30pm. Of course, we were often late, and Jack would lift me over the fence so that I could creep back to the Sergeant's Mess hoping not to be noticed. Whenever we had time off together we'd cycle round Northamptonshire, though my bike, brought from home, had a crossbar like a man's. It was all very well cycling around London in plus-fours, as I did, but another matter to do it when the crossbar was causing my regulation Army skirt to lift with every movement. However, decorum had to take second place...Jack's great sportsmanship meant that he was picked to run in the Inter-Regimental Sports. During the race, he was running so well that one of his competitors tripped him up deliberately, causing him to fall and break a big toe. To add insult to injury the perpetrator then spiked his back with his running shoes. Jack was so incensed that he got up and won the race. To great applause he was presented with a set of six Apostle teaspoons, which we used during the many years of our married life.

He had another mishap while riding in an open truck. The driver decided to back up to a wall, not realising that Jack had already jumped off and was behind the vehicle, frantically trying to get back in as the driver came too close to the wall and hit it, trapping Jack's foot between truck and wall. The driver was not qualified, so Jack had to cover up for him when the Medical Officer asked how it had happened. I'd felt quite sick watching the accident, which could so easily have been fatal if Jack hadn't moved so quickly. Even so, his movements were very slow for weeks after.

While we were courting he thoroughly enjoyed his drink, and no doubt he did the trial between young males to see who could hold the most without falling down. Many a time I met him following such a session and complained of his behaviour. Living opposite a pub as we did, I'd seen enough of drunkenness and brawls not to want it from Jack. Moreover I'd been brought up a strict Methodist. Heavy drinking offended everything I'd been taught. So I faced him with it. As his wife was still alive I could hardly say "it's drink or me." But I did make it clear that our friendship could not continue if he continued to drink. To my great relief, he took the warning seriously and gave up drink. I saw it as a kind of commitment, and our relationship grew steadily deeper as a result.

At the end of the summer season in our first year we managed to get a few day's leave together and headed for Tiverton in Devon, which was very enjoyable. Other, shorter leaves were spent with my family in Stratford, despite the frequent air-raids during which it was not unusual to occupy the Morrison shelter for part of the night before returning to our separate beds. I should mention here that Morrison shelters were like large, very sturdy tables with massively strong legs, all made of steel, that one could use as a normal table in the sitting-room. Named after Herbert Morrison, the Foreign Minister in the Coalition Government, they were designed to bear the weight of a roof falling on top of them. Many who would otherwise have been crushed were rescued unharmed from houses reduced to rubble. Anderson shelters, on the other hand, were dug into the garden and roofed with corrugated iron. People who used them sat below ground, where they enjoyed some protection against blast and shrapnel while the air-raids lasted.

During one of these 48-hour leaves I asked Jack if he'd been keeping in touch with his mother, and he assured me he had. I assumed that he'd also visited, but then the Commander of his unit received a letter from his parents stating that he'd had no leave at all for ages, and wanted to know why. The CQMS checked his records and sent back details of train vouchers and dates as eveidence that he had been granted leave, which came as a shock to them as it did to me. Whatever was going on? What was there to hide? For the first time I had doubts about our relationship. Soon I was introduced to his family as a 'good friend,' and was for the most part accepted. It came out that they thought his wife knew she had TB when she married Jack, but for whatever reason failed to tell him. When her condition was diagnosed, the doctor advised Jack not to kiss her under any circumstances. So far as I know, he stayed away from her after that.

His sister Margaret Ivy, who would only answer to Ivy, wrote me expressing her concern at any possible relationship between us. She was great friends with Jack's wife Ada and therefore felt that she couldn't continue to be friendly with me. While expressing regret, she believed it was best to tell me. I thought it showed integrity, and understood, though his other sisters showed no such qualms. However, village life being what it is, the place was soon alive with gossip of our 'affair,' which reached the ears of Mother Shaw. Only after intensive questioning of me was she persuaded that there was no abandoned baby in my murky past. Shortly after, my mother and father came to Aldwincle to visit Jack's parents, and the rumour was at last laid to rest.

I was on leave, staying with my parents, when Jack was posted to France. While with his convoy heading towards the coast he managed to call in for a very emotional goodbye. We said our tearful farewells and he went off, to return only weeks later having been with the forces retreating on the fall of France. Three days without food or proper shelter, waiting to be picked up from the beach at Dunkirk, had left him shattered in ways that took long to heal.

My parents accepted Jack as a friend. To them he couldn't be a suitor as he was already married, and therefore did not

The Smell On The Landing

constitute a threat to their plans. They remained convinced that I should marry Royalty, and it was only a matter of time before my Prince would appear and sweep me off my feet!

The day came when we had to close No 1 ATS Training Centre, Talavera Camp. Slowly each of the companies was wound up, and only a few women were left at HQ Company. My collection of keys to all the ablutions, huts and services, carried through many duties over three years, were handed over to a Major in the barracks on Barrack Rd. I was posted to a holding company in Brigstock, ostensibly for a week or two, expecting a permanent slot to be found for me. Jack did manage to cycle over from Aldwincle to see me, but this was an isolated highlight. Hanging around the camp without a proper job was extremely boring, and whenever possible I took a bus into Kettering. There I met a family who asked me to visit them, a typical gesture at a time when people were unreservedly generous to Service personnel. It was part of a common bonding that united people from all stations of life – a strong feeling that we were all in the same boat together, determined to win this dreadful war.

From Brigstock I was sent to Shirley in Southampton where both an ATS Regiment and a contingent of soldiers had requisitioned an infant's school, sharing the buildings and facilities. My bedroom was in a classroom, and it was my misfortune to be standing in for a popular Staff Sergeant in hospital. I did what I could to disarm the resentment, but was hampered by not knowing the names or duties of the Privates. On one occasion I found myself manning the PABX switchboard as the usual operator was off sick.

The soldiers who shared the school were most rude. When I took the girls for drill in the school playground they would cat-call, whistle and jeer in a very off-putting manner. Naturally it was not long before the girls began making excuses to be excused parade. I could never understand why they were not reprimanded, as discipline was beginning to break down.

More seriously, I was alone outside the school gates one day when one of the soldiers tried to rape me. He didn't manage it – perhaps because in the struggle he found that I was the fitter of the two! I could tell he was from our camp from his insignia, but in the dark I could not have been certain enough of his identity to report him. So, shaken and angry though I was, I let it go.

While at Southampton I came across a very zealous Private, working in the cookhouse. I don't know where she got the idea, but she decided to wash the butcher's block on which all the meat was cut - with Jeyes Fluid! The pungent disinfectant sank into the soft wood surface and flavoured the meals for some time. The place was in uproar. It's well said that an army marches on its belly, and this food tasted dreadful. The cooks went on strike, and I was the butt between the officers and lower ranks, trying to mediate and keep the peace. It was this incident that started me smoking.

An enjoyable leave was spent in Aldershot, where I fell hopelessly in love. It was in a pet shop that our eyes met, and I knew I could not leave without him. My beautiful fluffy Keeshond puppy cost me £25, just about all I had in the world, but I simply had to have him. I procured a cardboard box and a blanket, and "Keesh," as I thought it appropriate to call him, slept at my side in camp. He would grow into a big, powerfully built dog with a delightful temperament, quite happy to tag along at 6am when I took my troop for an early morning run before breakfast.

During a period between postings, when I was again back at Brigstock, he was run over by a motorbike. The driver came into camp to report the accident, but luckily the dog was not badly hurt. I didn't know how it happened because he almost

The Smell On The Landing

never roamed outside, seeming to understand that he was to keep within the boundaries of the camp. Keesh had quite a fan club, and looked a true aristocrat, with his black and grey coat and soft white underfur, very sturdy and strong, and a tail that curled over his back like a Husky or a Chow. No wonder he was made such a fuss of! Calling him was never a problem. I would only have to shout "where's that dog?" at the top of my voice, and he'd come running. Others tried to imitate this, but he was much too bright for that. He only ever came to *my* call.

My enthusiasm and love for him never dimmed, and he was a perfect gentleman. When he wanted to do his jobs he'd disappear behind a suitable bush or shrub, preferring not to be watched. When I had to go into hospital, Keesh settled happily with my parents until I could have him back, but there was a sad ending. During the unusually severe winter of 1947, the snow was so deep that there wasn't a blade of grass to be seen. Desperate for something to chew, he ate a piece of cotoneaster which stuck in his gut and led to peritonitis. I cradled him in my arms and prayed for his life, but it was not to be. I cried for three whole days after his death. We had been so close.

After Southampton I found myself in another holding unit in Steyning, Sussex, where I remember fire-flies dancing during the warm summer evenings. It would have been good to visit nearby Worthing and Brighton, but we were forbidden to travel to the coast and had to find other amusements. So with a friend on the camp I hired a hacking horse, and some enjoyable off-duty hours were spent riding over the rolling Sussex Downs with their abundance of primroses and cowslips. I was doing well until my horse reared at the sight of another horse's blanket lying on the ground. Somehow I managed to hold on, but the worst part was after dismounting. Unaccustomed as I was to riding, it took a few days each time to stop feeling stiff and sore.

The men in the Sergeant's Mess at Steyning were a lively bunch, and a certain amount of horseplay went on. Someone would take away your chair just as you were about to sit down, or throw your hat behind the bar or sofas. Once, when leaning over to retrieve my hat, I felt a sting on the buttocks. An irresponsible man had thrown a dart and hit his target! I vowed to get my own back, and sometime later I saw him sitting with his back to me. Gesturing to the others not to give my presents away, I crept up and bit into his left ear-lobe, yelling and laughing at the same time. Imagine my horror, when I finally let go, to find I had got the wrong man! He was actually a new posting, very similar from behind to the man I'd sworn revenge on, and his only mistake was being in the wrong place at the wrong time. I've never fled a room so quickly in my life!

The troops were becoming bored with the monotonous food served up to them, and I was asked if I could find ways to vary their diet. I scoured the village but without success until I spotted a field of rhubarb and picked as much as I needed. Thereafter we had rhubarb pies until we were sick of them, not to mention the frequent visits to the toilet brought on by the change of diet. This camp boasted a new-fangled bidet, especially for the use of women, housed in a separate brick-built edifice. Unfortunately it was watched with such curiosity by the men that no woman would be seen to go near it.

During this phase of the war, Radar was in its infancy. I had the interesting job of helping dismantle 'old' equipment and saving any usable parts for the next model. Progress was so fast in this vital piece of equipment that almost as soon as one version came into use, a more sophisticated one was under development. Radio was an important part of our lives. It kept us in touch with everything from the progress of the war (censored of course) to local news, talks and readings from selected books. One of these was about 'The Good

Life,' and included a section on how to preserve food by burying it in a tin with straw below ground. The author was a lady who kept goats and ran a café, not far from the camp, where I once had a curious meal consisting of sardines and mandarins, which was quite tasty. Inside the café was a small library where I would browse. On one occasion, on taking a book from the shelf, I found a pair of spectacles. Thinking they were hers, I handed them over. "Oh, they belonged to my father." After a pause she added, "he died years ago." This was a measure of her housekeeping. It explained why everything was so dusty. She turned out to be a great character, and I got to know her well.

It was here that I met Monty (no, not Field Marshal Montgomery!), a romantic episode in my life. We enjoyed a lot of free time together and used to take her goats for a walk – easier said than done, as they had an unsettling habit of butting our legs from behind. Monty and I were attracted from the start, and soon thoughts turned to marriage. Monty took the delightfully old-fashioned step of formally asking my father for my hand in marriage. Receiving a "yes," I wrote to Jack to tell him how happy I was. I had a reply that said he understood, as he had no right to me since he was already married. Reading between the lines I sensed his sorrow at my news. Then Monty asked me to go to Wolverhampton with him to meet my prospective in-laws, but the visit was not a success. They took an instant dislike to me, and following this meeting his attitude towards me changed. He had obviously been given a stern lecture by his parents. Perhaps they too were hoping for Royalty!

Jack was delighted, of course. He needed good news to alleviate the horror of his duties, travelling across Europe to help in the relief of concentration camps, seeing things that came back to haunt him years later. But at the time his letters said only that he was well, and how cold the weather was. The censors were still at work.

My next posting was to the charming village of Langton Green in Kent, our base a large requisitioned house in its own grounds that had delightful streams and waterfalls and an arboretum with lots of flowering trees and bushes. Inside the house were inglenook fireplaces and polished wooden floors, which by the time our Army boots had finished with it were anything but well-kept. Trees were cut down to make space for the concrete hard standing to accommodate small trucks, and some of the timber used to fuel the open fires in the house. One evening as we huddled round the inglenook a whole big burning log fell out on to the wooden floor. We were ordered out sharply while the male sergeants dealt with the potentially dangerous situation. Luckily nothing else caught fire, and only a long, ugly scorch mark remained as testimony to our carelessness.

The property had a resident cat, which had the misfortune to be run over by a reversing Jeep. The poor animal was brought to me in a filthy, oily sack in which it was rushed by me to the vet, who lectured me about the sack but operated to save the cat's life. On collecting the cat later I paid the vet's bill and decided that I would be responsible for the patient's recovery, and toilet-trained it in the various sand buckets dotted around in case of fire. The cat was quite a character and loved a game of hide-and-seek in my bed. But at the same billet another ATS sergeant was not so lucky with the 'heinz variety' brown and black dog she'd befriended. When it became ill I went with her to the vet, where we were told that the dog would not survive and should be put down. All the way back to camp she cried so much that in the open car the wind whipped the tears from her face straight into mine.

The Sergeant-Major and I would tour the camp together making inspections, he reprimanding the men and I the women as we scrutinised the work being done in the cookhouse, garages, house and gardens. We got on so well that we often spent our off-duty hours in each other's company. On one occasion, walking round the village, we found ourselves in what seemed to be an unnaturally quiet place. Everything was hushed and still. We both felt more at peace than at any other time. There was no obvious explanation, especially as we were only friends with no romantic attachment. All I can say is that it was uncanny and wonderful – a few moments of heaven that had to be accepted as it was.

Around this time I was asked to speak to a female sergeant on a rather delicate matter. She had been given permission to wear slacks as she undertook driving duties, and on one occasion in the Sergeant's Mess she sat down and cocked one leg over the arm of the chair. The men present found this offensive and asked me to have a quiet word. My suggestion that she sit in a more ladylike manner did not go down well with the lady in question!

Another temporary posting took me to Burgess Hill, under the flight-path of planes headed for France from a nearby airfield. They came in armadas, hundreds in the sky at one time, so thickly clustered that they looked like a swarm of gigantic locusts. Again, our base was a requisitioned house in its own small grounds that were very untidy and ragged from lack of maintenance. I sympathised with the absent owners having to leave their home for the war effort. What a lot of hard work would be needed to restore the place when the war was over. My accommodation was a tiny, cramped boxroom. I spent much of my off-duty time just walking around the country lanes, loving the cobwebs and the hedgerows covered in hoar frost. I also got to know two very nice ladies whom I visited for tea on several occasions, promising to come back after the war and bring my children, if any, to visit. I'm sorry to say that I never got around to returning.

Winter merged into spring, and with 20 girls to keep busy I hit on the idea of cleaning out the garden pond, overgrown with weed due to neglect. All went well until the frogs, disturbed in their habitat, began to jump out. The girls were not as keen on wildlife as I was, and the afternoon ended in chaos with the girls running away screaming. However, I found that I was not immune. One summer evening, enjoying a romantic moment with a boyfriend in the woods, I was startled by a loud rustling nearby. Imagine my surprise when a large hedgehog appeared to break the magic spell! I sometimes wonder if that boy is still alive and remembers…

Last of these assignments was in Brockenhurst, where I was asked by one of the officers to accompany him on an inspection of the Ambulance Unit. Apparently it was his duty to ensure the unit was manned at a certain hour, and we left the mess party we'd both attended to check that all was well. I'd been completely taken in by his ruse to separate me from the revelllers, and when we got to the ambulances he opened the back door of one and pushed me inside! I fought hard to repel him, and when he finally accepted defeat I found enough breath to tell him I would never salute him again, and that if I was court-martialled as a result I would make my reason public.

Dances given by the Bomb Disposal Unit were a welcome diversion, marred only by a ceremony that reminded us how dangerous the work of dismantling bombs could be. At a given moment all would fall silent while a huge bowl was passed round for each of us to take a sip from. It was a group farewell to members of the squad killed on duty. I found it very moving. When all had paid their respects, the band struck up again for the dance to resume. Though I didn't drink, I often helped in the bar.

The Smell On The Landing

My health was beginning to fail. I had a monthly period that wouldn't stop, and medical examination revealed that I was anaemic with a low blood-count – hardly surprising. The Medical Officer recommended me for discharge, which I certainly didn't want. I thoroughly enjoyed life in the services, and had even thought of signing on as a Regular once the war was over. But it wasn't to be. I became so weak that I could not carry out my duties properly, so I had to accept it and attend the cadre for discharge. From there I was sent to the Women's Hospital in Soho, where I was told I would never complete a pregnancy. I would lose the baby at about four months. With this daunting prospect I returned to civilian life.

Joyce

*Son Quentin with grandfather's
pipe (d. aged 4)*

Gladys aged 20-21

"Fifty Years On"

HQ Coy. No. 1 ATS T.C. 1943, Talavera.

*CQMS Cleminson (Gladys) with Sergeants
Cherrot, Jones and S/Major Ellis. Talavera*

Cookhouse staff, No. 1 ATS T.C
Talavera Camp Northampton 1942-3

Talavera Camp, No 1 A.T.S. Training Centre Northampton
The Warrant Officers, Staff Sergeants and Sergeants 1943

Back row,Sgt Carne, Sgt Leslie,S/Sgt Cohen,Sgt Elly,Sgt Power, Sgt Godfrey,SgtStanton
Sgt Fortey, Sgt Lebrun, Sgt Butler, Sgt Cooper, Sgt Cherritt, Sgt Thomas, Sgt Faulkner
Sgt Calcott, Sgt Stallworthy.

Front row, S/Sgt Harrison,S/sgt Jenkinson,CSM Munden,QMSI Daw,RQMS Lloyd,RSM Barley
CSM Lawrence, CSM Ayres, QMSI Ayres, QMSI HAMER, CSM Thompson, Sgt Miller, SgtHarvey.

Sergeants Mess, No. 1 ATS Training Centre,
Talavera Camp, Northampton Racecourse

ST. SEPULCHRES INSTITUTE CRICKET CLUB

NORTHAMPTON CRICKET LEAGUE · SEASON 1955

CHAMPIONSHIP WINNERS — FIRST SECTION — Played 14   Won 9   Lost 1   Drawn 4

L. Hillier   J. Haddon   D. Bonham   G. Bradshaw   P. Robinson   M. Summerford   G. Shaw   E. Law   J. Freeman   N. Green

H. Haddon   R. Stratford   H. Haddon   N. Hillier   W. R. Felce   C. Green   H. Marchant   R. Grooeman   H. Sutton
Vice-President   Captain   President   Vice-Captain   Hon. Sec.

St Sepulchre's Institute Cricket Club
(Jack's local team)

Jack in uniform (after Dunkirk)

Nurse Elsie Shaw (Jack's mother)

CHAPTER FOUR

After a three-month rest I got a job in Romford, working as a secretary for a firm called Redic. It was started by a Mr Whitehead, who spotted a bottle of cider on a café table and chose the name spelt backwards as the one for his new firm. I was very happy there until Jack was demobilised and my friend Violet took over my job.

Jack was employed with a printing firm in Broad St Northampton called Lea & Company. He lodged nearby in Royal Terrace during the week and would travel to Romford at weekends to see me. When he told me that his aunt, Mrs Eames, needed someone to look after her following amputation of a leg, we moved into her bungalow in Eastfield Rd, Brixworth. It was very damp, the mattresses were mouldy and the only heating was coal fires. The toilet had no flush, and we cleaned it by swilling buckets of water down the bowl. The garden was very long, with ample space for Jack to plant seeds to grow his beloved vegetables.

In November we learned that his wife Ada had died and we decided to wait until the New Year before marrying. On January 4th 1947 we attended the Registry Office alone with the staff as witnesses. I had discovered I was pregnant in November and the marriage was much against my parents' wishes, but we had to put up with that. I wore a blue woollen costume and white lambswool coat, topped with a magenta feathered hat I'd bought for the christening of a friend's child.

I had changed my name by deed-poll to Shaw, but insisted before signing the marriage certificate that 'née Cleminson' was inserted.

After the ceremony we went to see a film, emerging into the beginning of the worst winter for years. The snow continued until all transport in the county ground to a halt. It seemed interminable, and in fact was still on the ground in May, with snowdrifts in places reaching the tops of telegraph poles. Here I was, almost marooned in the icy house, looking after a woman who was cruel and demanding. It would have been bad enough without the pregnancy, which caused me to pass out most mornings around eleven and come to feeling horribly sick. Needless to say, I had no sympathy from Mrs Eames who was a most unlikeable and ungrateful woman.

At the six-month stage I went to stay with my mother's sister, Aunt Dolly, in Forest Gate. Mother had 'excommunicated' me on the grounds that Jack and I had been 'living in sin' before our marriage, but Aunt Dolly had no such prejudice. She could not have known what she was letting herself in for!

Because of the pregnancy I needed to visit the toilet several times during the night. Aunt Dolly suggested I had a pot in the bedroom to save the journey downstairs. One morning on my way to empty this I fell and landed on my face and stomach. Consternation! Aunt was hysterical. If I had not killed the baby already the fall would have induced rapid labour and a child within minutes. The doctor who was summoned had first to calm Aunt Dolly before turning his attention to me. While waiting for him I had assured myself that the baby was alive by the simple expedient of eating something. I had noticed before that the baby became more active when I'd eaten, and this was the case now. I was able to assure the doctor that I could feel movement and so both I and the baby were pronounced unharmed. The accident had its positive side. It broke the uncomfortable silence between mother and daughter, and our relationship continued as before.

During the same stay with Aunt Dolly I went to see her mother-in-law, who was also my great-aunt and who gave me two beautiful rose-buds from her garden. On my return I proudly showed them to Aunt Dolly, whose reaction dumbfounded me. Snatching them from my hand she put them straight in the dustbin, saying "nothing from that house is coming into mine." I knew that she and her mother-in-law were always rowing and bickering, but I felt strongly that their dislike of each other should not have deprived me of a gift lovingly given, and I mourned the loss for ages. The incident had an extraordinary sequel a few years later when I attended the Spiritualist Church. To my complete astonishment the medium came to me and said "I have in my hand two gorgeous rose-buds. I believe they belong to you. You lost them." I ceased to regret their loss from then on, for I felt that I had not only recovered them, but the love that came with them too.

The dire predictions regarding my inability to carry a baby to full term had not so far come to pass, though I wasn't going to tempt fate by presuming that I had proved the doctors wrong. Towards the end of the pregnancy I returned to my parents' home in Hornchurch, Essex, looking forward with confidence to the birth. I came under the care of Mr Spiers, a consultant at Queen Mary's Hospital, Margaret Lyle Maternity Unit. Having read my notes he was taking no chances and decided that I should be induced early. So it was that on 11th August 1947 I was delivered of a beautiful baby girl whom I called Josephine. It was a hard labour on one of the hottest days of that year and I needed stitches to mend the tear her 6lb 6oz entry into the world had caused. But it was a small price for such a wonderful event.

The Smell On The Landing

Jack had fallen asleep sunbathing in my parents' garden, and when he telephoned the hospital for news he was amazed to be told that the baby had already arrived. Jack visited me most days until my discharge from the hospital. He maintained that his new daughter had the biggest lungs in the world, since from the courtyard below he could hear her yelling in my upstairs room!

I went home with the baby to my parents' house, and Jack to his digs in Northampton, until we found lodgings together with a Mrs Watt in Broad St Brixworth from whom we rented two furnished rooms. I then had to travel there from Essex, and while I was on Euston station, struggling with luggage and a new-born baby, a woman approached me and offered to take the baby if I didn't want it! I felt very vulnerable standing there alone, afraid that she might take the child, but my worst fears were not realised. In those days, baby-snatching was quite rare.

A stipulation of our tenancy with the elderly and poorly-sighted Mrs Watts was that we would move out when Josephine started to walk. This didn't give us very long, but Jack and I plannned ahead and pooled our money from the Army together with some savings and put a deposit on a plot of land in Weston Favell. The contract stated that a local firm would build a house for us which was due to be finished by the time Josephine was mobile. Imagine our horror when we received a letter one day to say that the firm had remortgaged the land, had then been unable to pay instalments on the loan and had subsequently gone into liquidation.

This represented a total loss of our savings, which had taken years to accumulate. We weren't alone. About 30 of us in a similar position formed a group to fight for recompense via the Department of Fraud, but it all failed. Somehow we had to pick up the pieces and make alternative plans to find a house we could afford on Jack's wages of £8 per week. We looked at everything at all likely – small dingy houses in depressed areas for the most part that we wouldn't care to live in. I decided to look for a house too big for our immediate requirements that had potential for the future, and finally found one that we could just afford to buy. Josephine took her first steps at 14 months, requiring us to leave the house in Broad St under the terms of residence while the conveyancing of our new house proceeded. Our daughter was 17 months when we finally got the keys to 32 Boughton Green Rd, Kingsthorpe, on the outskirts of Northampton.

The house, or '32' as we always referred to it, was built by a reputable local firm called Chowns. It was a spacious four-bedroomed late-Victorian townhouse, purpose-built for a family of means who could afford live-in help. Five of these tall, red brick and stone houses had been built at the same time, and their distinctive appearance got them known as 'doll's houses' by the locals. There was a sturdy panelled outer door to the porch, closed only at bedtime, which opened into a classically tiled porch from which a second door, half-glazed, led into the hall. The front room was entered by a door on the left of the hall and the staircase ascended immediately ahead. The passageway or corridoor was directed around the staircase to the middle room, and then changed direction again, passing the door to the scullery and a back room which would have been the servant's kitchen and which had an enamel, coal-fired range.

Upstairs the rooms were arranged as below with a bathroom and separate toilet over the downstairs scullery area. A second enclosed steep staircase led to a very large attic bedroom, still with the wooden holders of the gas brackets on the wall. The meagre iron fireplace could never have heated the huge room for the servants, who must have suffered in the winter, poor things. The space was sufficient to allow both a double and a single bed, plus the large wardrobe and glass-fronted bookcase we later installed.

The principal bedroom on the first floor overlooked the front of the house through a large rectangular bay window and sported a magnificent Victorian fireplace which today would be a desirable collector's item. There was space for two double beds and a large dressing-table. A huge fitted wardrobe had been built into one chimney breast recess, leaving plenty of floor space. Downstairs through the scullery was a second toilet, and outside the long narrow garden led to a gate giving access to an alleyway.

What we didn't know was that while waiting at my parents' house for the purchase arrangements to be completed, Josephine's cousin and playmate Christine had been going down with measles. We had only been in the new house a matter of days before Josephine contracted it, and became seriously ill. The doctor who was called was horrified at the conditions in which we were living – no furniture, a few kitchen utensils, an orange-box full of oddments, bedding and personal clothes and making the best of a cold, draughty house.

Josephine would not eat and was losing weight at an alarming rate. All I could coax her to take was the juice squeezed from navel oranges. She sustained a prolapsed bowel, and her legs were not strong enough to hold her weight. The doctor ordered me to take her to the Manfield Clinic at the bottom of Hazelwood Rd. Here she was fitted with surgical boots to provide support for her feet and ankles, and slowly she began to regain her health. It took years to get my once bonny baby back to normal, and even then her growth was stunted, leaving her smaller and thinner than girls of the same age almost until adulthood. I managed to get into town to order a bed-settee so that Jack and I both had somewhere to sleep and a place to sit during the day and gradually brought other furniture. My idea from the beginning had been to let the spare rooms. The terms of the mortgage prohibited this, but I reasoned that as the repayments took a week of Jack's wages every month, there'd be nothing over for emergencies, and we needed that extra income. So we arranged the upstairs back bedroom as a kitchen/diner and the attic room as a bedroom, let the accommodation at 30/- per week and negotiated an agreement to keep the stairs and hallway cleaned.

My first paying guest was a lad who worked with Jack as a printer's apprentice. Alan was only seventeen and a fitness fanatic. He kept weights under his bed and would use them each day as part of his fitness regime, but tended to drop them on the floor with such a thud that I feared for the ceiling. If he left them out, it was impossible to move them to clean the room properly. A bigger problem was Jack's attitude. Working with him by day and then accomodating him was very irritating, and he was jealous of the boy, picking on him unnecessarily – what dreadful ties he wore, and those awful shoes… Then the lad wanted to entertain his girl-friend in his room. What could I say? I felt a responsibility to his mother, who might well not have approved of any 'hanky-panky' at his relatively immature age. Eventually things took their course, he married the girl and he and his weights moved on. I had lost my first paying guest, though I still get a card from them every Christmas.

There was always some decorating and alterations to be done between tenants. This was often a time of stress for my husband Jack and myself. Times were hard, reduced as we were to only his wage coming in and the mortgage to be paid. Looking back over the myriad of people who have shared our house, it seems that all of them in some way have created a different 'smell on the landing'. The prospective tenants who answered my advertisement often had to be assessed on sight. How had they presented themselves? Did they look clean, tidy and considerate? Would they be quiet when my baby was in bed; was their speech coherent; did they swear? There was so much to consider, and it all boiled down to whether or not I liked the look of them. Jack left me to make all the decisions regarding tenants. He was at work for many hours a day, doing overtime if it was available. He accepted any new tenant as having passed my scrutiny.

Two young girls came to the door one day. I took to one of them instantly, but unfortunately she was not the hopeful tenant. The one I had taken a shine to was merely the spokeswoman. I was told that the quieter of the two would soon be marrying and was looking for lodgings for both her and her American fiance. My questioning began. "When are you wanting to move in?"

"I'm not sure. I must ask him first".

"Can you both come together to view the flat?"

"I don't know"

"What will your surname be when you are married?"

When she again said "I don't know" I repeated incredulously, "you're getting married and you don't know what your name will be?"

She was squirming but managed to answer "yes." I terminated the interview immediately, thinking it was a pity the chattier girl wasn't my prospective tenant, and thought no more of it.

A relative of mine and her husband lived in a nearby Northamptonshire village. For the sake of anonymity we'll call them Bob and Pat. Bob was out of work after the war and wished to come to Northampton to look for a job. They asked if they could stay in the vacant flat while he hunted for work, which Jack and I agreed to.

Bob was not very sure of himself. He needed a big push to go for interviews, and his wife and I walked with him to the gates of the iron foundry, as they had been advertising for labour. He managed to get a job on the furnaces, but before long had an accident with molten metal and burnt his back very badly. I nursed him through this ordeal, changing dressings etc, and then he fell ill with pleurisy. His wife and I helped him to recuperate and he went back to work.

By now Pat and I had come to an agreement. She would clean the house – her background was in domestic service – and I would do the cooking for all of us, sharing the evening meal. I had arranged for separate meters to record the consumption of gas and electricity in the tenanted part of the house, and we had separate living areas. With 'personal space' if we needed it, the arrangement worked well and suited everyone.

Pat and I would go to the Repertory Theatre once a week for 1/11d and sit 'in the gods.' I very much looked forward to these outings, and we got to know each other quite well. One day she confided that she hated sex and would not allow her husband penetration. For relief he would rub himself against her thigh. I tried not to be judgmental. It was their life after all. On our evenings out, I would first make sure that Josephine was safely tucked up in bed before leaving for the theatre, with Jack watching TV downstairs and Bob upstairs doing likewise – or so we thought. Everything was going well when Josephine began wanting to help Pat clean the house, mimicking her movements. Pat was clearly annoyed, saying that the child got under her feet. I felt our harmony was beginning to falter, but we continued our weekly theatre outings. Then Josephine let something slip about 'treats' while we were out, and after much questioning the awful truth emerged. Bob had been taking my daughter from her bed and sexually abusing her. I went into shock. What can one do on discovering a paedophile under one's own roof? First I had to tell Jack, but being quite incapable of doing such a thing himself he couldn't believe it. After all, they had known each other for many years. I began to wonder if Bob was simple, or retarded, so I went to see his doctor and confided my problem. He treated me as though I was an over-protective mother, dismissing my claim by saying that young people often made up stories. So neither my husband nor his doctor would take me seriously. I was furious and felt forced to confront Bob himself. When he denied it I tackled Pat, who was dumbfounded at first and then seemed to blot it out completely. By then I'd had enough. I ordered them to leave the house immediately. I knew my child was telling the truth, whatever denials the culprit had made. Some of the things she related were outside the normal scope of experience for a girl of such tender age. I should have told the police, but even though Bob had betrayed my trust in the worst possible way, knowing the background of his unfulfilled sexual life with his wife, I felt I could at least understand what had driven him to behave as he did. I have often wondered whether their marriage was ever consummated. A few years later I heard that Pat had died. Within weeks of her death Bob had married again and emigrated to New Zealand with his new wife. There is an amusing postscript. On the day of his wedding he was lying on his bed when a picture of Pat, hanging on the wall above, fell down for no apparent reason, narrowly missing him. I laughed to think that Pat may have been trying to get her revenge from the other world. Some things we shall never know for certain…

Another young couple, just married, arrived. Each time I engaged a tenant I would ask them to sign a formal agreement, which was drawn up by a solicitor. Having accepted them as suitable, my stipulation this time, as well as the hall and the usual landing-cleaning clause, was that the agreement must terminate if she became pregnant. Ironically it wasn't her, but me, who conceived. We could manage with a first child, now 6 years old, in the middle room and the baby in with us in the very large front bedroom. This was fine for a long time but eventually my tenant fell for a baby. They'd been saving up and had already decided to buy their own house. The contracts were not signed and I was asked if I could wait until their house was ready before terminating the agreement. We got on so well that I was happy to agree. She went into labour before their house was ready and her husband was beside himself. Frantic with excitement and fear, not knowing what to do next, he was blaming himself for her being in pain. He couldn't make up his mind whether to call a taxi or pack her suitcase first and he dropped things everywhere, constantly complaining "oh dear, oh dear!" I'd never seen such a performance.

Eventually the baby was born in hospital and they returned to the flat for two weeks. Now he was at a loss. How could he pacify a baby that wouldn't stop crying? He was worried that they hadn't yet got the keys for the new house, and his condition was exacerbated by lack of sleep. Once in a desperate moment, holding the baby at arm's length, he said. "If it was a cat I'd throw it out of the window!"

I cannot remember how Annie came into my life. She was a widow when she moved in, and out of respect my children called her 'Auntie Annie'. She was 55, a warm and loving human being who soon became part of the family. She would take great care of baby Hazel, cradling her gently as she showed her the 'pretty flowers' and 'dicky birds' in the garden. While she was talking sweet nothings to the youngest member of the family I got on with washing nappies and making meals for all of us.

The Smell On The Landing

Annie was quite eccentric. I sometimes wondered what made her tick. She was what would be called 'laid back' in today's parlance, as nothing seemed to worry her. She had taken to life at *No 32* so completely that she felt safe and relaxed in our company. In the evenings we'd gather in the front room round a coal fire, she and I both with our knitting, but she always seemed to be undoing what she had done the night before. Sometimes she completely forgot what she was making.

Her husband, daughter and grandchild lived further along the same street, and made it quite clear to her that she was not welcome in their home. Sometimes this became very awkward when she was repeatedly snubbed. A particular problem was the time she devoted to preparing for the day. Dressing and washing seemed to take forever, although she prided herself on how quickly she could wash her naturally curly hair, saying it only needed a shampoo and towel dry to bounce back to shape. When she emerged from the bathroom there was often an odd look to her clothing, and I would realise that her jumper was on upside down!

Small wonder she'd had problems with her family – and they with her. They'd announce they were going out for the day in the car, but not wait for her to be ready. While she was completing her endless ablutions and dressing rituals, they'd hurry through breakfast, jump into the car and go without her. As she became an integral part of our family, we thought it only natural to invite her out with us. But having been disappointed on so many occasions by her own kith and kin, she'd reserve her seat in the car and be sitting waiting in it ages before the appointed time. Her cardigan would almost certainly be inside out from her haste not to miss an outing she invariably enjoyed.

Annie was one of the kindest and most generous people I have ever met, and her great misfortune was to meet a man who married her for the cash in her bank. I never got to meet him – he was too cunning to risk anyone seeing him for what he was – and poor Annie was like a lamb to the slaughter. He took her to Ireland, where he soon spent all that she had and then abandoned her. It was too much for such a trusting person who saw no evil in anyone, and I'm sure her death shortly after was from a broken heart. She was a great loss from our household, especially at meal times when we'd remember her fondness for lettuce leaves sprinkled with suger, and very over-ripe bananas.

Kitty and Paul came to live with us through cricket. Paul and Jack both played for St Sepulchre's Cricket Club. When matches were on Kitty and I would sit watching and chatting about life. She happened to say that she and Paul needed accommodation and I offered part of our house. Kitty moved in first until she and Paul were married, and to begin with were both out during the day, as they both worked Then Paul broke his leg and Kitty, being the kind and loving girl she was, volunteered to get Paul to his place of work in St James by sitting him on her bike and pushing him. She walked all the way to Church's Shoe Factory and back pushing the bike every day for six weeks until his plaster came off. I marvelled at her staying power, as Paul was a 'bonny' man and no lightweight.

He loved cooking and tried his hand at pastry-making, with limited success. I was summoned to help one day and found that he'd managed to cement the pastry to the board when rolling it out and wanted to know how to remove it. How we laughed at his antics in the kitchen, especially his attempts to get the flattened pastry over the apple pie dish. It was lovely sharing with such pleasant people, and I was really sorry when they moved out to a home of their own.

Another couple, whose names I forget, came to us when they were just married and sex-mad. The girl was also very

The Smell On The Landing

keen on housework, which suited me, and cleaned all day until everything shone. She often spent so much time polishing she forgot to prepare a meal for her husband on his return from work. Waiting for the food to cook was the occasion for some noisy sex, and on Sundays their enthusiastic cries of "yes," "yes," from the attic bedroom would echo through the house. It was as well they were only short-term tenants.

Sheila came to the house in answer to another of my advertisements. She had fallen out with her mother and was thinking of marrying her boy-friend Alan in the near future, so the upstairs flat was occupied once more. In due course the couple got married and I took Josephine and Hazel along to the wedding in the church on the corner of Edinburgh Road. Sheila was radiant, having got her man against his parents' disapproval.

From the beginning she was very open and easy to talk to, and although she hadn't acknowledged that we'd met before it didn't bother me. She was delighted at my choice of colour when arranging for redecoration of the attic bedroom prior to her arrival. It was a pale lavender shade, and I'd bought a lovely lilac and white counterpane to match the wallpaper. She was quite artistic and so much appreciated my efforts that she used to say she felt like a princess, waking up each morning to such a beautiful room. Her pleasure in it made me feel good too.

Alan was called up and went off to Vietnam. Before his departure Jack had asked him if he'd mind him taking his wife a cup of tea in the mornings. Both she and Jack needed to make an early start for work, and it would also be a kind of alarm call. Alan could see the sense of this and was quick to agree, so it became part of the house routine in Alan's absence.

Sheila loved cooking and laundry, so a succession of monumental lemon meringue pies proceeded from the basic gas-oven in her quarters. Her washing, done in a large pan on the same stove, was more accident-prone. One day she forgot it altogether and it boiled over, quickly forming a damp patch on the ceiling of the room below. I dashed up to find the room full of steam, the floor awash and no sign of Sheila. Another *Smell On The Landing* to cope with!

It all passed off without rancour, though the ceiling and floorboards took a while to dry out. Sheila eventually confessed that she'd been the talkative half of the duo who had previously come to enquire about accommodation, and she was the one I took to. Her rather secretive companion had been about to marry an American soldier without knowing his surname! So it all worked out well. I ended up with the more agreeable girl, and Jack and I grew enormously fond of her and Alan. Our long and continuing friendship has been a great joy to me.

With the best will in the world, one's judgment cannot always be relied upon in the business of letting rooms. One couple who presented themselves as prospective tenants were dressed up to the minute in fashion. Looking so well groomed suggested that they would treat the place decently, so I welcomed them to the house. Appearances were deceptive, however. When they moved out I could hardly believe what I found. They'd managed to cover just about everything in grease. Walls, stove, floor, the lot. Everything felt too dirty to touch, but it had to be thoroughly cleaned before I could re-let, and I had to use a screwdriver to get the grease off the walls. It would be nice to think that this was my only error, but that would not be strictly true.

Simon was a teacher and a diabetic. He lived with us on a full board basis and had a penchant for tripe which to his delight I cooked regularly for him. In general, though, he chose to eat all the wrong food for his condition and neglected to have his insulin injections at the correct time, resulting in him frequently becoming 'hypo.' As he ran the school football team and played himself he was fond of drying his wet clothes on top of the storage heater in his room, despite a large notice saying DO NOT COVER. I can't think of him without remembering the unmistakeable smell of wet washing steaming.

He asked if I would undertake to wash the team kit after each match, but I was too busy with other things to shoulder such a large task and refused. Simon got round this by waiting until I'd gone to bed and then pushing numerous jumpers, often caked with mud, into my washing machine. These would then be dried piece by piece on the long-suffering storage heater. If a match was imminent and they weren't dry, he would try to speed the process by steaming them under the iron.

Resting in bed one night I realised I could hear running water. I popped on a dressing-gown and went down to the kitchen, thinking there must be a leak. Imagine my surprise to find the kitchen had turned into something resembling a pantomime laundry, with the whole team's football kit in various stages of processing. I lost my temper and gave him notice to quit, which he did the next day. As he still owed rent I had the foresight to confiscate his typewriter, saying I would hold it until he paid the arrears. He never returned, and I've since puzzled how he came by it. Was it school property, or lent by a friend? Did its loss pose difficulties in explaining away? Whatever the answer, I made great use of that typewriter over the years, and the embryonic life-form of this book sprang from its keys.

One day I noticed that a "mature lady" was advertising for accommodation in the local newspaper. I liked to keep abreast of the local scene and the advertisement continued to appear until I replied, and there she was on the doorstep. She was delighted to have found the right location at last and handed me two weeks rent in advance. How I blessed her! My money had run out completely, and her deposit was like manna from heaven.

We got to know each other pretty well. Sadly she had a grandson who suffered from cystic fibrosis. When I met him he was quite aware that his days were numbered, despite his gandmother's coaxing him to live. We all felt his death at only fifteen, but his grandmother seemed comfortable with us until a falling-out one day. Soon after that she moved away to live with her daughter.

Rosalie came – a student who wanted only a bed-sitter. That was all she could afford, as I found out when a Bank employee called to see me about her overdrawn acount and other matters. She didn't stay long after the Bank had apprised me of her circumstances. It was best for her to move and try to overcome her money worries.

In that busines it would not have done to take on just anyone for the sake of their rent. You have to imagine the person trying to make an impresssion on you actually living in your house, sometimes in fact eating with your family. One such couple turned up one day, a truly weird pair. The man was small, hardly more than 5ft in height. Skinny with it, characterless and with an insecure air about him, he wore a black plastic macintosh tied with a contrasting belt and dirty brown shoes. She must have stood more than 6ft, very thin, in a long old-fashioned brown coat down to her ankles topped with a cloche hat over straggly hair. An extra-long cigarette – probably one of those then advertised to last a full fifteen minutes – drew attention to her deathly pale complexion and staring eyes. They got as far as the attic, where her head almost touched the ceiling, when she looked down at him. "Alright, ain't it Fred?"

The Smell On The Landing

to which he replied "yea, yea," or words to that effect. That was enough for me. I got them downstairs and ushered them out of the house in short order.

I was approached by an Irish Catholic lady who wanted to rent the kitchen upstairs for only two hours a day – an odd request to say the least. It seemed that she worked split shifts and needed somewhere away from work to relax in her time off. I agreed she could do this, and on Christmas Day I met her on the landing. She had brought a pot-roast with her for lunch, and the enticing smell drifted from the open door behind her as she wished me 'happy birthday.' Momentarily puzzled, I suddenly realised she meant Christ's birthday, so I answered her in the same vein. Later that day, of all days, a plumbing problem developed. If a tap was turned on a loud banging sounded. An air-lock was causing the water tank to move on its housing above the bathroom. It was a potentially serious situation, so I asked my part-time tenant if she could avoid using any water for the time being. The request must have offended her because she left abruptly, without saying goodbye, and I never saw her again.

One early evening, a harassed-looking social worker arrived on my doorstep. Could I possibly accommodate two students? They were due to attend a course on Leather at the University College and she was becoming desperate to find somewhere for them to stay. Upon my telling her I'd be glad to help, she almost fell on her knees with gratitude.

My two black students – a new departure for me – turned out to be really nice. One was the son of an African chief from Ghana, the other his manservant! They were extraordinarily clean and tidy, with the quaintest etiquette. If I wished to speak to the 'Revered One' his manservant would ask that I be granted an interview. I would then be allowed to enter the room and address him. Everything was subject to this ritual.

When Jack saw our new tenants he was not happy. Had the social worker asked him to take them in he would have invoked a colour bar and refused. Inevitably we had words about this letting, but I was adamant that all men are equal, and had no qualms about later accepting another black man. My new tenant, from a humble village in primitive Africa, was more of a challenge. Used to bathing only in the river, he found our bathroom a very complex place. I had to go back to basics and explain the concept of separate hot and cold taps with an ON and OFF facility and provide him with a towel and flannel. He thought the flannel was for drying himself! As to the gas stove, it flummoxed him completely. He would turn on the gas but not light it, so that I was on the constant alert for the smell of escaping gas. Thankfully he didn't stay long and returned to Africa, where perhaps he suffered the occasional bad dream about the strange and noisy ways of the western world.

My neighbours also were not happy with black tenants living in their 'upper class' area, and Jack's views didn't mellow over the years, though my children grew up accepting that people of all colours fell into two two categories. They were either nice and to be accepted as friends, or they were not and best avoided. My husband got a great shock one day. One of the children had invited a friend to stay the night and Jack, essentially a hospitable man, took the friend a cup of tea first thing in the morning. He was not at all prepared for the sight of her ebony skin contrasting starkly with the white sheets and the incident did nothing to change his views which were as radically racist as Enoch Powell's. I'm glad my children did not share them, and as a result have had many rewarding friendships with people of other or mixed races.

Another couple absorbed into our household were teachers, she of music. I was glad to let her use my piano to to practise and I did enjoy their cheerful presence until they took jobs in the Nottingham area and moved away. I went to visit them soon after the birth of their first baby, and a few years later moved to Germany, having then two children to take with them. We've kept in touch over the years, and I understand their children are now talented adults. As with many of my ex-tenants we enjoy each other's news, particularly at Christmas when many round-robin letters drop through my letter-box and make me feel part of that larger world beyond the family circle.

Taking people at their face value, as I usually had to, was fraught with risk. On one occasion I asked myself seriously whether I had been accommodating "the enemy." But *which* enemy? The war with Germany was over and the Cold War with Russian Communism had begun. So what were these German people actually doing in my house? She was very personable, with good English, and I had no reserve about taking her in. Then who should turn up to collect her for trips in his car but a 'sugar-daddy,' also German. Nothing wrong with that, you might think. But when out of politeness I asked where their travels had taken them, it always seened to be in the vicinity of an airfield or military installation. Was my imagination running away with me? Then I found some electrical components dropped on the stairs up to the attic bedroom – an ideal place for radio transmissions? Could they be spies? My finding the electrical bits was apparently the spur for them to move on, but I'd like to have known…

Another rental was to a pair of pensioners, who had the large front bedroom. She was in poor health, her husband her carer. They opted for full board, and I frequently had to enter their room to serve meals, etc. On these occasions she would clutch her handbag to her chest. The opening of the door triggered the reaction, as though she had something of great value. Whatever it was, she certainly didn't trust me near it and was generally hard to please, complaining regularly of this and that.

Her husband decided to take her to Devon, ignoring her doctor's advice that she was not fit to travel and would never survive the journey. I felt obliged to add my voice to the protest, but he was adamant. On the day, we had to carry her out on a chair as she couldn't walk, or so it appeared. Was her husband trying to rid himself of her continual carping? Did she live to tell the tale? I can only guess, as we neither saw nor heard from them again.

I was asked by a local entrepeneur if I would accommodate him and his partner for a few days, which I did. They were an odd couple, she much younger than he was. With his demeanour I found it difficult to believe the man was as successful as the image he liked to project. I asked what they would like for breakfast and was told – eggs in vinegar to alleviate the effects of his drinking bout the night before! Whilst with me they had an enormous row one night just before bedtime. The next morning I took the usual egg in vinegar into the breakfast room only to find that as a result of their quarrel the wife had been banned from the bedroom. I found her curled up on the kitchen mat, having spent the night without any sort of pillow or top cover. Other people's lives are so interesting they can make one's own appear dull by comparison, though I certainly didn't envy the life this woman had with her entrepeneur.

Sophia was my clerk during my ATS days, and she'd settled in the neighbourhood with her husband. When I heard she had suffered a nervous breakdown I volunteered to nurse her back to health. Since she would only eat milk puddings, feeding her was something of a challenge. I tried to encourage more variety in her diet, but she didn't care for my cooking and after only two weeks declared she wanted to go home and almost ran out of my house. What had I done? Was she cured? Later they visited me regularly for a game of cards, but her stay was never mentioned. Eventually they moved up North, I can't remember in what circumstances, but I did hear later that they'd both died up there.

Old acquaintances continued to turn up, and none was more welcome than my dearest friend of childhood days, with whom I recalled many happy hours in the Girl's Life Brigade. Rose now lived in Rothwell together with her husband and daughter. They were only a bus ride away, making it very easy to renew our friendship. It was arranged that their married daughter and her husband, looking for work in Northampton, should stay with me in the meanwhile. Both young people were members of the Church and she became a lay preacher or Sister of The Church, much to my admiration. They've since had children of their own, and I hear that those children have now left home and made their way in the world.

José, my neighbour and dear friend developed cancer and needed care while undergoing radiology treatment. I nursed her over one Christmas when her husband and their two boys, respectively six and four at the time, moved in too. It was a worrying time for all concerned, though she was responding to treatment and at the end of the two-month course felt well enough to leave. She sent me a lovely 'thank-you' letter, which I still have, and we remained friends for the next fifty years. Alas, her cancer was only dormant, and returned, so both her family and mine were bereaved. We loved her very much.

I seem to have spent much of my adult life looking after people in various ways, often in the closing stages of their lives. For a short time I nursed Jack's parents. He had cancer of the testicles and she was simply frail. Both died in St Edmunds Hospital and were buried together in Kingsthorpe Cemetery. I thought it odd that his grave was worried for a long time by rabbits, since he must have shot many hundreds in his career as a gamekeeper, and even stranger that during his committal service a light- bulb burst, sounding just like the report from a gun. Maybe I'm just fanciful, but it was a fitting tribute anyway.

After 39 colourful tenants, I had a growing family of six children, and in 1965 I decided that alterations to the Victorian property were overdue. The outside toilet had to come in, the icy scullery had to go, and behind it the space occupied wastefully by the passage would be incorporated into plans for the new kitchen. Now that we had the whole house to ourselves (but lacking the income its tenants had brought) we moved upstairs while the £3,000 worth of aleration went ahead. The money was found by extending the mortgage (which took more courage than I'd imagined) and at times we had to put up with brief periods of being without running water and electricity but the result made it all worthwhile.

It was much warmer, for one thing. Also I had a serving hatch in the new kitchen from which I could keep an eye on the children playing in the newly enlarged front room. They seemed more secure without having to share their home with others. While they slept soundly, I often lay awake wondering how we should manage to pay the increased mortgage on a reduced income, but somehow, when I was shaking out an empty purse, help arrived. It might be a bag of apples, sticks of rhubarb, a basinful of gooseberries. Occasionally birthday money was donated to the kitty, and we got by. We had our groceries delivered by Turners, the local shop. Our budget was flexible enough to allow for my owing the value of one week's goods. Bad times, when a fortnight's provisions were owed for, were accompanied by sleepless nights. How many people can escape the influence of their upbringing in such matters?

The Smell On The Landing

CHAPTER FIVE

Two doors away from our house on the same side of the street lived a family of three boys and a girl. The girl Madelaine was a playmate of my own girls and would often be invited to stay with us for a tea-time meal. Her mother and I would frequently stop and chat in the street, and on this particular day she was most distressed. Her middle son Vernon had been taken to hospital with Mengingitis. She did not stay long to talk but hurried to the hospital to be with him.

The neighbours and I were very anxious for the little lad and kept asking for news, until eventually we heard he was out of danger. He was kept in hospital for many months, and on his return I noticed he was wearing a caliper on one leg. Obviously there must have been complications.The lad became a bit of a pest to other children, sticking out the calipered leg to trip them up among other naughty tricks, so my children avoided him whenever possible.

Some years later I learned something of the family background when his mother and I were having a cup of tea in my house. She gave me to understand that her married life was not just unhappy but violent too. In fact she was leaving home to take on a house-keeper's job for a man outside the town, taking Madelaine with her and leaving two of the boys, 15 and 11, with their father, the eldest boy having left home by now. The night before their mother left she and her husband had an almighty row. Unbeknown to the boys she'd arranged for her household belongings and personal clothing to be moved next day when the family carried on in their daily routine, the boys going off to school and father to work. But today was different. Mother and Madelaine packed their belongings and left for their new life.

The boys came home from school to find their mother gone. The shock affected the middle son Vernon most of all. He was convinced it was all his fault that she'd gone, and blamed himself with such remorse that it affected his whole character. He became a recluse, an agoraphobic and avoided people as far as possible. He would shy away from crowds and queues, or riding on a bus, and wouldn't go anywhere unfamiliar. He took to going for walks alone in the dark and sleeping during the day. Hence he couldn't keep a job. His father failed to understand the cause of his son's problems and continued to badger him to find work. At last Vernon could stand his father's rages no longer and got a job with a furniture removal company, which was bearable as he had only one man to work with.

Later he worked for the Electricity Board, but always walked to and from work so as not to mingle with other passengers on the buses. The job was quite solitary, driving around with a mate repairing the electric signs in the street, and he kept at this into his early twenties. Meanwhile the motherless family had learned to cope. Father cooked wonderful cakes and meals, bedsheets on the line were whiter than white and he worked very hard for those two boys. I extended a welcome to our home, but that didn't work very well. I was invited into their house now and then and became aware of the tension there.

In early summer 1968, I was trying to level some ground prior to seeding a lawn. Jack and I had bought a car, and in putting up a garage at the bottom of the garden had messed up

The Smell On The Landing

the lawn. Raking it over wasn't the answer. It needed something heavy to flatten the soil. Then I heard a thudding noise coming from Vernon's garden, where he was re-laying their lawn and had made a ground flattener which was just what I needed. He brought it along and did the job for me, and after that became quite a regular visitor.

Georgina was almost three years old then and irresistible at that age. Vernon felt quite at ease with her, and would often come and read to her, which certainly helped me to get on with other things. He was there for Ginny's birthday in October, also at Christmas and by now I was getting used to him helping out. I felt that this was therapeutic for him, and as Jack didn't mind him coming into the house that was fine. Christmas dinner that year was much enjoyed with Ian and my eldest daughter Josephine in their house. We had a lovely time until Georgina and Geoffrey, aged 3 and 5, grew very tired and fractious, so I took them home while Jack stayed on enjoying the atmosphere of Xmas.

I put the little ones to bed and sat alone, knowing that Vernon was also by himself. I asked him to join me until the rest of the family came home from the party and another chapter started in our relationship. Although I was 27 years older than he, we realised that this was deeper than just neighbourliness. We had come to mean much more to each other and wanted to be together as much as possible. All went well until he wanted to interfere with the running of the house and how I brought up the children. My way was wrong in his eyes, and we began having endless arguments about such things.

Even so he was still a great help. He loved putting the children to bed, and in later years meeting them out of church in the evenings after Girls Life Brigade so that their journey home was a safe one. Jack considered this a woman's task. In any case he was always very tired from working overtime, and could be found asleep in front of the TV in the back room downstairs. Vernon took over other functions of a husband too. If any of the children came back with tales of upsets at school we'd discuss it together and decide what was to be done.

Jack's isolation came about also because I didn't want to watch sport all the time. We agreed that I would use the front room TV and the radio, so that he didn't have to listen to my music. Consequently after his evening meal Jack would disappear into his domain, leaving Vernon and myself enjoying the classical music we both loved. He became like a surrogate father to the children, bringing us closer all the time.

Eventually Jack came to realise what was happening, and asked me outright if Vernon and I were having sex. I could not lie to him, and when I admitted to it he reeled, as though I had struck him. This was obviously a bitter blow. He'd trusted me, and I'd betrayed him, though to be honest I felt more married to Vernon at this time than to Jack, who was by now having slight strokes.

Perhaps I expected too much of him. In 1965 he'd had a severe stroke at work, which took 14 weeks to recover from while I nursed him at home. After that he was given a more sedentary job but the stroke had sapped his strength. It hurt me that Jack thought I had stopped loving him, which was far from the truth. I loved him in another way; for the long extra hours at work, for his love of the children and his pride in them and for the care he took in his appearance, always looking smart and clean. I admired his will-power in giving up smoking when money was tight, yet when all was said and done we never talked and discussed problems. I always dealt with them alone until Vernon came along.

Vernon had inherited a violent streak from his father and there was always trouble if I didn't take his advice. Heated arguments led to blows. On one occasion he held me hostage in the bathroom, and when I would not give way, punched me hard on the jaw. Twice I was forced to tell him to leave the house and get out of my life. When he was banished I was very lonely, with no adult conversation and only the children, to talk to. After the second time I asked him to come and visit again. He was always repentant following our quarrels, but I felt, and said, that he should get himself a glrl-friend and regard me as a kind of role model as to how to behave in a relationship. It was some 20 years later that he told me about a lady he was attracted to who kept dogs, and I really was very pleased for him. It had taken a long time for this to happen and I hoped he would establish a satisfactory relationship with her.

All this time the children were growing up, each trying to stamp their own individuality on their environment. I particularly remember Hazel as a very sensitive child during her early babyish years, who as she entered puberty showed herself to be very artistic and began to dress in what seemed to me an outrageous collection of clothes, dressing in the late sixties like the flower people with sparkles stuck on her face, and underwear showing, short sleeved cardigans over long-sleeved blouses, which to my conventional tastes seemed wrong. We all went to London on a day out with her dressed like this, but she blended in with others that also had knicker-bocker lace showing below their skirts.

At sixteen Hazel went to Art school in London. It almost broke my heart as I felt I hadn't finished the job of directing and mothering her. This was a college of Art and Design – not quite what we'd expected – where they taught structure of buildings and furniture design. Hazel and her friend Wendy were both accepted so it was natural for them to get accommodation together. Then Wendy left the course and Hazel stayed on, possibly because of a young man named Alan who was also in the class. After a while the two of them decided to get a flat together. They tried to keep it a secret from Jack and myself, until we decided to visit her to give her new accommodation the once-over. Arriving at the address given, we called the lift. When it came a very flushed young man emerged, glanced our way and ran off.

When Hazel let us into the apartment she was doing her best to act normally, though in fact she'd had a culinary disaster. Intending to make us dinner she'd placed a tinned meal in an old fashioned iron oven, without following the instructions to first puncture the tin before heating, The inevitable had happened and chaos greeted us. Remnants of meat pie, gravy and suet were spread over the double bed and bedding, the floor, the ceiling and the walls. The cooker door hung loose, and the inner shelves were buckled. I'd never seen anything like it.

By some miracle Hazel had been a safe distance away when the explosion occured. We looked at each other, said hello, and set to work cleaning and laughing about it for hours, it was so bizarre. No wonder the young man we met at the lift was so flustered, though we didn't actually meet him – Alan – until a long time afterwards. I was not very happy about their relationship, though they lived together 10 years and had bought a house in Kingsthorpe, Northampton, until Hazel realised it was not working. They agreed to part and she settled his part of the mortgage with him, putting herself in debt for some years. Alan departed one springtime amid much rejoicing on our part. We filled the whole house with daffodils in celebration!

Josephine, Hazel, Frances, Zena, Geoffrey and Georgina, were all popular and had many friends. I used to say the house was like Euston station, with all the comings and goings. When boy friends started to call I treated them with great caution and wouldn't let them into the girl's bedrooms, unlike the girls' same-sex friends who were always welcome. Hazel's best friend Roberta lived only a few doors away. We'd known her since a very young child and had photographed her and her sisters playing in my garden in bathing costumes, jumping in and out of a bath of water being sprayed with a hosepipe. Hazel and Roberta continued their deep friendship even when young men appeared upon the scene. One evening Roberta and her friends went out in a car that belonged to a young man enthusiast. Tragically he'd fitted the wrong-sized tyres to the wheels, which at speed came off. The car left the road and poor Roberta was killed. She was only seventeen.

It was a dreadful shock to the neighbourhood. Everyone rallied round. Vernon and I called on houses collecting money for her devastated parents, to help with the funeral expenses. One tragedy soon led to another when her father died too, and the family moved away, though we have maintained contact over the years.

When Ginny started school at the age of 5 I decided to apply for a job as an auxiliary nurse at Harborough Road Hospital, about a quarter-of-an-hour's walk from home. I was accepted and at 1.30pm I walked on to the isolation ward in a pair of black stockings and brown shoes. I had no money for black ones, but although I felt I stood out like a sore thumb, parents and children would address me as Nurse. I was not used to that, and more or less ignored them. Then when I was working with a Staff Nurse, a parent approached us and called to "Staff ". I immediately answered, much to the annoyance of this senior nurse. It was a natural reaction for me, as I had been used to that address as a Staff Sergeant in the ATS. Trying to explain was no use, as the nursing sisters were mostly Irish or Scottish. I couldn't understand their brogue, so had to ask them to repeat orders, especially concerning the patients, which made me look stupid. One sister in particular took great delight in making one feel small. Her physique was as enormous as her rudeness, so that most nurses under her direction feared her entrance on to the ward. One day I had to confront her and must have given a good account of myself because thereafter she treated me with more respect and consideration.

The isolation ward was infested by silver fish, especially in the store room where all the baby food and dried milk was kept. Usually this room needed the light on for reading measurements of quantity for the sick babies. The moment the electric light was switched on, the whole floor seemed to move as the silver fish took cover. At times we got cross infection in the ward even though each patient was isolated in their own room. The nurses were trained in how to avoid taking infection to another patient. Bowls of disinfectant stood outside each room, outer clothing was changed and as a further precaution, patients' soiled dressings were stored for burning. Yet those silver fish got everywhere. Could they have got inside the cartons of dried baby milk that were covered with cellophane? We the nurses always took the blame, but nobody had the answer. I also worried about the anthrax patients, whose outdoor clothing was stored in the room with them, ready for discharge. I felt it should have been destroyed or at least fumigated, as anthrax can live for many years. But as I was told when I raised the point, I was merely a nursing auxiliary…Inevitably there were deaths. It was especially hard when a baby failed to respond to all our efforts, and at the other end of the scale to watch elderly patients succumbing gradually to severe infections, wanting to die, and be unable to help them painlessly into the next world.

Admitted to the isolation ward was a tramp with a severe skin infection all over him. Each day I was given a tube of Cortisone cream to spread gently over his body, naked on the bed. This went on for a week, and when he fell asleep during my treatment I had to wake him up to spread what was left in the tube about his private parts. The Ward Sister got quite worried when his treatment was due, and kept a beady eye upon me, just in case I was attacked. She needn't have worried. My healing hands soothed him to sleep each time and he was the perfect gentleman in that respect (or else he didn't fancy me!)

The wards were very hot to work in, and walking home after duty one winter's day I caught a chill in my kidneys – pyelitis – which ended my work at the Hospital. While on duty there Vernon would call at my parents' house nearby and make them a cup of tea, ensuring that all was well unitil I got back home at 7.30pm. He would then look after the children until Jack got home from working overtime and would spend hours helping them with homework, drawing graphs and answering their questions wherever possible and even help to bath and put them to bed.

Whenever it was possible financially and weather-wise, we took the family on day trips. One such was to Kew Gardens in the car we had managed to buy with money from an injury payment that Jack suffered when moving heavy stock at work. Entrance to Kew gardens then was 3 pence each for adults, and I was looking forward to seeing the lovely green of the lawns contrasted with the gorgeous colours of the flower beds, the great pagoda and the lakes. We set off to enjoy ourselves, but Jack was as miserable as sin. He didn't want to explore with us and sat down gingerly on the slatted park seats, refusing to move. When I lost my temper and tore off a string of abuse, he groaned "My piles are killing me." It seemed he was alright driving, but walking about on a very hot day was too painful. MEN! Why on earth hadn't he told me? We could have got some relief for him, or not gone at all until he was better.

Another time I took the children by myself. Hazel was about 15 years old and a great help, so we loaded a push-chair with food and drink to last the whole day. This time we went to London to get a boat along the Thames to Kew on a beautiful day, happy to watch the scenery and landmarks sliding by. Lunch time came around, we unpacked the food and found that some bread had gone mouldy inside the plastic bags overnight. Some was alright and the children ate that, but Hazel and myself had no choice but to tackle the mouldy ones or go hungry, as I had no money to buy more. Ever after that when mould was mentioned, it brought back the taste of that bread!

Another day's outing was at Armistice time in November. We all went to see the Cenotaph and the wreaths surrounding it after a walk to Horse Guards Parade where we watched the immaculately-uniformed soldiers mounted on lovely horses. The children had wandered a little distance away when I heard a familiar call in Barrack Square style. My sister Joyce had recognised one of the children. Within moments we were in each other's arms, not knowing that both families had decided to visit London that day. Meeting up by accident like this was quite miraclulous, as she lived in Hastings and I in Northampton and rarely visited. A later visit to London took in St Paul's Cathedral, memorable for the 365 stairs we climbed to the very top of the Dome. Exhilarating and a wonderful view, but the effort was a little too much for me and it took me some time to recover. But it was well worth it.

1969 was the year of my parents' Golden Wedding Anniversary. It was decided that they should come to Northampton for this special day, for which preparations began a long time beforehand. Invitations were sent out early, which was just as well, as we found that 14 people would need a bed that night. Others could travel back to their homes after the event at Boughton Green Road.The caterer was booked well in advance to prepare the meal in my kitchen, which meant we'd be spared the chore of washing up after. I felt really good about that bit.

We did it in style. The menu was prepared and printed on cards for the table, with congratulary expressions on the front of the menu cards with a large 50 yrs prominent in gold. This theme was repeated on large gold cardboard bells I'd made myself, to spread around the room. I'd thought of another novelty too. When we were young enough to need correction, father used to talk pointedly about his "little black book" in which all our misdeeds would be recorded. So I ordered the cake to be made in the shape of a book, which caused some merriment.

I felt that those who could not attend and those now deceased should be remembered with their photographs displayed on the wall. We then raised our glasses to them during the ceremony, speeches were made and applauded and many photographs taken of the table and particularly the cake. Later we all assembled in the garden, as the weather was lovely that day (August 16th) The whole thing was a great success, and for rememberance before splitting up we each signed the others menu card.

Ten years later for their Diamond Anniversary we hired the Ballroom of the Moat House Hotel in Northampton, when I'd arranged for a telegram of congratulations to come from Her Majesty the Queen. We had a small orchestra, and I remember being afraid that one of my parents would fall down during the waltz, as mother's balance was affected by Ménières disease and father could not move his feet very well. But he did his best, clutching the Queen's telegram in his hand all the while. He was so proud to think that *she* knew it was their anniversary that day. He thanked me profusely for arranging everything, little knowing that as I had Power of Attorney over his affairs, he had paid for it all! His Altzheimers disease would have been too far advanced for him to understand how I could spend his money.

Shortly after, I realised that my parents' health had deteriorated to such an extent that I felt I must give up my work at a Day Centre for the Blind in order to look after them. So although I've tried to maintain a fairly strict chronological sequence for the events I'm relating, I now need to go back to 1973 when I took a job at one of the Blind homes. Here I was amazed to discover what power the Matron had and how she abused it. At first she seemed easy to get on with, but that was to change. My duties were not just those of a Care Assistant, I soon found out. I was expected to clean and polish, serve at dinner, also bathe the residents, sort out dirty washing, scub it clean etc. I was to be a general factotum, or all-rounder, apart from waiting on Matron. The blind people were even worse off under the Matron's control. I did what I could to protect them, but had to watch I didn't overstep the mark.

One partially-blind elderly man seemed to get more favours than the others. Why, I asked myself? Months later I found he had quite a large bank balance, and Matron wanted it. She eventually managed to get him to change his Will in her favour, and having done that he used to take advantage of the other residents while she still favoured him with treats. Her deceit became clear when he told me in confidence that Matron took him to the solicitors to sign his money over to her. Another resident had stashed away about £100 in his wardrobe. He had told another Care Assistant it was for his friend who took him out. This resident took ill and died, and the Care Assistant whom he'd told about the money took it to Matron, with his instructions as to where it was to go. The money disappeared, and Matron accused one of the young volunteers of stealing it, which was flatly denied by the young lad, who stopped giving his services and left extremely upset at her accusations.

The travelling salesmen would call for orders, particularly cleaning materials and replacements for the Home. A great fiddle went on about the orders. Matron was considered a good customer to them. If she over-stocked, a gift would arrive from the firm, such as a lovely pouffe or stool, sheets and lace covers for chairs etc., which went into her own home. Also I can remember looking at her car laden down with a heavy load of coke and coal delivered for central heating for the home, going for her own use. To balance this deficit, the heating was restricted in the Home and the residents would get cold. She'd tell them the system had broken down, so that the theft was not noticed. Meal times were a disgrace. The residents would have a meal of sub-standard quality, sausages, mince topped up with extras that the cook herself provided, ie herbs etc, while the good meat, steaks and joints were sold out to other homes, as extra to requirements, or eaten by Matron and her family.

On cleaning, we the staff had to provide our own rubber gloves. The toilets as you can imagine were always a mess, because blind people, especially men, could not aim straight, and we were told the allowance for cleaning was used up, so we the staff must buy our own. I also had soiled knickers and pants to clean, as the elderly blind could not see what state their underwear was in. They were allowed clean underwear only once a week. This was disgusting to me, so I wrote independently to the Executive Committee of the Home, stating that my job was unhealthy and unhygienic without the protection of rubber gloves, and asking why were they not provided.. At the next Committee Meeting which Matron attended, my letter was read out. Matron immediately vomited and had a fainting fit. I knew she could vomit at will when in a tight spot, but the Committee did not. She was excused the Meeting and sent home unwell, to rest. I was furious, but we got our gloves.

From then on she hounded me, and when she couldn't find an excuse to get rid of me, she decided to upset the residents, one of whom we (the family) had befriended. We would call for Bill on a Sunday afternoon and take him out to visit open spaces and country houses and homes. We also took him to the theatre, which he enjoyed very much until Matron put a restriction order on him to return to the Home before any performance was finished. The doors would be locked, she told me, and I must put him up for the night. Bill also had made friends with one of the women residents, who became very ill with cancer and was dying in a room of the Home. Bill asked to be allowed to visit her before she died but was refused. How could she do this to him? I marched into her office and accused her of many wrongs, some of which I have written about here. We shouted at each other, she banged her hand in temper on her desk and I did likewise and so it went on, first her, then me. The staff on duty at the time had gathered outside the office to listen, until I emerged. I then learnt about other matters such as not banking the residents' money. She used to collect the pensions from the Post Office, and was instructed to bank some, but the amounts didn't appear on their books. When relatives did have a word with Matron about the discrepancy, she would say "Poor dears, they often make up stories like this when they get old." So nothing was done. Often the staff were asked to change her bed, which was unpleasant for various reasons. We shouldn't have had to do it.

One day the Committee informed me that they knew what was going on and that soon the residents would go into Council Residential Homes as they were closing the Day Centre for the Blind and would be using it instead as a training and rehabilitation centre. Until then a lady detective had been sent in as overseer.

One of the residents in the blind Home – let's call him Albert

– was a small man with crippled feet who had to walk leaning on a stick. Totally blind, he could nevertheless find his way along a path in the park to await someone on the pavement of the adjoining busy road to ask him if he needed to cross. A good samaritan would often cross the road to buy him cigarettes or sweets with his pocket money.   Unfortunately some school boys had noticed him, asked if he needed help, and when given the money simply ran off with it. He waited… and waited…in vain. Poor, trusting Albert.

When he was taken ill and admitted to Northampton General Hospital, as it was policy for the staff to visit residents in their own time, I entered the ward and came upon a strange scene. Other visitors were obviously very embarrassed, judging from the barely suppressed sniggering that could be heard. Albert's bed was in a very prominent position, placed at the end of the room opposite the door I'd come in by. What all patients and visitors could see quite clearly was Albert sitting on the chair beside his bed, his pyjama trousers gaping open, amusing himself by gently fondling his genitals and totally unaware of the minor sensation he was causing. There was only one thing to do. In my best parade-ground voice I shouted "Put that away Albert..NOW!" He reacted promptly and my visit continued as though nothing untoward had happened. The under-Matron always seemed very concerned about Bill, and asked me to take extra care of him when we took him out on Sunday afternoons in the car to visit parks and houses open to the public. As we walked around these estates I would describe for him the shape and colour of the buildings. Inside, the guides were very helpful.   Sometimes he was allowed to run his fingers over the beautiful furniture and artefacts, especially if it was too complicated for me to describe. Bill had gone blind in later life through diabetes, so could recall the colours and shapes of many things. The guides allowed him to touch objects inside the guide ropes at times, and for me it was a joy to be allowed so close to these acknowledged treasures. When in the grounds of the estates, Bill loved to walk faster than when tapping his way with a white stick. Sometimes we would even skip and run on a straight path, linking arms, and we had great fun, until news came that the Blind Home was to close for residents.

Bill was approached by the under-Matron, who suggested that he went to live with her. He saw this as a better alternative than going into accommodation where the blind and partially-sighted mixed with sighted people, which would mean constantly falling over furniture which would no longer have its designated and remembered place. So Bill decided to marry her. When I asked him if he was happy about this he replied that it was the best thing for him to do.

We all went to the wedding but sadly Bill died eight months later. At least he was spared the ordeal of the other blind residents on entering their new homes. Not knowing where the toilet or anything else was, they fell over chairs, walking sticks and other unaccustomed obstacles. When I visited them they told me how miserable they were, because the sighted residents got annoyed having to guide them about, and perhaps this simply heightened an awareness of their own disability, for which there was no cure. Within about 6 months most of them had died. It was very tragic, but perhaps death was better than the deep despair of their hostile new environment.

I applied for another job. Matron had warned me that I would not have a reference fom her. This didn't matter, as I had a good one from the Hospital as an auxiliary Nurse, so when St David's Day Centre opened I became a Care Assistant there. The Unit Manager and myself sorted out the kitchen a week before any clients came, then Kitchen Hands and other Care Assistants arrived. The purpose of the Centre was to offer respite care to clients who suffered all manner of complaints, which we learnt to cope with, although I felt those with advanced Dementia should have gone into the Day Care of Princess Marina Hospital as they often wandered off into a neighbourhood unknown to them, and got lost. We could not lock all the doors to keep them in, so we frequently had to search for them in the nearby streets. Some were so "out of it" when we caught up with them that they struggled to escape from people they saw as hostile strangers. Our Unit Manager decided that his staff would represent all classes, so that they could relate to whoever came for Day Care. Some Assistants had great people skills and others none, not even the concept of tender loving care, so the staff were not happy with one another.

Somehow I was ostracised, accused of something unrevealed to me. Was it because the Unit Manager would call me into his office to discuss a certain matter, or ask me how to spell a word that he wasn't sure about? I shall never know.. It was my job to look after those in need of some kind of nursing (diabetics and leg ulcers were most common} I also did chiropody for those who couldn't reach their feet, cut fingernails and bathed and showered them as required. I was also asked to look after the plants for decoration and sale and the Craft work, which I enjoyed and which brought me into regular contact with the Manager.

One lady of about 70 came in the same dress every time, which needed washing very badly. We asked her husband if she had a change of clothes so that we could wash the dress for her. He was most uncooperative, so we contrived to spill something over her at meal times, much to the annoyance of her husband whose general cleanliness left much to be desired. This same lady took a fancy to one of our other clients, and he to her. We found them together in the ladies toilet with her hair down and all gooey-eyed as he was embracing her. Whoops! we got there just in time.

The blind clients that came made some wonderful cane trays and stools, so dexterous without sight it was wonderful to watch. The newly-blind could not cope so well and needed more help, but were able to make bobbles around a cardboard frame, which were used by the ladies who had knitted some poodle dogs for sale.

Most of our clients needed help in the toilet, especially the wheelchair-bound. Those new to a walking-frame had to be taught how to walk with it. The placing and distance from the body was most important. At first they couldn't manage it. They tended to carry it in front of them, putting them off-balance when they moved, so it was a matter of coaxing and practice until it became natural and could be accomplished without conscious thought.

The knitting that was encouraged was helpful to those with arthritis in their hands, even if we did have to re-knit their work after they'd left to make it perfect for next time they attended. This made them so proud of it that one lady wanted to take her knitting home. When I explained why we liked to keep it and tried gently to retrieve it, she tightened her grip and began stabbing me with the points of the steel needles. It was quite scary at the time.

When I re-dressed wounds and ulcers on legs for those who were in need of a clean bandage, some were so grateful they would try to press money into my palm. It was policy to hand such monies into the office, to be shared equally among the staff, but I generally refused the offer. However, a Mr and Mrs Mann were so impressed with my attention to their needs that when they died I found they had mentioned me in their will. I duly received their gift of money through their solicitor.

Another lady, who said she couldn't get her shoes on, shuffled about on her heels in slippers. After some weeks of gradually gaining her confidence I was able to see what the problem was. Her toenails were so long they had rounded about her feet, sidewards, causing intense pain. I cut her toenails, and the next time I saw her she came skipping in in her shoes, free from pain and quite delighted. It became a dream of mine to go peripetetic, just doing simple chiropody for the elderly, but fate had other plans for me...

Daisy was more intelligent than her appearance suggested. She was about 65 yrs old, with the body of a girl of 14 yrs. Her legs were like two clothes props, not much flesh upon them or on her arms. She walked painfully with the aid of a walking frame, was usually docile in character and just sat on her own staring into space. As she was incontinent, others didn't want to be associated with her. Walking to the toilet she left a trail of urine on the floor, the Care Assistants would find her and replace any wet underwear, pad her up, and guide her back to her seat. She appeared to have no interests, so as we passed her we would call out "Are you alright, Daisy" rather than ignore her. She would answer YES. This routine was repeated, time after time, by each carer, until one day she'd had enough. In a squeaky voice, she took the rise out of us all. "Are you alright Daisy? Are you alright?"she mimiced. "I'm sick of it. Is that all you can say to me?"

We were dumbfounded. How else could we address her and show that she was not ignored? It was soon back to the old routine "Are you alright Daisy?", when she'd answer "YES" or not, according to her mood. I used to attend to her feet, for which she was grateful, but getting her to the loo before her weak bladder leaked was another matter. Always conscious of it, all too often she would cry "too late again."

When a client was unable to attend and sit in her usual place, those who had befriended them became very upset at their absence. Death was never far away from this group of elderly people, and when it came the Care staff had to cope with weeping friends. Most of our clients liked to be addressed by their Christian names, which they preferred, and they appreciated little things that others take for granted. The majority lived alone, and to be offered a cup of tea they hadn't had to make themselves was a real treat. At dinner time we had to ensure that the diabetics didn't get a sweet pudding. For them it was biscuits and cheese instead. We also had to see that people who needed tablets before or after a meal got them. All in all there was a lot to think about by the staff.

We visited a lady in Oxford who was recovering from a nasty accident. Striking a match in her home had set off a gas explosion that left her with extensive severe burns to her hands, face and arms. Her hands were in plastic sheeting and she was in a critical condition for many weeks. She was popular at the day centre and returned to a rapturous welcome, though it was some time before she could make anything for the yearly sale, despite her efforts. This annual event always went very well, with the money left after expenses going into a fund for clients outings. It was a very well run and organised Centre and I loved the job, if not the unwelcoming daily reception from the staff which I dreaded. But I would have stayed on if my parents hadn't needed me more.

While working there I managed to save a few pounds and felt that life was a bit easier, so I booked two chalets at Bacton-on-Sea and took grandchildren, daughters and son Geoffrey for a holiday with friends Florrie and Stanley. It was the year of glorious sunshine and happiness, 1976. We had self-catering, taking it in turns to carry out certain duties. Stanley had contributed teamaking equipment for the beach in the back of his car, which was driven as near as possible to where we sat and the children played. I bought a large kite that had two strings to pull, one that could perform aerobatics. Geoffrey became adept with it and more than once frightened the life out of Florrie, making the kite dip until it nearly hit her before soaring up to the heights again. All went well, and this was one holiday I returned from feeling fully refreshed. I was soon to need all the strength I could muster…

CHAPTER SIX

The failure of my parents' health happened gradually. Sister Joyce and I both lived approximately 100 miles from the family home in opposite directions, she on the South Coast and me in the Midlands, and from 1974 we took turns to visit the homestead fortnightly. Mother was suffering from Ménière's Disease, which affected her sense of balance. She couldn't go shopping without rolling around like a drunken person and sometimes she dare not cross a road as she found it impossible to walk a straight line.

Her illness progressed so that she suffered bouts of noises in her ears, sometimes so severe that she would bang her head against the wall in an attempt to gain some relief. From my parents' point of view my going to visit once a week was hopelessly inadequate. From my own point of view it was difficult to make the trip so frequently. Both Joyce and I took with us cooked food and supplies for the following days. We worked hard during these trips, returning home in need of a rest only to have to catch up with the tasks we had not carried out because of our absences from husbands and children. Joyce then needed surgery to her arthritic hands and knee, which meant she was unable to make the journey at all. One weekend my husband refused to look after the children on his own, and the financial strain of frequent train fares was taking its toll on the family budget so I had to lessen the frequency of my visits. All this and the deterioration in my father's mental health directly increased my level of worry.

My daughters were now old enough to make the trip independently but found their grandfather in a sad state. He could not remember what day it was, or even recognise which grandchild was visiting. My mother was giving father his medication at the wrong time, or at the wrong intervals. They had both lost a lot of weight and my mother, still trying to carry out such mundane tasks as hanging out washing, or visiting the local shop, fell over alarmingly often. Their doctor became concerned and called in the Social Services. The neighbours reported that the daughters "don't care what happens to them and hardly ever come to see them," and so it was decided without any reference to Joyce, Ken or myself that our parents would be separated and put into homes. The old couple didn't want to be apart, but were ill equipped to fight the system.

We three had a conference over the telephone, and it was decided that I would invite mother and father to my house on the pretext of a holiday, as we all acknowledged that father would never willingly consent to leave home permanently. So commenced their temporary stay.

Their clothes and bodies needed great care after years of neglect, and their home was filthy. The decision to keep them in Northampton was not made lightly. My husband disliked his in-laws, and resented the time I spent looking after them, so although our family home was spacious enough it would have been a disaster to have us all permanently under the same roof. The obvious answer was to sell their property in Hornchurch on the outskirts of London, buy an easy-to-heat, well maintained property close to my home, and install them there for the foreseeable future. The main problem now confronting Joyce and I was how to sell their home. My parents had insufficient funds to finance a new house purchase without arranging for the sale of the old one, so Joyce came up to Northampton and went house-hunting while I looked after the old folks, doing my best to reverse the circumstances which had left mother weighing only 6 stone.

Father had also lost weight, and it was heartening to see his Alzheimer's stabilise as he picked up in health. Unfortunately, his improvement meant he seemed to know more about what was going on around him, and after a time he announced that as his wife was now so much better they would go home. Part of me regretted his return to fitness as arguments followed. He got so angry one day after dinner that he lashed out at me, catching me with a fist to the jaw that really hurt. To aggravate matters, the rift with husband Jack, who couldn't wait to have his house to himself again, was becoming serious, so Joyce and I put our heads together to think of a way we could get father to sign the papers for the sale of the London house. All this felt horribly dishonest but I had to tell myself it was for a good cause. It took two days to get his signature on the conveyancing documents, by trickery. As soon as the sale became a certainty, my sister went to London and packed up the house. It took her a week to do alone, while I was trying to pacify father who was now truculent enough to say he would go home without his wife if necessary. I wasn't sure if he was capable of trying to carry out his threat so a strict watch had to be kept. The doctors in Northampton were a great help regarding his state of mind and supported me in a bid to get Power of Attorney.

Getting him to sign the papers to put this into operation was essential as Joyce had now found a house at 40A High St. Kingsthorpe, just three or four minutes walk from Boughton Green Rd. After much cajoling and some deceit he eventually signed. Within a few weeks their furniture was brought from the store in Kettering, Vernon and I spent days washing everything that came into the property and arranging the furniture, and at last my parents were installed. Our efforts were rewarded, as father didn't seem to notice that he was not

The Smell On The Landing

in his own house. It was only if he went outside into the street that he became disorientated.

I called in daily to make sure all was well until one day I found mother slumped in a chair in great pain. The doctor diagnosed a strangulated hernia requiring urgent attention. I immediately arranged for her to go to St Matthew' s Hospital as a private patient, where Dr Cronin, who turned out to be a former medical school colleague of brother Ken's from way back, operated successfully. The surgeon was delighted to receive news of his old friend, and carried mother in his arms from the operating theatre back to her bed – an honour, I suspect, not given to many of his patients. When she recovered and had gained a little weight Joyce and I decided to send them both to a Bournemouth nursing home for convalescence. The rooms were booked, and Hazel and myself took them by car to the south coast, where we made sure all was well before leaving them.

Two days later I got a 'phone call from an angry Matron, who said they must be collected as they were not "settling down". In fact they were a nuisance, and she refused to keep them any longer, so Hazel and I made the journey again to find out what was wrong. Mother complained that tea-making was not the home's speciality. They were not allowed to have a pot of tea straight after dinner, only at allotted times. Their routine was apparently sacrosanct, so mother had made a nuisance of herself. Father was convinced that the TV didn't work. He'd forgotten that it was possible to operate the set by remote control, and when reminded, found the handset impossible to comprehend. Then they said the beach was too far away to walk to. I'd told them to call for a taxi, to avoid having to cross a busy road, but father's inability to spend money got in the way of my advice. Soon after our return I had a bill for the whole two weeks which I paid out of father's account. He'd have had a fit if he'd known!

I continued to visit my parents in their Northampton home on a daily basis. I did their shopping and mine, did their cleaning and mine, made their beds and mine. I tended both gardens and continued with my part-time job, as thankfully mother was able to continue with cooking, which gave her a sense of satisfaction. I'd been looking around for a smaller house because with only two teenaged children remaining at home it seemed sensible to move to somewhere which would be easier to maintain and cheaper to heat. The one I decided on at 62 North Western Avenue seemed very suitable, although it took me slightly longer to walk to see my parents each day.

It soon became obvious that more time was needed with them. Father was getting worse, trying to leave the house, insisting that he had a meeting to go to. His diminishing co-ordination also meant that he dropped much of his meal on to his clothes. Mother's Ménière's disease continued to be a problem. Despite my efforts they were not always taking their respective tablets at the right time. It was obvious I had to be in attendance at lunchtimes as the old couple refused to eat their main meal at any other time of day. Eventually I had to give up my own work to spend all day with them. Father had continually to be restrained from leaving the house as he was liable to wander the streets, unable to remember his current address and not knowing where he was. He was also very prone to falling down.

I took them both for a walk every afternoon; quite an achievement for a woman of my small stature. Father would repeat endlessly "where are we going?", "what time is it?" or "what day is it?" No amount of answering could satisfy his curiosity. Despite having eaten a cracking meal, he would accuse me of not giving him any dinner. The pressure of spending all day in their company was building up alarmingly.

When I returned home in the evenings to seek respite, I certainly didn't get it. Nothing was done in the house, as Jack felt it wasn't his concern to do anything domestic. He expected the children to take my place – to cook and clean and run about after him. They were doing O and A-levels at the time with a lot of homework and didn't share his views on their potential as his servants. More rows, more upset. It was impossible for me to meet everyone's needs.

Mother then began to complain that she couldn't sleep. She said father was up in the night, still anxious that he was missing his imagined meeting. He would be totally disruptive, coming downstairs looking for his clothes, falling over and not being able to get up. The house was in uproar. It now occurred to me that I should also sleep at their house. My life had taken a nasty turn. The waves of animosity from my family were probably justified, but sometimes a problem is so consuming it's impossible to see a way out. I thought of the elderly couple lying on the floor at night, unable to get up, and worried about them suffering from hypothermia in their light nightclothes, possibly undiscovered for hours. During the night father was now trying to go out into the street, completely naked, still determined to attend that pressing meeting. I didn't feel I had any option but to move in.

I put two beds in the lounge and slept down there with him, determined that my mother would be able to get some sleep upstairs. I barricaded his bed with chairs, but he'd lost none of his determination and climbed over them, only to fall over again. No-one was getting any sleep. The doctor came next day, only to find father clean, well-fed, sitting quietly in his chair. He was unimpressed by what I told him and assessed father as a "nice type of man," obviously well looked after and not in need of help. Never mind that only seconds after he'd gone, father couldn't remember that the doctor had been. I phoned the Social Services and drew a blank. Nobody wanted to know what a mess I was in, and things were about to get a lot worse.

Only those who've struggled to look after two self-willed, ailing parents can imagine the day-to-day problems besetting their carers. For most of the time I kept a diary, which when I read it again makes me wonder how I kept going so long. Here are some extracts, taken at random, for the years 1979/80:

June 22nd   Dinners not good. Father intolerant about tough meat (two turkey drumsticks cooked twice) Given to the dog.

June 26th   Alistair arrives. Father doesn't recognise his grandson. Very sad. I call at Police Station to see if anyone has handed in the missing £100 in case father took it out with him that day. No luck. Then he produces from somewhere the money to replace the saucepan mother burnt dry!

July 23rd   Safe door is stuck. I call in key expert to open it. Father's legs are locked and useless – too long on his knees wrestling with safe door. We get him up somehow, then I find he's put £40 into the organ. I take £20 of it to the bank, hoping he won't notice. TV still changing from colour to black and white. More knob-fiddling by father, who can't understand.

July 24th   Caught him urinating in milk-bottle, tipping it down kitchen sink and rinsing out. Why? Then he goes into the garden and does it in the drain. He's only four steps from the downstairs toilet! I want to tell him, but what's the point if he doesn't take it in? When I give them their weekly bath, mother comes willingly. Not father. "I had one yesterday," he insists. I have to con him to get him out of his dirty clothes into fresh ones. No wonder I've got that rash again. "Stress," says the doctor, but what does he do about it? Nothing, while I'm still on my feet.

July 26th   Mother burns out saucepan again. Gas too high, not enough liquid, as before. Nurse arrives to syringe her ears and discuss a walking aid.

August 4th Mother's 86th birthday. Josephine takes them to her house for the celebrations. She has made the traditional cake with candles, only to have mother tell her that she never before had a cake with candles to blow out. Is her memory failing too? Vernon and I stay behind at 40A to clear up the rubbish in the garden, erect a trellis and generally get some peace. Josephine and Ian have laid the new carpet in the dining area ready for the expected visitors on August 16th, their 60th Wedding Anniversary.

We take them to Holmer Green to visit mother's sister-in-law known as Billy, 91 and extremely deaf, in a home for the elderly. Mother thrilled, very tear-jerking re-union though conversation limited to pen-and-paper messages. Picnic on way home.

August 7th Home help cannot come today. Local paper *Chronicle and Echo* ring to say they'll be here on 15th to take Anniversary photos. Josephine has arranged for a telegram from HM the Queen to be sent. My nervous rash worsens. Am so glad when Hazel takes me to Bath for a break while Joyce takes over my duties at 40A.

August 14th Find plenty to do on my return. Cut father's hair, trim his moustache ready for photographer tomorrow. Also wash mother's hair, scrub out sun-lounge, replace plants, go into town to buy net curtains for front door and side windows.

August 15th Photographer arrives early. Neither parent ready. Can't be helped. Hazel helps me change bed ready for Ken and **Elaine** (real name Elsie, but we've been instructed to use her new name from now on) Tom and Edie, parents' oldest friends, can't make it here due to ill health. Such a pity. They'd gone on holiday together and visited for so many years.

August 16th   Anniversary Day. I'd hired space at the Saxon Hotel with catering for 18 people and a small orchestra to play light music. Somehow mother and father dance the last waltz together, but seem overwhelmed by it all, especially with Joyce and her family arriving from Hastings. Father comes to thank me but doesn't offer anything towards cost. He doesn't know the £288 bill was paid from his account, but a gesture would have been nice. Ken and Elaine return to Peterborough, Joyce and family to Hastings.

August 21st   All over now. Everyone gone home. Father reverts to being disorientated. "What day is it?…where's the Post Office?…the shops?…my pipe?…my dinner?"   "You had dinner an hour ago, father."   "No I didn't. I know I didn't."   So it goes on. A few minutes later he'd start all over again, until I could scream. The really strange thing is, when the doctor comes he's LUCID. How can that be? When the doctor's gone, father says to me. "Who was that? What did he want?" It's incredibly wearing.

August 23rd   Father wakes mother in the night and insists someone else is in bed with them. He requests that she shake hands with them! In the morning he makes the bed, most unusual. Is he looking for the intruder? Mother very annoyed relating this to me. "I even put the light on to prove no-one was here," she says at breakfast. She needs undisturbed rest at night and rarely gets it. Advertise for home help.

August 25th   Mother cuts her hand between thumb and forefinger. Bleeds a lot, but won't let me look at it. Sue comes in answer to my advert. Good references. She agrees to clean 32 Boughton Green Rd on Mondays, 40A High St on Tuesdays. Makes a good start bleaching all white surfaces.

August 30th   Mother has burnt her arms on the oven again. Dress them with Savlon and Melonin pads. Cut hand improving, but teeth a problem. I call in a peripatetic dentist. Meantime provide her with a snug protector and she eats an enormous dinner at mine at the weekend. Alistair calls to see them. This time father recognises him. "You're Joyce's son," he says. Hooray!

September 10th   Discover that while I was out, Porch salesman has called against my specific instructions and told father what the porch will cost (£825.00) Father nearly has a fit. Says he doesn't want it, and if he had it the rent would go up! I'm the one who goes up. I was so cross I phoned the company to complain and cancelled the order. They wouldn't, saying the agreement had been signed and was binding. Contacted our solicitor, who was looking for a chance to get his own back on this particular firm. Said he'd be delighted to take up the case, no charge to me. One more thing I don't have to worry about. But the business of the porch has brought on another of mother's trembling bouts. She wants me to say Ken is paying for it, to stop father going on and on, so I tell her I'll put it through her account next time.

September 22nd   Joyce is here to take our parents to stay with her in Hastings for two weeks. What a relief it will be to me. I await news of their arrival, then at 9pm Joyce phones to say they broke down in Tunbridge Wells and had to wait for another car. Father very disorientated, can't think how he got there.

September 25th   I have a letter from Durolitum Lodge, requesting £20.00 for father's demit. I comply and tell them he's not well and won't be able to attend Lodge meetings again. Considering his long service to Freemasonry and the money he's helped raise over the years I would have expected something more than this curt demand for £20.00.

October 14th   Father is worried about his property, but for the wrong reasons. He keeps asking about uncle Stan. Is he still collecting rents from his houses? I lie again and tell him all's well. Uncle Stan died several years ago, and as to the property, father has been as close about that as with all money matters. We had no idea until he moved here and we saw the papers that he'd sold his houses to a rogue he'd trusted, having read the contract price of £20,000.00 each as *£2,000.00*. His trusted "friend" had resold them at a huge profit, and when I consulted our solicitor he said it was too late to do anything about it. Some inheritance!

October 29th   It's getting very cold in the house. I alter the thermostat setting, which unfortunately father notices me doing. In my absence he has a go himself, so when I come in next day I find an atmosphere like a Kew gardens hothouse.

November 28th   TV licence due, £25.00. It goes up to £34.00 in two days, but I'm too ill with 'flu to go and get it so will have to pay new price when I'm better.

December 8th   Central heating breaks down. Fowkes man comes at 3pm, does job, mother pays out of housekeeping to avoid a row, though father has £70.00 in his wallet, and although he's paid nothing, still expects a receipt.

January 3rd 1980   In bed with 'flu again. I seem to be susceptible to anything going around. Skin rash very itchy, so I warn mother not to come too close until it clears.

January 6th   High winds and the cold have affected mother's ears badly. Can't sleep well and father still walking about at night.

January 13th Am finding it increasingly hard to write this diary. Life at times seems almost impossible. Jack cannot grasp my predicament and the conflict of loyalties I endure every day. He gets so frustrated with our situation he's confessed to having to fight an impulse to push mother down the stairs and finish her off when he stands behind her on the landing. I tell him later we should move to a smaller property. 32 is too big for our present needs and is costing too much to maintain. He doesn't agree, but I have to do it so I look around and find a smaller, three bedroomed house in North Western Avenue. Meantime things at 40A are going from bad to worse, father still prowling around at night and falling down. I move in downstairs for the nighttime vigil, but father defeats my every move. There'll be no peace for anyone until we can remove him to another place. Mother's nerves are on edge. She drops a casserole that was for dinner, all over the floor. From now on, she says, she'll cook no more. More trouble. "Little Thing," the cat, is not well. I take her to the vet, who has to put her down. Then Ronka the dog gets knocked over by a car that splits his leg open. Back to the vet, carrying the heavy dog. Where will it all end? Georgina, left behind at our home with grumpy daddy, can't face it any more. She runs away. When the doctor at last sends a specialist to assess father's condition, I tell him the true situation. Trying to cope with my parents has put another nail in the coffin of my marriage, our teenage daughter can no longer bear to live at home, and I cannot carry on. Once I start to cry, all the frustrations I'm enduring come pouring out.

Faced with my nervous breakdown in full flood, the specialist has said he would place father in a mental hospital. Two men in white coats came to take him away but I could not escape a feeling of guilt. Mother was not happy about it, but I took her to visit him twice a week until it became a ritual and seemed part of normal life. Joyce by now had recovered well from her operations and came to Northampton to relieve me for two weeks at a time. How I welcomed that help! I could get up when I wanted, go on holiday or just sleep, sleep, sleep. That was what I needed most.

Then mother started being troublesome at night. She refused to go to bed until long after I was ready. She would say "you die in bed," and seemed intent on delaying bedtime for as long as possible. Once in bed, she needed turning during the night as she said she couldn't lie on the ear affected by Ménières disease. Just as I would be dropping off again, there'd be a crash and I'd find her on the floor. She couldn't get to the toilet without falling, so I then had to listen to try to anticipate her getting out of bed. The weeks wore on, with me getting more and more stressed and fed up with being spoken to worse than a slave. She began hallucinating, and on the first occasion when I heard her shouting, she told me she could see naked Japanese men jumping about on the bed. I didn't treat it seriously and commented "you lucky woman," but she was in no mood to joke. The bedclothes were in disarray from her thrashing legs. I decided to go along with her. "Come along gentlemen," I said in my command voice, "it's time to leave." I held out my arms like a policeman directing traffic and followed the imaginary offenders out on to the landing, where I instructed them to shut the door behind them. Perhaps I was going mad too. Mother was quiet as I took her to the toilet and tidied the bedclothes. She settled for the rest of the night.

Another time she awoke me to insist she was being poked by a horde of children, wincing and ouching convincingly the while. Again I shared the delusion and spoke sternly to the chidren to go home. In mother's mind they had gone too and she slept. Not for the first time I wondered how much was play-acting and attention-getting and how much genuine mental unbalance. Father with his Altzheimer's I could at least divert and persuade.

Mother was already proving a far tougher proposition, and she had a few more weapons in her armoury that I was soon to be made aware of.

Meanwhile Jack, alone in an empty house now that he'd retired, and without the means to amuse himself, sank further into depression that developed into a nervous breakdown. Of course, I had to take some of the blame. Having earlier decided that my parents needed me more than my husband and children at that stage of their lives, I now had to live with the fall-out. It was a bitter pill, but perhaps I wasn't put on this earth simply to have an easy time! Jack, when he'd pulled himself together after the breakdown, may have thought he was helping by calling in on me daily at 40A. True, he learned to cook, which I appreciated, and took mother in her wheelchair when she could no longer be trusted to walk on her own. But he'd never got on with her, and the many rows became quite wearying. Mother had decided that she was in charge. She chose the TV programmes she wanted to watch and ignored anyone else's wishes. Brought up as I was to respect my parents, I gave way until it suddenly struck me that it wasn't just herself she was pleasing. It was me she was *displeasing,* which appeared to give her satisfaction. The worm turned at last, and I asserted my right to choose the programmes I particularly wanted to watch from time to time. In retaliation she thought up all sorts of ways to ensure my compliance with her wishes. Her legs were not comfortable under the bedclothes. I bought a clothes support. Then she was too cold. When extra blankets were put on, they were too heavy. Her feet needed attention, her bra was too tight. She wanted ear drops, nose drops, suffered from sore throats and aching joints. When the doctor came, all she wanted to do was kiss him, making matters between myself and the doctor rather strained. Then came the "going without so as not to be a nuisance." Her ploys were endlessly cunning.

When I went back to see how things were in my own home, the state of it was horrifying. Jack obviously couldn't cope. I found a warden-controlled flat nearby which seemed to meet his requirements and sold the house – just in time, perhaps as his health was deteriorating and arthritis had set in. He still came to see me every day to 'help out,' but imagined he had some kind of right to lay down the law in the house, and made a grinding task all the more difficult.

Three and a half years after father had gone into mental care he died. One day soon after the funeral all the accumulated stress caught up with me again. I collapsed with what was diagnosed as a psychosomatic illness. The community nurses came to look after mother and the doctor suggested she should go into respite care for a fortnight to give me a rest. She reluctantly agreed, so I stitched name-tags into all her clothes and took her to view the prospective home. I warned the staff of her walking difficulties, even with a Zimmer frame, and left her there with a huge sense of relief. Two weeks without responsibility for her would be as near to Heaven as I could expect.

It wasn't long before I had a call from the home. She'd had a nasty fall, so I went over to see how she was. I found her in tears, bruised and shaken up. No-one had helped her to dress or wash. Without support for her breasts or stomach she was uncomfortable, and she hadn't been able to put on her stockings. When she'd asked for help she'd been told that the home's policy was for old people to do as much as possible themselves. I didn't know to what extent she was responsible for her own difficulties but she was quite capable of using the situation to her advantage. I set my heart against taking her back with me and went home alone.

My peace was short-lived. There was a phone call from the home. Mother had fallen again. Later another call told me she was in hospital from a second fall that had brought on vaginal bleeding. When I got there I found she was bruised all over. This was just too much. How could the staff have let it happen? I took mother away and lodged an official complaint, which caused much ado and investigation by officials. If I had expected gratitude from my mother for rescuing her from a place she hated, I had much to learn. Mistrust and hostility towards me simply oozed from her. Whenever the subject cropped up she'd point an accusing finger. "You did it," she'd say. "You put me in there." It was pointless to offer my own side of it. She knew exactly how to play on my guilt complex.

It took months to resume anything like "normal" relations. Jack continued to visit and help where he could, until a stroke left him with movement in his arms and legs impaired. With help from the warden and care from the community nurses he made a good recovery, but by now mother was suffering from what the doctor said were small strokes which took longer to get over each time. On several occasions I sent for Joyce, thinking the end was near. Between us we pulled mother round. I was glad of Joyce's help because Jack could no longer do jobs about the house. One Christmas morning walking to see me he'd fallen and broken his wrist which never set properly and made it hard for him to do even basic things like cutting up his food. Mother capped it all one morning early when she accused me of neglecting her by leaving her in bed. Such was the adrenalin rush accompanying her anger that she did what I'd thought was impossible. She got herself out of bed unaided, only to collapse on the floor and injure herself to the extent of requiring two months of hospital treatment.

Until I noticed an article in the local paper about "carers," a new word to me that was coined to describe people in my situation, I'd thought I was alone. On telephoning the contact number given I learned that a meeting of carers was to be held in Kingsley at the local church rooms. The idea was for those with the burden of care to meet regularly to discuss their respective problems. The first meeting was most helpful and led to others. For me it was a marvellous way to keep in touch with other carers, and in the course of time I talked myself into being co-opted on to the committee of the Northampton branch of the Carers National Association. As in any organisation, people are always willing to let somebody else do the real work, and since the group urgently needed a Chairperson to direct their affairs, the choice fell upon me. Along with my good friend Nuala Fitzgerald who was Treasurer, we ran the Carers group with a dedicated committee of five or six others for some 15 years. The Treasurer and myself served on many a committee to bring our cause to the notice of GPs, the NHS, Social Workers, the National Association for the Blind, homes for the elderly and many charities whose members may have needed support in caring. Each year in June we ran an information stand in the Grosvenor Shopping Centre, which also gave us an opportunity to rattle our fund-raising tins. Following the death of my mother in 1993 we were out and about most days proclaiming the aims of the Carers National Association. I have answered many calls from the general public, spoken on Northampton Radio, and in 1988, when mother was 95, I appeared with her on Independent Television.

To round off this part of our family saga I should mention that during a later Carers Conference I was presented to Princess Anne, and was able to speak about the problems that children have when caring for their parents and other relatives or siblings. She seemed very interested in what I had to say, and I felt that she was well aware of and sympathetic to the problems of carers in today's society.

The Shaws. Mother and father with Geoffrey
and the five girls.

Geoffrey (1972)

Zena at school

Georgina with Keeshond (Ronka)

Josephine, modelling, 1964-5

Frances in school uniform

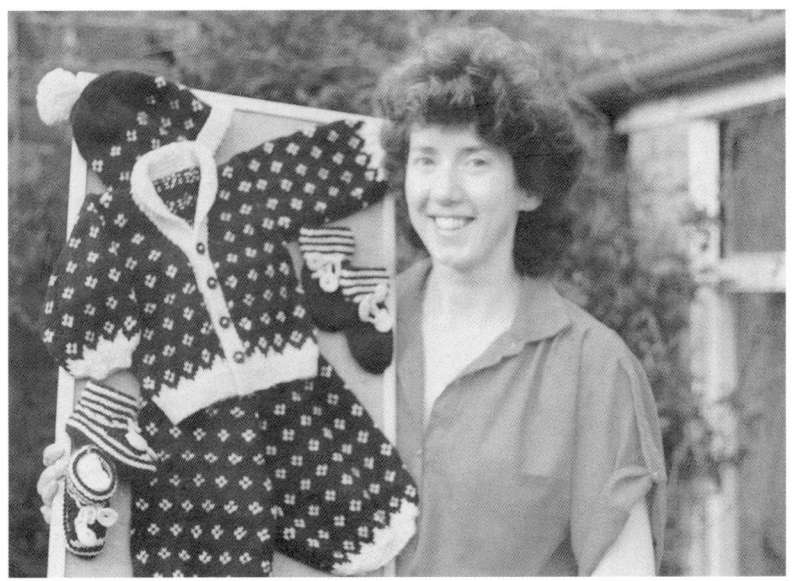

Hazel with one of her creations

Graduation Day, Carnegie Hall.
Frances and Gladys

Bride Josephine and groom Ian

Josephine with father at her wedding

Bridesmaids (from top) Hazel, Frances, Zena, Donna and Georgina, with pageboy Geoffrey

Another view

CHAPTER SEVEN

As my family of young girls moved towards becoming young women it was inevitable that they would attract the opposite sex. This was a period of my life that I found hard to handle. Exactly how is a mother supposed to act towards strangers calling for her daughters? While wishing to protect them from a broken heart, or harm from the wrong sort of young man, I was aware that my assessment of their suitors did not always coincide with theirs. The correct balancing of the scales is very hard to achieve when the codes of conduct laid down for my sister and I in the 1930s and 40s were so very different from those that my children find acceptable among their contemporaries. Yes, we had the heartache of believing puppy love to be the real thing, and I had to cope with several unwanted sexual advances, but with the prevalent moral laxity I feared for my daughters. True, there was sex education in schools, which is more than we had, but is that enough?

I well remember as a child my mother's feeble attempt to warn me of the dangers posed by men. "You wouldn't allow a man to put his finger in your eye, would you?" she said to me one day.

Without the least idea what she meant by it I pretended to be grown-up and replied "Of course not."

"Well, then," she said in a very meaning tone. "*Of course you wouldn't.*"

Some years later I guessed that this was her way of trying to explain the mystery of sex. At about sixteen a young man brought me home, and in kissing me goodnight pressed his body against mine. When I told mother that he seemed to have a bottle of beer in his pocket and couldn't understand why he wanted to press it against me, she could have taken the opportunity to elaborate. Instead she made no comment. For my part, I was relieved. At least he hadn't put his finger in my eye, so there was nothing to worry about. The thought reassured me.

I could hear myself saying to the children. "There have been enough babies in this house. Please don't bring any more. You're on your own if you get pregnant." I was frightened and worried as my own resources had been used up in raising this family of six children. It had been years devoted to babies and their care, and I had cried for three weeks when I knew my youngest was on the way.

I felt I just could not cope with the aftermath of their mistakes. So imagine the shock when it was brought to my notice that one of the girls was "indulging." I might have expected that Jack would share my concern and point out to this young man the possible consequences of their actions and that the practice must stop. But his philosophy could be summed up as "anything for a quiet life," and he did nothing. I turned to Vernon and we discussed what to do, but it was me who visited the boy's parents to put my view. Another visitor to our house was a male student nearing 20 years old, who had taken a fancy to another daughter. He was unkempt and demanding, helping himself to food and my cigarettes without asking. I was pleased when he disappeared from the scene, taking his bodily smell with him.

Why is it that teenagers like to sprawl about on the floor? Maybe the advent of central heating and wall-to-carpeting has made it more comfortable than in my day. Now the older members of the family (mums and dads especially) are obliged to step over them – no easy task for Jack after he'd suffered a slight stroke that impaired his balance and left him with a weakened bladder. His pacifist nature stopped him from complaining, but sometimes I showed my annoyance when visitors couldn't be bothered to move aside for him. Some of the young men struck me as suitable for potential sons-in-law. I could have welcomed them more, but dared not allow myself to get too fond until it became clear that they intended to stay. Josephine, then aged around 19 to 20 was becoming serious with her boyfriend Ian and wanted to show off her cooking skills. Having made out a menu she asked if she could entertain him alone in her bed-sitting room which we agreed to. The first thing she asked me to do was to make a table decoration including a candle for the small dining table. On the day of the event she went into town to buy some prawns and other ingredients, while I took the flowers into her room.

Come lunchtime, Josephine returned from town quite agitated. No fresh prawns. The menu would need to be changed. She had a quick bite to eat and was off to town again in search of something different for 'starters'. While she was away I laid a coal fire in the grate so that it would only need a match put to it. Josephine returned with ingredients for the evening meal and left again, late as usual, to have her hair done. 1 looked at the food she'd brought in and realised that some of it needed to be prepared before the meal, so lit the downstairs oven and got on with it. Later I lit the fire in her room to warm the place up.

Josephine returned, beautifully coiffeured, and went up to her room . The moment she opened the door she was met with a haze of smoke and sooty cobwebs that festooned the walls, ceiling and furniture. Unbeknown to us, the chimney was blocked. We learned later that when a previous tenant had tried to sweep it, the brush had come adrift and was stuck., causing a blockage. They hadn't realised that the chimney flue veered sharply to the left part-way up, and had to be accessed from a grating near the ceiling for cleaning.

Panic stations. What a mess! The hot coals were transferred to the grate downstairs, the whole room had to be spring-cleaned and time was of the essence. Fortunately the bed had been folded up, and a cloth covered it. We worked really hard to clean throughout until all was shining and presentable again, after which Josephine took her usual leisurely bath and I returned to the kitchen to finish cooking the meal, knowing that she wouldn't have time now to do it herself. When Ian came, looking somewhat strained I thought, he was ushered upstairs to the accompaniment of much giggling from the younger children. The loving pair were left alone for a few minutes, I served the meal, and the children, each carrying a dish like a line of waiters, trooped up the stairs to the couple seated at their candle-lit table and warmed by the heat of the electric fire.

Next morning, dirty plates and a half-eaten meal were strewn about the floor. Ian had been suffering from a stomach bug and only wanted to be sick and lie down, so he'd left early. Josephine had tried to eat after he'd gone, and then had managed to put her foot in the leftovers by her bed. And the polished table had acquired a scorch-mark where the unattended candle of the table decoration had burnt down. In more than one way it was a day to remember.

Ian and Josephine were married the next year, and as I write this have enjoyed over 30 years of happy togetherness. As eager as Josephine had been to show how well she could cook, it is Ian I consider now to be Head Cook of their household. He is very adept in the kitchen and his contribution makes all the difference, especially at party time. As they both work full-time, he often has their meals either prepared or ready if he arrives home first. I rate theirs as a very successful partnership.

Hazel, the second eldest, was short of money following the purchase of her first house. To begin with she shared the house with Alan, whom I've mentioned earlier, but the relationship didn't work out and it became obvious to everyone that they had to part. With mortgage rates at an all-time high of 15% she needed a second job if she was to keep the house. Jack, while proof-reading at work, happened to notice an advertisement due to appear in the paper the following day for bar staff at a pub in a nearby village. He rang Hazel, who applied and was taken on, subsequently working three or four evenings per week and thoroughly enjoying it. In due course she met Ray Gammage, a self-employed builder, and they began going out together. History repeated itself when she asked me to do the flower arrangements for a meal to entertain Ray and his family.

As a builder, Ray was always on the lookout for properties to convert and improve, and had spotted a redundant chapel in a local hamlet. A bidding battle then ensued with a determined would-be purchaser which Ray eventually won. From then on most weekends were taken up with work on the chapel in which Hazel soon became involved along with Ray's father George. It took five and a half years of spare-time work to strip the place back to three walls, add an extension, create an upper floor and make a home that could be admired by all who saw it. Hazel's earlier experience of building construction at college and a flair for design was a key factor, and her various office jobs had enabled her to keep accounts, do tax returns and be an active partner in their business.

Frances and Zena, my next two daughters, shared a flat in their teens. I would visit occasionally, and on one occasion noticed that the pet goldfish were swimming frantically to keep up with the flow from a very aggressive oxygenating pump. When I pointed this out and the flow was adjusted I couldn't help thinking that this was how these two children were leading their lives – at top speed with little time to rest and reflect. Here they were, burning the candle at both ends, trying to work, study and entertain at a frantic pace with frequent quarrels over boy-friends or clothing. How long could they keep it up? In fact they stayed in Kingsthorpe Hollow until Frances found someone she wanted to marry, and Zena decided that she, too, should enter the housing market. She took out a mortgage on a small house in Kingsthorpe and began to entertain freely, both girl and boy-friends. All appeared well until, on a day in 1982, she let herself into the house (each of the children had a key to the family home) and came upstairs to where I'd retired feeling unwell. What she'd come to show me was a photograph which I quickly realised was an image of an ultra-sound scan. She was pregnant. How on earth would she manage with a mortgage, living apart from the father of the baby and having to work to support themselves? At a family conference we all agreed to do whatever we could to help. The father had undertaken to pay maintenance until the child was 16 (he soon disappeared from the scene)

One January morning in 1983 my telephone rang in the early hours. Zena's waters had broken. Luckily I'd passed my driving test in my sixtieth year, so I dressed quickly and went out, to be met with torrential rain that soaked me before I'd got the car out of the garage. Having picked up my daughter we were soon on our way to the maternity hospital and I was reminded of another January day, when Zena herself was born. I was in great pain during that taxi ride through slushy snow, and the driver who was something of a comic commented "if it's a girl you ought to call her Thora." I didn't appreciate the joke at the time.

Zena was taken into the labour ward and I was left outside with an anxious expectant father who restlessly paced the length of the room. I was relieved when a nurse appeared and he followed her, but there was no news of Zena. Daylight broke, and I could wait no longer. I had to get back to my parents, dress them and prepare breakfast. Later that morning there was reassurance from the hospital. Zena had given birth to a lovely little girl and had given her my middle name Laura, which was also my paternal grandmother's name. It gave me a wonderful feeling of family continuity. Zena found evening work as a waitress in the town centre, when Jack and I shared baby-sitting duties. To ensure that she could continue to work, several family members including the child's great grandmother paid for Laura to go to a private school that had a crèche after hours from where she could be picked up as necessary. Laura went on to attend Northampton School for Girls where she was a popular and talented pupil. Meantime Zena met Vincent who moved in with her. Their first son, named Jack after his grandfather, was followed by Harry in their new, larger house. We shall meet them again a little later.

My only son Geoffrey was blessed with an outgoing personality that made friends easily, though I was not aware of any special romantic attachment until the girls told me of Michaela, with whom he was setting up home. On meeting her I had to agree with their enthusiastic approval. She had a very lively personality and modern outlook, and there was something about her that made our age difference immaterial as we found it so easy to communicate. She and Geoffrey set about modernising the house they'd bought in Semilong. Out went the old kitchen, in came the latest fitted model. They revamped the bathroom and generally gave the house a 'cared-for' feel. Soon they decided to sell the house and buy a more modern one nearby.

I loved visiting the house in Brixworth where Geoffrey and Kala, as she liked to be known, co-habited for six years. Her domesticity and decorating skills were a joy to behold, and we were all made very welcome. Geoffrey loved cars, and spent most of his spare time tinkering with them in the garage so he was always in a mess, as was the garage. This caused friction between the pair, since Geoffrey was a procrastinator, always putting off necessary jobs about the house. Kala was a 'doer,' and the gloss was fading on their domestic bliss.

One day Kala was devastated to hear that her father, with whom she was very close, had died suddenly from a heart attack. Estranged from her mother (her parents had long since parted company) the shock affected her attitude to Geoffrey, whose apparent indifference to household chores now infuriated her. She began to give him ultimatums and then, as these failed to produce an improvement, told him to leave. She'd intended it as a further threat to make him conform, but he saw it as a final statement. In despair he went to his eldest sister for advice and comfort, taking his belongings with him.

This brought home to Kala that she'd gone too far, beyond her intention. There seemed no way out and she began drinking, which only made her depression worse. To Jack and I she had become a surrogate daughter, and I was called upon to help if I could. When I entered the house, I found her vomiting, reeking with drink and fully dressed, lying in an empty bath. After some hours of trying to reassure her I got her to the hospital, where they kept her in for tests. Her mother, having learned of her condition, called to take her away with her. Michaela said she preferred to convalesce in our home, and mother went off in a huff. Her daughter responded gradually to my care and we remained the best of friends. But her relationship with Geoffrey was over. The house was sold and they went their separate ways.

When Geoffrey had got over the worst, I began to notice changes in him. From being careless about his appearance he developed a dress sense, buying smart clothes and knowing how to carry them off. His attitude to work improved too, all of which I attributed to Michaela's lasting influence on him. One day, alone in a hotel reception lounge, he was approached by a girl who thought she'd met him when they were at Sheffield University, though he looked so much smarter than the lad she'd known. They struck up a friendship and in due course I was introduced to Clare, a slim girl almost as tall as he, who seemed very agreeable. As the romance continued, it looked as though Geoffrey had at last found the right partner, but if I was hoping for an early commitment my hopes were not to be realised...

Josephine and Ian were married at the church of St John the Baptist in Kingsthorpe on 7th December 1968. While it wasn't a 'shotgun' wedding, the preparations were rather rushed, to say the least. At the end of October Josephine turned up at the house and announced casually "we're having a white wedding in December, mum. There'll be five bridesmaids and a page-boy, all dressed in royal blue velvet."

Before I could open my mouth to register amazement she went on. "As we're short of money, could you possibly make up the dresses and page-boy suit on your machine in six weeks, please?" There was a moment of silence as I digested this new shock. "All right," I said. "When will I have the material?"

"Right away." With that, off they went to the shops, to return with the patterns and material. I was somewhat relieved to find out that the urgency was due to Ian's having been unexpectedly offered the tenancy of a cottage in Hardingstone. As he would be paying rent on it from December it made sense to him that they move in as a married couple, so he popped the question to Josephine, who wasn't at all prepared for it but quickly accepted.

Now began my apprenticeship in sewing velvet, which at first seemed impossible until I learned the dressmaker's trick of using a tissue-paper sandwich between the two sections to be joined, preventing the fabric from moving about on its pile and causing mismatched seams. There was enough material left over to run up muffs for the girls to keep their hands warm. Just as well in the circumstances. Their headdress was to be swansdown which would sit around a bunch of their hair like a halo, tied by matching blue ribbon which would hang down their backs. The page had a white lace jabot at the neck, just under his chin. Luckily I escaped having to make the dress for the bridegroom's mother, Edna, who went to a dressmaker, and Jack's need of a new suit, beyond our budget at the time, was generously met by his eldest daughter and her husband-to-be.

The morning of December 7th dawned clear and bitterly cold, free from snow. With the bridesmaids needing their hair to be piled in a bun on top of their heads, and so much to do before the wedding at midday, Josephine returned from the hairdresser with her hair still wet, and we were simultaneously trying to fasten dresses while forcing sandwiches on the children who wouldn't be eating again until the wedding breakfast at three. When the bridesmaids left for the church I was still not ready. I dashed upstairs to put on my glad rags but found that the tights just wouldn't go over my bottom. Panic! At that moment a call from downstairs told me the taxi was waiting. I had no choice but to dab powder on my shiny nose and leave, the tights still perched uncomfortably on my thighs.

The Smell On The Landing

Josephine arrived at the church with Jack. She looked radiant, having been dressed by 'Aunt Betty' our good neighbour who was a perfectionist. Jack by contrast looked worried and failed to smile for any of the photographs. Was it the reality of giving away his eldest child, or the bitter cold, or simply feeling unwell? He was not a man to volunteer anything about himself or his feelings, and I never did know what preoccupied him that day.

The bridegroom was waiting tensely for his very late bride. Drawn and pale, he went through the ceremony trying to speak through clenched teeth. In contrast the children were relaxed enough to be enjoying themselves thoroughly, although somewhat in awe of the proceedings. Despite the rush to get to the church on time and the groom's nerves, everything went splendidly. I walked back down the aisle on the arm of Ian's father Don, very conscious of the restriction around my legs. The tights had not yet fallen down but I had hours to go yet. Outside in the bitterly cold wind one of Josephine and Ian's friends had thought to bring some shawls to put around the children, and my sister Joyce gave up her fur coat to put around Hazel's shoulders. An amateur who belonged to the local Photographers Club took photographs. He snapped away happily, not realising that his camera was not working properly. For many years we relied on snaps taken by visitors for a record of the occasion, except for one photograph of the bridesmaids and page boy, which was recommended for an award by the Club.

We arrived at the reception very cold and hungry, not helped by the slowness of the Italian waiters. Georgina decided it was time to go to the toilet and lifted her dress so high she exposed her tummy, which caused a laugh. After that she asked to go often down the many steps into an outdoor courtyard at the back of the restaurant. Each time someone had to go with her (she was only three years old) so missing the speeches which were hard to hear anyway as some of the guests were seated so close to the front of the building and the traffic noise that they couldn't catch what was said. They were also cold, as was their meal when it turned up. Fortunately Josephine's cousin Christine could speak Italian, which helped to save the catering situation from becoming quite impossible.

Ian sent the wedding negatives away to a specialist laboratory, hoping some of the images could be rescued. On their return, he promptly forgot about them, as they were both very busy setting up home in their little cottage on the farm. The story of those photographs had an unexpected conclusion. Thirty years later, with three grown-up children, Ian came across the damaged negatives. He sent them away again, hoping that in the intervening years technology would have moved on. It had, and so he arranged for them to be framed as a surprise for their 30th Wedding Anniversary. The restored photographs now adorn the sideboard of their living-room, for all to admire as a memento of the beginning of a long and happy marriage.

Frances and Duncan's wedding took place at the United Reformed Church in Northampton's Abington Avenue, on 2nd August 1981. As they had known each other such a short time, I felt they were rushing into marriage. It was hard for me to understand the attraction and the haste. Were there things I didn't know? She was an impulsive girl, given to snap decisions, and I couldn't help wondering whether she'd fully thought through the consequences of such a major step in her life. I counselled them to wait, and when Duncan came to see me and I was honest about the way I felt. But young people in their situation find waiting irksome, and they chose to go ahead with the wedding without my blessing.

The Smell On The Landing

Frances and Zena had by this time been living away from home for several years in their shared flat, and as such had been free from parental control. Knowing how I felt about the wedding, Frances decided to go to a friend's house to dress for the ceremony. I visited her there before she left for the church. She looked lovely but defiant when we had our photograph taken in the little garden together. Her father was willing to give her away, but I was not ready to part with her. Our difference of opinion caused ill-feeling between myself and Jack and there was a noticeable coldness in the atmosphere for some time. Strangely he never asked the reasons for my not wanting to attend her wedding, but everything passed off well and the couple spent a short honeymoon in Cornwall.

Ray proposed to Hazel in January 1986. They calculated they needed until late summer to finish the chapel conversion at Teeton, and set the date for Saturday 27th September. Georgina and Laura were to be bridesmaids and Josephine's seven-year-old son Nathan would be page-boy. Hazel was encouraged by Ray to have a beautiful dress made by Catherine Davighi, a local designer, and Michaela happily agreed to make the bridesmaids' dresses and page boy outfit. Hazel purchased some pretty apricot-coloured fabric to pass on to Michaela, at which point she was told by Ginny that she would unable to be a bridesmaid as she would be six months pregnant by September. Michaela made a beautiful dress with an embroidered bodice for three year-old Laura and a miniature replica of the groom's suit for Nathan to wear. The surplus bridesmaid fabric was made up into an Austrian Blind. The weather in the days preceding the wedding was awful, but the day itself was ideal – warm and sunny with a slight breeze.

Hazel came to 40A High Street on the big morning to dress. Knowing that she planned to do this, I'd purchased a full length mirror so that she could see herself in her full regalia before leaving for church. At the time I was caring for my mother after father had died, and my good friend and neighbour Dorothy Cork stepped in to carry out my carer's duties while I attended the wedding. She pushed mother down to the village green in her wheelchair, leaving me free to dress myself and help the bride. We were both very aware that one phase of life was ending and another beginning, with the future holding who knew what?

When Hazel reached the church she was greeted in the porch by the vicar and a very patient Nathan and Laura. She stooped to speak to her little page-boy, telling him that she had chosen him especially as she thought he would be wonderful at looking after his younger cousin Laura. He took her words most seriously, and I noticed him holding Laura's hand throughout the ceremony.

It was a great feeling to relax and enjoy the happy day after all the hard work of planning the wedding and getting the converted chapel ready to be lived in. The reception for 122 guests was held at the Derngate Centre in Northampton, where Jack surprised me by producing a hand written speech from his jacket pocket and delivering it well. There was plenty of laughter and a wonderful time was had by all. For the honeymoon Ray had arranged a trip to Venice on the Orient Express. In true dramatic fashion, the tickets did not arrive at the travel agent's office until the last minute, and Ian went to collect them on the day of the wedding on their behalf. When Ray took out the wallet to show the tickets at Victoria station a shower of confetti fell around their feet, prompting more congratulations, by the staff and fellow passengers. The travel agent had thoughtfully told the train operator that they were on honeymoon, so another celebration took place when the guard presented them with a bottle of champagne in their sleeper.

The Smell On The Landing

Andrew their son was born in 1988 and was a great joy to them. It has to be said that Ray was over-protective, not allowing him to sleep round at his cousin's when he was old enough, and generally restricting his freedom unduly. It was not until the lad was about twelve that he was able to go on school outings, and not before time. Hazel fell pregnant again, but this time things went wrong. An ultra-sound scan showed that the baby was not forming properly, and had to be aborted at 18 weeks. Hazel's sisters and myself tried hard to support her during her grief, making sure we attended the Hospital at the time of the abortion. When we had all left the hospital Hazel nursed the foetus, a little girl, for two hours before Holly as I called her was taken to the mortuary to await interment. The service, with the little white coffins laid out in a row at the hospital church, was a very moving time for other mothers whose child was aborted or born dead. We continue to remember Holly each year.   Over the years Ray continued to buy properties for conversion, until his health began to deteriorate. As I write he is teaching the trade to youngsters at college, and Hazel is having to care for an ailing man who is not happy in his work and baulking at the restrictions that hamper the imagination, as everything must be done according to the rules of the Education Authority. It must be very hard on a man so used to being his own boss.

Geoffrey finally married Clare in the same church as his sisters Josephine and Hazel had wed, namely St John the Baptist, Kingsthorpe, on 10th May 1997. It seems extraordinary that this month should have seen another family wedding, three weeks later, when Zena and Vincent Brown, who after years of co-habitation and two grown-up sons, felt the need to tie the knot.

As is the custom, most of the arrangements were made by Clare's family, as was my privilege with my own daughters. It felt odd not to be involved. Their wedding was to be traditional, with-all colours co-ordinated, and I had received advice about what colours not to wear, so that we didn't clash. Hazel and I scoured the shops in Northampton for an outfit that was suitable for me. At 76 1 was anxious not to show any crinkled skin on my arms and neck. We were lucky enough to find a very helpful shop assistant who helped us to pick outfits in the permitted colour range. I settled on a pale yellow costume teamed with navy accessories that I felt happy with, and on the day of the wedding had the luxury of dressing at a leisurely pace – so different from the hectic rush I associated with the giving away of a daughter.

This was my only son, at 34 ready at last to settle down, all fears of unwelcome commitment vanished. I was still living at 40A High St Kingsthorpe with its memories of nursing my mother and father. Geoffrey left from this house for the church, and had made a point throughout of involving me in everything he could. Rushdi, his best man, was a marvel. When they remembered that Geoffrey's wedding shoes had been hidden in the boot of the car to keep them from the attention of pranksters, it was Rushdi who dashed off in the nick of time to retrieve them.

During the wedding ceremony I was very conscious of Jack's absence. He'd been very fond of Geoffrey and Clare, who sat in vigil with him during his last weeks, but he had died six months earlier and only days before our 50th Anniversary. Clare looked wonderful in a dress decorated with beige lace in a pattern transferred to the decoration around the cake. The setting for the reception was the opulent Sedgebrook Hall, where the décor of peaches and cream as we entered seemed just right for the occasion. All the family were there, including Georgina's ex-husband Darren, who although he had ceased to be a family member and had not been invited nevertheless expected to be seated at table with his children. Rushdi resolved the problem in his gentlemany manner, and persuaded Darren to wait outside for the later festivities. The happy couple had kept the venue for their honeymoon secret, but it came out later that they'd had a wonderful time in Italy.

Hardly had they returned when all attention became focussed on Zena and Vincent, whose wedding was to be at Northampton's Guildhall on 31st May. All appeared to be going to plan when Zena called at the Squash Club in Dallington to check the reception details with the proprietor. His hands flew up in horror. "A hundred and fifty people? It can't be done. There's no way the Fire Regulations will allow it." She pointed out that everyone had been told of the arrangements and it was too late to alter them. "It's no good," he said. "I'll have to cancel your booking."

There began a series of frantic telephone calls. Again and again she was told "we're fully booked." Hope was running out fast with two days left when a friend suggested she try Northampton Cricket Club, which had no match that weekend. Yes, they assured her when she rang, they'd be happy to take the booking. More phone calls to tell people of the change of venue, more stress. Family and friends rallied round. The room allocated was in fact a gymnasium whose walls were covered with records of achievement in the form of plaques and trophies, together with practice nets. It was certainly a challenge to give the place a festive atmosphere, but the pipes that ran just under the ceiling gave us an idea. Helpers were asked to bring along any spare white sheets which we were able to secure to the pipes and decorate with greenery. For flower arrangements I used crepe paper tied with ribbon around jam jars, but the driving force behind the ensemble was Josephine herself and her friend Mo. The tables were placed around the perimeter to leave floor space for dancing, and then it was time to leave for the Guildhall. When I saw the happy couple on their way to meet the Registrar I had great difficulty in suppressing my tears.

Zena and Vince looked suitably relaxed at the wedding breakfast, where the food was laid out in buffet style. Guests kept arriving – many more than we expected – and the bar did a roaring trade. The room rapidly became too warm for comfort, so the huge patio doors were opened wide to reveal the beautiful cricket ground beyond – an   invitation to enjoy the open air and fine weather from the seats outside. When it was time for the cake-cutting ceremony, somebody noticed that the wonderful colonnaded creation, complete with decorative figures of a bride and postman groom, letter in hand, was leaning to one side. Happily, order was restored when the heavy top tier was removed, to everyone's great amusement. The shoestring wedding ended with the bride and groom's departure for Skegness, where as a wedding gift they'd been given the use of a caravan. Nobody had told them the van had been neglected by the previous occupants, but they set to with a will to clean it thoroughly and it became a family honeymoon with their own two children plus mother and father-in-law, all accommodated there. When I think of how well they coped with the setbacks along the way I feel reassured that they have a loving, well-founded relationship to carry them through the years ahead.

CHAPTER EIGHT

I am still wondering why the life of my youngest daughter Georgina should have taken such a different path from that of her brothers and sisters and caused such anguish to everyone. To what extent was I and her father responsible? Did we fail as role models? If so, could we have done differently in other circumstances? These are among the many questions I ask myself repeatedly, since both she and her ex-husband Darren are currently outside the family circle.

I suppose the first indication that something was amiss came when she left home at fourteen and was out of touch for days. It was a bad time for her, left alone a lot with her elder brother Geoffrey and father Jack, who expected her to run about for him as I did, clean the house and prepare meals etc, when she needed to study hard for her school exams. I was involved with caring for aged parents and assumed that Jack would buckle to and do his share in my frequent absences. Not a bit of it. Each time I returned to the house in North Western Avenue it was clear that no housework had been done. If Georgina brought a boy-friend back, Jack asked no questions, and I later discovered that she'd been sleeping in the house with one of them.

Trying to keep two households and gardens tidy while maintaining my caring role eventually became too much, and when Jack retired and began having slight strokes that worsened over the years my conflict of loyalties intensified to the point of having a nervous breakdown. Meanwhile Ginny was doing exactly as she pleased. I returned once to find the place smelling strongly of smoke and discovered that she'd invited some boys in who clearly were not house-trained. They set fire to some decorative Pampas grasses that I'd arranged in the living-room, damaged a prized statuette, rampaged through the house and stole money they'd found, leaving a smoke trail on walls and ceiling. To say I was stunned would be an understatement. Whatever was she thinking of? And what was Jack doing? It was as though he didn't care what happened around him.

When Georgina took off with Darren, whom she'd been sleeping with periodically at North Western Avenue, she asked me for blankets which I handed over without questioning her as perhaps I should. It turned out that they'd rented a garage nearby and slept there at nights. They were soon evicted, and there began months of hunting for accommodation, Darren unable to get and keep a job and increasingly in debt, leaving a trail of rubbish and unpaid bills behind them. Several times I bought them secondhand furniture, and everyone hoped they'd settle in the house at Lutterworth Rd which they'd acquired without a deposit. Living in squalor, they were evicted a year later by the building society, having paid not a penny in mortgage. Next stop was a council flat ten floors up in Claremont Court, where they threw a party complete with barbecue on the verandah which attracted the attention of the Fire Brigade. Shortly after, Georgina produced a baby, Simon, and the trouble really began.

Shortly after Darren's 18th birthday they decided to get married. Georgina was four years older than Darren and the wedding was arranged for 4th June 1987 at the Northampton Guildhall Registrar's office. I didn't attend as I couldn't give the union my blessing. Darren embodied just about everything

I didn't want for my daughter. Her sisters were more supportive and went, but it wasn't long before my forebodings became reality. Darren had no idea how much time a mother needs to spend nursing a baby and his feelings of neglect came out in violence towards the baby, to such an extent that the Social Services placed little Simon on the 'at risk' register, arranging for him to be taken into the care of his grandparents Terry and Anne.

Terry's sudden death caused a serious upheaval. Simon was now given back into the charge of Ginny and Darren. After five years without him, Darren resented the attention given the boy and began to abuse mother and child, both verbally and physically. Georgina, who it had seemed would take almost anything from this man, plucked up courage to report him to the police, who arrested him on a charge of grievous bodily harm. Subsequently she applied for divorce, and removal from the high-rise flat to a council house in King's Heath. When her sisters turned up to help with the move, they were appalled at the state of the place, especially the bedroom strewn with empty cigarette packets, half-chewed food, dirty socks and knickers and the inevitable empty bottles and beer cans. It was all too much for the removal men, who simply scooped up everything and delivered it to the clean house so that the whole process of neglect could start again.

We all hoped that when the *decree nisi* arrived Georgina would be able to begin a new life away from Darren. We hadn't allowed for his persistence and her apparent inability to resist him, for they continued to share a bed. Soon there was another baby on the way, which we only heard about from Darren's mother Anne. When their new son Martin arrived our family rallied round to supply food and clothing. Money was very short in their household as Darren was out of work as usual and there was no baby food in the house. We helped with this as well, until we realised that the money was going to buy cigarettes for Darren and feed his addiction to one-armed bandits in the pubs. We took it in turns to supply something towards their family needs every week, and at Christmas a large hamper. The intention was to continue to support them with the basics until the boys started school and Ginny could start earning money, but she had to take work before that.

Her sisters helped with looking after the children until the long summer holidays when they had their own to amuse. Now Darren, unemployed during term-time, decided to get a job in the school holidays, which meant that Georgina had to give up her own work, and the family budget took a tumble again. Darren was supposedly working part-time as an electrician's mate, but so far as we could tell spent much of his time sitting about the house in his dirty outdoor clothes with a glass of beer in one hand and a cigarette in the other, looking after the dog he'd brought into the house which had puppies on the baby's bed. The puppies were rehoused, but one was later brought back, so there were now two flea-ridden dogs in the household with the children. The flea spray we provided seems not to have been used.

We stopped going inside when we could see that no effort was being made to clear up the empty bottles, the stacked dishes with remnants of food left on them and the unwashed clothes that littered the kitchen. Ironically, Ginny had found a job cooking and serving food in a café. When visiting, we stayed only long enough to hand in our offerings at the door and run. The months went by. We felt helpless, having to watch from afar their family lurching from one crisis to another, Darren still knocking her about, regular visits to hospital, and always making excuses as to how she received the injuries. Then when Simon was about thirteen and as tall as his father he began to defend her and himself became a target for

The Smell On The Landing

Darren's violence. Ginny had managed to prepare a meal one Sunday, despite the mounting tension following a drinking session, when the arguments turned ugly."Grab your coats and get out!" she shouted to the boys. Somehow they escaped together, leaving their meal untouched. I got the news via a hysterical call from Ginny, phoning from a public box, asking if I could put them up for a few nights. "Just come," I told her. The rain was pouring down, so to save them getting soaked on their walk from the other side of the river I rang Geoffrey, who turned out straight away in the car to pick them up. They were in a state of shock, with Georgina vowing that this time she'd had enough. I could not do very much, being still weak from a hernia operation, but Geoffrey organised a meal and I'm congratulating myself on keeping two single beds made up for such an emergency. They all had a shower, and while the boys enjoy the luxury of a clean bed each, Ginny had to share my double. But what a sleeper! She was all over the bed, digging her knees and elbows into me until I became aware in the early hours that she was gripping my hand tightly. At seven everyone was awake for the Monday schoolday but Ginny couldn't get her head round the idea of breakfast. Did they usually miss out on this important meal I wondered? I made sure they ate before they left for school.

Georgina called at the Council housing department, to be told that she and Darren owed £1,000 in back rent. Until this was paid, they would not re-house her and the children. Meanwhile something had to be done. I found a Refuge home for £65 weekly, to which Ginny and Martin moved after three days with me. Simon had decided to stay with his grandmother Anne who had looked after him until Frank, the new man in her life after the death of husband Terry, found it too much of a trial.

This arrangement appeared to be working well, though not a permanent solution. We held a family conference, from which

Georgina was necessarily absent. How could we help her make the transition to a more ordered and healthier life without Darren? We'd become increasingly aware of his hold on her. Part of her desperately wanted to get away, yet whatever she'd done he'd been able to frustrate. Is there a way forward, or would his influence always be too strong? It's as though he's put an evil spell on her, stalking her constantly with impunity.We were determined to explore every avenue for her benefit, but without her co-operation all plans must fail. She seemed to have lost her own individuality and the power to act decisively. When a professional counsellor recommended that she take deep breathing exercises and some pills, I could only despair.

After a month at the Refuge Centre, Ginny came to see me, head high, eyes brighter, quite different from the cowed creature of earlier. We all began to hope that at last she was finding her better self, but it wasn't to last. Darren had appeared again, to look after Martin two or three times a week while she indulges her favourite pastime of drinking in the local pubs. Her attitude towards her son was that if he got a hot midday meal at school, all he would need is a sandwich in the evening which could be taken at his father's house and save her the bother. It was hard to watch the lad suffering from his parents' neglect. The school had told us he was nearly always late and smells so fusty that other children were reluctant to mix with him. He also had head lice. Another conference, this time with Ginny present.

We could see that soon Social Services would catch up with her and take Martin into care – something that she hadn't thought about. Zena offered a solution. She and Vince would take Martin into their household on a temporary basis. He would be company for their own sons Jack and Harry, if he wanted to stay. Under pressure from her family, Georgina agreed to sign a Protection Order so that Martin could at least have a break from his parents.

He arrived at Zena's without a change of clothes, pyjamas or toilet things. We surmised that he must often have been put to bed fully dressed, to rise next morning, have breakfast if he was lucky, and set off for school. By Friday he must have been smelling awful. We learned later that when his clothes were discarded they joined a pile waiting to be washed, and when he needed to dress next day his mother would select items from the pile and give them to him with the assurance that they'd "get clean as you wear them."

The new arrangement worked well once Martin had been taught how to use the lavatory properly and not object to being kept clean. Zena and I bought him £100 worth of new clothes, at which Ginny protested that he had plenty of clothes already. Needless to say, they never materialised, nor did the Family Allowance she was supposed to hand over for Martin's upkeep. Four months after he'd joined Zena's household, only two lots had been paid. Martin's stay should have been made official, but as his mother wouldn't stir herself to attend solicitor's meetings to arrange this we were stuck.

We began to suspect she was playing us for fools, and when we heard that she'd been visiting Darren in his home and they'd been seen together in pubs for boozy evenings, Zena and Vince were appalled that she'd shrugged off responsibility for the children. Ginny's application to be re-housed was stalled by the problem caused by the arrears of rent, and until this could be resolved, the family must continue to help, if only for the sake of the children. Trying to record all the ensuing ups and downs and day-to-day disappointments would be tedious for the reader, so I shall attempt to summarise the saga to date that has affected and involved everyone in our family.

Christmas Day 2001   Went down with 'flu yesterday. Today it's developing with a high temperature and vicious cough. I don't feel well enough to go out, even if I still had my car, so reluctantly I phone Hazel who was due to pick me up in hers to spend Christmas with them and their children. While I was feeling miserable and trying to catch up with some sleep, a drama was beginning at Zena's when Ginny called to take Martin to Darren's, where Darren's mother Anne and Simon were gathered for Christmas. They were to be away for no more than a couple of hours, until the dinner was ready at Zena's. Time passed, the dinner was spoiling, and still no sign of Martin. The family could wait no longer, the meal was eaten and cleared away, and in the late afternoon a drunken Darren brought Martin, Simon and his mother back. Zena was furious with Ginny for spoiling his Christmas treat, having to sit alone eating a warmed-up meal and being offered only a couple of biscuits while away. Vince then had to take Georgina to the Refuge Centre and Simon to his grandmother's in his car.

February 2002   Zena has brought her two children and Martin to see me. While they play she lets out some of her rage at Georgina's neglect and brings me up to date. The dentist has told her that Martin's baby teeth have no enamel coating and are rotten, so it will be difficult to save his adult teeth. He should be drinking lots of milk. His nervous cough has been diagnosed as asthmatic so he needs an inhaler. His lack of interest in books can be partly attributed to imperfect vision, requiring glasses, but he may also be dyslexic like his mother and brother. If this were not enough, when the discharge from his ears is examined a hearing defect is found. His mother knew about it and did nothing, and now she has shut herself off from the family. No wonder Zena is furious.

Young Harry is beginning to resent Martin's presence in their household, and thumps him when nobody is looking. The solution agreed in the family is that he should spend weekends alternatively with one or other of my children to give Zena a break. The alternative – private foster-care to the age of 16 – would entail my taking a loan on the house to pay for it and seriously diminish Georgina's inheritance. To consult Social Services would be useless with their policy that children are better off with their natural mothers, so we have to work it out ourselves. Hazel, Ginny and I met here without the children. We pointed out that when she is re-housed – it's now six months since she entered the Refuge Centre – she will need to take better care of herself and not let the place deteriorate into squalor again. She should not be bullied by her ex-husband into handing over money, and his paternal rights to see the children should be decided in Court. Georgina retaliated by demanding where Martin was at weekends – this despite not having visited either child for weeks – and turned on Hazel who had done her fair share of ferrying them about and generally showed more concern than their mother. This upset Hazel, who left in tears, and with nothing resolved.

26th February   A day I would rather forget. While Ginny was with me, Frances telephoned. For the best part of twenty minutes she gave her sister such a verbal lashing I cringed. She related all her shortcomings; failing to keep crucial appointments, neglect of the children, expecting her sisters and brother to take responsibility for what she should be doing herself. It all came out, leaving Ginny tearful and at times speechless. While I knew that she'd brought all this upon herself, I felt Frances should have tempered her anger. My youngest daughter needed help to overcome her problems and constant depression. She needed to regain some self-esteem, and I felt this was not the right approach to the problem, however justified.

27th February   Frances comes to apologise for giving her sister such a hard time. When I tell her it's for Hazel to deal with as it was she who was upset at Ginny's accusations, Frances' reply was. "Hazel's too nice a person to speak out." Now there's more bad news. Vince has had enough of the disruption to his household. If Martin is still there at Easter, Vince will leave!

2nd March   Georgina telephones to say she's been offered a three-bedroomed maisonette in Broadmead Avenue when the council have carried out some repairs. She should have keys in a month or so and has already looked at it from the outside.

3rd March   It was Frances' turn to have Martin for the weekend. She brings him to mine. Ginny comes along for lunch, Zena calls to pick up Martin later, and Ginny and I have a long discussion. She says she's completed a counselling course that has helped her and also signed up for No Smoking therapy. Could this be the beginnings of a change for the better? I hardly dare hope. During her visit she ignored many calls on her mobile phone from Darren, who she tells me regularly rings twenty times a day or more. It turns out he is still stalking her, like some evil Nemesis, which brings back all my doubts. She could so easily change the mobile number if she wished.

Easter   What will happen when Georgina moves into her maisonette and Martin lives with her? Geoffrey and Hazel have seen a solicitor, who tells them that a "shared care" order can be made, whereby the family could remove the child upon signs of neglect. But to where? Social Services would simply put him into care, which we're all against. Georgina visits me with Simon to discuss what he wants to do. He'll be staying on at the Duston school to take O or A levels and will need a bus pass from Broadmead Avenue. She's arranged for him to have counselling, which I'm sure he needs with all the upheaval there's been in his life. The Court has decreed that Darren alone must pay the £1,000 arrears of rent on the King's Heath house, which is a big boost to Georgina as it gives her the chance of a fresh start.

10th April   Georgina rings to say she's at last been handed the keys to the Broadmead Avenue property along with paint and wallpaper etc to redecorate. She's arranged for Martin to attend Arbours school, for which he has to have a uniform, but transport may be a problem. Will grandma Anne be willing to drive all that way there and back? The boy has thrived with the attention he's been getting from his relatives and had a great time at the shooting range at Holdenby House during the holidays. Also Frances has enrolled him for football training. Unfortunately Ginny also decided to take him to visit his father at King's Heath, but when returned to Zena in need of a good wash and change of clothes and Zena asked whether she'd been in touch with Darren, she made a vigorous denial. What on earth is the point of us talking about injunctions when she takes Martin to see him and then denies contact? Why do we bother? At least she had a conscience about the money Zena is laying out on her behalf, and brought round to me out of the blue £180 she'd received in arrears of Family Allowance, which Zena was glad to accept.

19th April   Georgina comes to tell me that she's having trouble in getting a bus pass for Martin. They're due to leave the Refuge on Sunday and move to Broadmead Avenue tomorrow ready for his new school. Ginny didn't turn up in time to collect Martin's new uniform, so Clare goes for it rather than have the boy feel out of place among the others on his first day. Georgina can't seem to grasp the concept. She thought he'd "blend in in his mufti." How strange. She's made no effort to book a removal van, so Ray has offered his.

20th April   8.30am sees Hazel and Frances begin emptying the contents of my garage into Ray's van. A few weeks ago my 86-year-old neighbour died and I bargained with the relatives to buy his furniture, having in mind Ginny's pending move. Now it's upon us, and these two sisters are marvellous, working as one to move beds, sideboards and other household items into the open-top van and secure the load with a safety net. Geoffrey comes along to help with the heavy things, but it takes three loads up and down the stairs to install it all in the maisonette. Hazel isn't satisfied that the place is ready for Martin. The fridge and cooker promised by the Charity hasn't arrived and the redecoration isn't finished. So she takes him back with her, and in so doing commits herself to a round trip of 16 miles twice daily for the school run.

One week later   We've explored the possibility of getting counselling/psychiatric help for Martin, and I learn that Hazel would like to take him into her family on a permanent basis. I feel that Georgina should be given the chance of looking after him herself (though I'm in a minority among the family) She seems to have been making progress in the nine-week counselling course, but at the cost of learning some hard truths. Her last assessment shocked her. As a result of abuse going back in her life with Darren, she'd become *a non-entity*, someone who had *ceased to think for herself*, having an existence rather than a life of her own. While this had been abundantly clear to the rest of us, it has only just struck home to Ginny. She was sobbing uncontrollably on the telephone, and asked me if I'd tell the others, as she couldn't face doing it herself.

Reactions to her 'official' assessment among the family who subsequently visited me were mixed, as were opinions on how she would cope living with her children in the future. My view that she should have the chance of coping during one school term initially without our intervention or support was not popular.

On visiting her later in the newly decorated maisonette, I find it's been carpeted by Social Services grant, and the gas cooker, washing machine and TV are all working. The bad news is that Simon has fallen out with his grandmother Anne's partner Frank and is now with Darren, a repeat of the problem 10 years earlier that so disrupted his young life. Martin has come off better. His bedroom is strewn with clothes and toys from Zena, and the walls are hung with paintings and drawings from his last school.

MAY   Why is it there's always a fly in the ointment with this household? Simon spent a night with them but let himself down with awful table manners. He lounged awkwardly at table, slurped his liquids, talked with his mouth wide open, and lacked the social graces his younger brother had acquired. Simon is torn between living with Georgina or returning to his father, who lives much closer to school. She wonders how she could cope with a fourteen-year-old, taller than herself, with uncouth manners, a boozing habit and a temper. Like father, like son?

Back with Darren, Simon is invited to spend a weekend at Georgina's to try to rebuild the relationship, while Martin is with Hazel and Ray, but he fails to arrive, which leaves Ginny alone. I'm thinking about the pub opposite and wonder if she'll see that as a refuge from her problems. Frances and I have been to the Child Development Centre and have been asked to bring Martin there the following week, when it is agreed he'll enrol for a course in Art Therapy.

There is a wait of several weeks before the boy can start. Meantime he's living with his mother and the family are doing their best to leave well alone. However, Hazel attends classes each Monday at Booth Lane, next door to Martin's school. On collecting him in the car she has a chance to check on how things are going. When asked where he's been that week he usually says "to the pub." As they chat, Hazel learns that Georgina has arranged for Martin to stay with his father every other weekend. We're all shocked to think that the boy will again be exposed to the filth and unsavoury life-style he's needed to get away from. Again, Georgina has put her own needs before the welfare of her children. She has a new relationship with someone called Terry, which in principle we're pleased to hear because she needs loving to replace all the bullying she's endured and hopefully it will keep Darren away. But why, oh why, can't she see what she's doing to Martin? This latest development throws doubt on the sincerity of her recent remark that she "wants to be a mum again."

To compound her problems, the Council are bankrupt and cannot issue a bus pass for Simon, so his decision to stay with his father in King's Heath is hardly surprising. It's much nearer school. Darren of course has lost no time in applying for the Family Allowance to be paid to him. We can imagine how *that* will be spent.

AUGUST The six-week school holidays are upon us. I'm regularly asked by her sisters what news I have of Georgina.

The Smell On The Landing

The fact is, I havn't seen her for three weeks, and a few days later I telephone. Her excuse is that Martin has a nasty cough that has turned to croup, but the children have had outings to Twycross Zoo and the Northampton Balloon Festival. When I remind her that she does have a telephone, her excuse for not using it to contact us is that she's like her father – "just laid back" – and has not realised that we are concerned about her welfare. When at the end of the telephone conversation she says "I love you, Mum" I get quite emotional.

The **sixteenth** is a bad day for me. Dashing outside to retrieve some partly-dry washing from the line before the rain comes, I fall and injure myself – blood everywhere. I manage to contact Geoffrey, who comes to nurse me. Eventually, after a two-month absence, Georgina turns up at mine to collect some clothes Josephine had left for Martin to wear in the school holidays. Too late. The holidays are over, and she's missed the boat again.

OCTOBER Ginny's birthday. I go with Zena to her flat, which I look over with her permission. Clothing is heaped in the bottoms of cupboards, but overall I've seen her living in much worse conditions. Simon, who's back with her, has few clothes she tells us, but as this family has kept both boys well supplied with this and other basics, we're at a loss to know what's happened to them.

One Saturday Georgina stands on my doorstep looking dejected and bursts into tears. Darren had been stalking her again. Somehow he'd got into the flat uninvited, used her bed, and refused to leave until her friend called the police, who evicted him. The arguments upset Martin, who hid shivering under the bedclothes.

Later Hazel comes to see me to say she's given Martin a lift from school, when the lad starts to tell her what's been happening. Then he clamps his hand to his mouth in alarm and says. "oh, no. I'm not supposed to talk about dad." We speculate it's probably because Darren is living with them again and Martin's been primed not to let on. Shortly after this, Frances was driving through King's Heath and noticed that Ginny's old house has been boarded up. I need to know if it's possible Darren could still be living/squatting there, but when Hazel drives me slowly past the house I can see for myself that it's been completely sealed. I imagine the mess inside, and feel sorry for the council workmen who'll have the job of clearing it out and making it habitable again.

MARCH 2003   Hazel has a brief note from Georgina, who has not been in touch for weeks. The note confirms that Darren is living with them again, but adds that he'll be moving out shortly to a bed-sit in Kingsthorpe, which will enable her to "become part of the family again." As usual, she's kidding herself. She had every opportunity and support from family and Social Workers to break clear and purge this man from her life. I can only conclude that she doesn't want to do this. Perhaps she needs his dominant and perhaps evil presence in some way that we cannot understand, and will tolerate a great deal rather than lose it. I can't help remembering my mother's words on the first occasion I went to her in tears about a crisis in my marriage with Jack. "You've made your bed. Now you must lie on it." Harsh words, but probably justified. Georgina's problems are her own. We intervened with the best of intentions, and failed dismally – perhaps even made it worse for her. At any rate, the hard lesson has been learned. We are resolved to do no more, and events must be allowed to take their natural course, for better or worse, without our contribution.

Georgina's remark about being like her father gave me food for thought. Was this her get-out for behaving differently from her siblings? Wasn't it possible that other factors were at work? Being the youngest child, born at an age when most mothers had long since given up child-bearing? And what about Jack himself? Working in the print industry for most of his working life, he was exposed in the early days to the lead used in making up founts of type that were laid by hand into a "bed", and later to a lead-based ink, sprayed on to the rollers while printing. This process was apt to release tiny droplets of lead-infused spray that hung over the machine and which Jack inhaled each time he leant over to remove or replace a bed of type. Some months later, he fell ill and I called the doctor, who stood on one side of the bed with me on the other. The doctor naïvely assured me that Jack could not have contracted lead poisoning in this manner, while I was convinced that he had. The poor man looked awful. Any doctor nowadays would have recognised the symptoms – face distorted from swelling, lips enormously puffed up and other unmissable signs. In a moment of levity, not realising the gravity of the condition, I'd remarked that he looked rather like Andy-Pandy! Jack was not amused, and could not have smiled anyway because of the swelling. He did in fact receive treatment and was soon back at work. As a precaution, the firm suspended the lead-based spray process, but perhaps the damage had already been done. Today the effects of lead-poisoning on the functioning of the brain are much better understood. Lethargy could be one such symptom. Who is to say that the early onset of strokes in a previously fit man might not have been directly connected to the nature of his work?

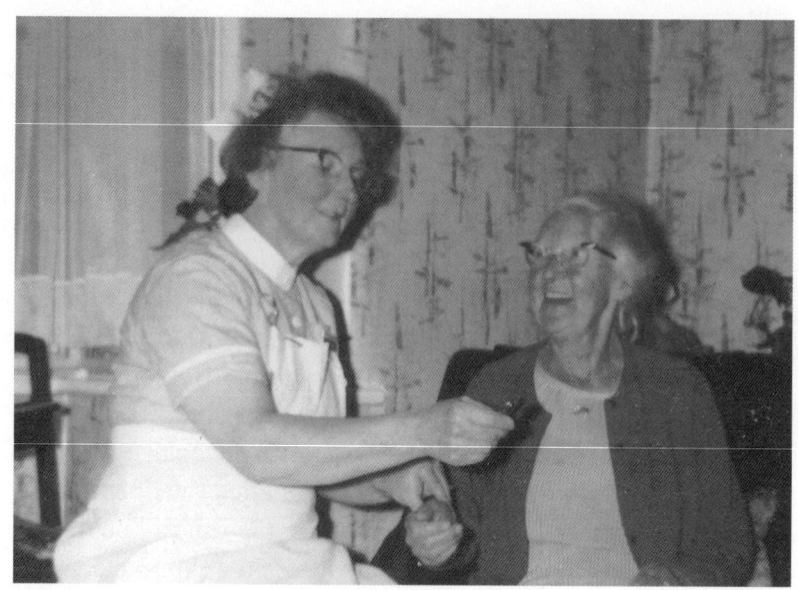

Nurse Gladys

Gladys again

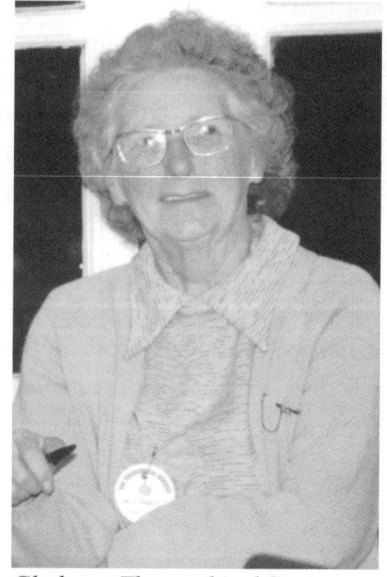

Gladys at Theosophical Society Summmer School 1990

Leonard in Masonic Regalia

Adeline 1950

Adeline aged 92

Ladies' Festival Piccadilly Hotel, London

THE DUROLITUM LODGE No. 5613
(President W.Bro. L. J. CLEMINSON, W.M.)

The Master, Wardens and Brethren

request the pleasure of your company at

THE LADIES' FESTIVAL

AT THE PICCADILLY HOTEL,
LONDON, W.1

ON SATURDAY, 9th FEBRUARY, 1957

38

Reception 5.30 p.m.
Dinner 6.15 p.m.
Carriages 12 midnight

Durolitum Masonic Lodge. Adeline's invitation to
Ladies' Festival 1957

*Leonard and Adeline presented to Duke of Gloucester
at consecration of Chapel at St Mary's Hospital, Stratford, London*

St Mary's Hospital with Matron

Adeline and Leonard. Diamond Wedding 1969

Adeline with Gladys as carer

Adeline with great-grandchild no.1 (Kos)
and Gladys

100th birthday telegram from Queen 1993.
Adeline with Gladys and Mayor of Northampton.

CHAPTER NINE

Jack's retirement was something of an anti-climax. At work he'd had a series of illnesses, and the trend continued with small strokes that increased in frequency to the point where he needed more care than I could provide with my ongoing commitment to aged parents. I felt he would be better off in a warden-controlled environment, so it was arranged for him to take over a flat in nearby Garfield House following the sale of the house at 62 North Western Avenue.

He was much attached to Ronka, who had to stay with me, and calling each day while he could manage it, to take the dog for a walk, gave him a welcome break. He needed to feel useful, so I taught him to cook. His Yorkshire puddings were a great success and he also kept the garden tidy, cutting the grass and weeding and even taking on another garden in Gillsway. These were good times for him until his legs gave out. I noticed it one Christmas, when we drove round the area delivering. While I stopped the car by the house, expecting him to get out and post the cards through the letter-box, I was surprised to see the difficulty he had in getting in and out, clearly in great pain. On Christmas morning, having celebrated with too much whiskey, he fell and broke his wrist on his way round to see me, so Christmas Day was spent in the hospital outpatients department from which he emerged with his arm in plaster, unable to cut up his food when we sat down eventually with Frances and family for a belated Christmas dinner.

Next stage was an electric-powered wheelchair, which caused complications. There was no convenient charging-point at Garfield House, so the wheelchair battery had to be charged in my garage overnight, necessitating my moving out the car each day to accommodate it. Then he couldn't get into the wheelchair unaided, so I had to leave my parents at 40A to pick him up at Garfield House, get him into the chair, and take him back at night. Quite a performance with everything else I was trying to cope with! He began falling out of bed at night, and since he was to heavy for the wardens to lift, the decision was made to move him into Residential care at Obelisk House.

The children were a wonderful help in making his room ready and bringing in familiar furniture to make him feel as much at home as possible. His stay at Garfield House had been full of disappointments for him. He expected the wardens to do much more, such as cooking his meals, and could not seem to realise that this was not their function. He wouldn't join in with any activities or go to morning coffee-breaks in the communal lounge, claiming that they were "all OLD people who can only talk about their own complaints." Now at Obelisk House he had other problems, especially when some residents suffering from dementia entered his room and removed his belongings.

The ratio of care assistants to residents was one to ten – not sufficient for a man now incontinent, who would try to reach the toilet using his Zimmer frame without help and would collapse and injure himself before he got there. Each time I visited him his plight had worsened, not least because the care assistants were no more able to cope with his falling down than at Garfield House. So it had to be a Nursing Home for the more intensive care he needed, and I was lucky to get him into Collingtree Nursing Home, where the nurses became quite fond of him. The Home was beautifully situated alongside a golf-course and he enjoyed regular trips in the grounds, pushed in his wheelchair and cared for by friendly staff, who on his birthday in June would prepare a birthday cake which we all shared with him.

Photographs taken at the time showed a happy man, but inevitably he suffered a massive stroke that damaged the brain stem and left him without speech, sweating profusely and doubly incontinent. For seven weeks the family took turns to mount vigil until his passing in the morning of 14th December 1996 in the presence of his son Geoffrey. The funeral was held at St Columbus Church Collingtree on 20th December and conducted by the Chaplain to the Nursing Home who knew Jack's favourite hymns and allowed us to arrange the service in our own way at both the church and crematoriam. The following year on his birthday, 17th June, we scattered his ashes in his native village of Aldwincle, and a year later held a memorial service which most of the family attended. The text of my address may be found in the Appendix at the end of this book.

My visit to Australia in 1994 was first proposed by brother Ken, who had settled there and returned briefly for mother's 100th birthday. Sadly she didn't recognise him, and he returned to Australia with my promise to accept his offer to pay my fare and all expenses for a three-month stay. At the airport Geoffrey handed me £100 for "spending money" as he put it. (I didn't discover until my return that the money was in fact the sum I'd lent him months before and had forgotten about)

The flight from Heathrow to Brisbane was a stressful twenty-three hours as I found I suffered from altitude sickness and needed the devoted attention of an air hostess who offered iced water to drink and iced blocks for my forehead. The cool stream of air directed at my face from the air-conditioning system was also very welcome and helped me through an uncomfortable time.

Excitement at seeing Ken on my arrival at Brisbane airport compensated for the tiredness. It was still dark at 6am when we set off for his home in Maryborough. In the opposite carriageway I was amazed to see a virtual unending stream of lights from the traffic converging on the city and which stretched for miles. Some of the roads seemed to have been cut from the solid rock, that occasionally towered above us. The broadening daylight showed other details. The stark outline of certain trees gave them a ghostly appearance, especially those that had died from lack of moisture. Others had snapped off and littered the ground like so many straws. I noticed that a number of living trees carried black knobbly cankerous growths about the size of a carrier bag – wasps nests I learned later. Varieties of the native eucalyptus are seen everywhere.

Now and then we passed through residential areas where the houses, well spread out and separated from their neighbours, seemed oddly different. It took me some time to realise that the reason the rooflines were all uncluttered was the lack of chimney-stacks and aerials.The wood-burning stoves that heated the houses in colder weather had their flues on an outside wall, so no chimneys were needed. TV aerials were mounted on long poles in the garden, to receive signals that would otherwise be blocked by the mountains in between.

From time to time along the way, white-painted wooden posts reminded oncoming traffic of the site of a road accident, though from what I had seen so far drivers were more courteous than in this country. The quality of the light seemed clearer than I was used to, partly because I had arrived in their winter, when typically between about 10am and 3pm the temperature would rise to as much as 70F in a brilliant blue sky, and after dark at 5pm fall rapidly to Zero with virtually no twilight.

Ken's house, reached after a three-hour drive, was Queensland Colonial in style, mounted on three foot high posts with lead caps of dinner-plate size to discourage water entry and unwanted creatures, though cockroaches, small lizards and the occasional red-back spider whose bite can be fatal would get through.

But we were soon to be on the move. Ken was mourning the loss of his wife and had sold the house, so I was not idle for long, with the date for moving up-country looming and much sorting and packing to be done. He and his wife had lived in the same house for twenty-five years and brought up a family there, so it was no easy task. He had an extensive library and an enormous amount of cut glass, particularly vases and wine glasses, which needed professional attention, but at least we could make a start with the books and going through personal papers. We worked every other day so as not to get tired of it, and the off-days were most enjoyably spent at beaches such as Hervey Bay, Maroochydore or Rainbow beach. For a change we would visit a bird sanctuary where there was a variety of large, brightly coloured and noisy native species, from the pelicans with their great wingspan, Ibis Geese and black swans, to parrots of all kinds and budgerigars. Galahs were both spectacular and comical, congregating in flocks that wheel to expose first the pink underside to their wings, then their lovely green and red backs. A favourite meal is fermented fruit. They blanket the chosen tree to gorge themselves on the heady brew, with the result that they become quite drunk and fall out of the trees, to squabble interminably.

Black swans in the nearby park had become accustomed to being fed by visitors. If you weren't generous enough you could find yourself being sharply pecked by a swan hanging on to your clothing, so persistent were they. Geese were annoying in another way. They seemed to have a special liking for hot tarmac. When the sun had warmed the road sufficiently they would waddle into the middle and warm their bottoms on the crown of the road, refusing to move at the approach of traffic and requiring drivers to make a careful detour round them. Snakes have been known to behave similarly.

The roads themselves are much easier to navigate than in England, once you've got used to the idea of driving in the wrong lane. The inside lane is for turning left only. Road signs often give warning of another road sign ahead, as where there is a pedestrian crossing or traffic lights. These lights have a smaller set attached for those wishing to turn right. On slip roads the signs *ask* you to proceed with care and join the main stream when the junction is clear. Where there are road-works, a man with a red flag gives the first warning before traffic lights. Drivers seemed more patient and orderly than in Britain, and I imagine road rage is rare indeed. At bus-stops drivers automatically give way to buses drawing out, and being in the left-hand lane means that you are supposed to turn left at the next junction. The other two lanes are for through traffic. One of the big surprises was to see the number of women working as navvies and paviers on road maintenance. Australians don't share our view that such work is strictly the province of men – a welcome sign of a more egalitarian society.

The house at Maryborough, like others of the same Colonial style pole-mounted, utilised the three-foot space beneath the floor for storing tools and other items not suitable to be kept in the house. For some who enclosed it with wire netting or a fancy fence with a gate it made an ideal dog-run. It also served as a shelter for lizards and snakes, the cooler air trapped there making the house above more comfortable in summer. This type of timber-framed house is also very adaptable. We learnt that the new owner had plans to enlarge it, but when he was advised not to as it had already been altered, he arranged for it to be cut into sections and transported to a site some 25 miles away for reassembling and connecting to the mains services, ready to be rented out. The wide load, moving at about five miles per hour with a police escort front and rear, would have been unpassable and the subject of much vitriolic comment from motorists on the road behind it.

Ken's new house at Currumbin Waters had no such problems. Built of brick on conventional foundations, it was laid out in extended bungalow style. Seven years old, it had patio-door windows that could be used for going in and out, and left open in summer behind fly-screens to take advantage of every cooling breeze. However, before we could move in, there were certain things to be done, above all the de-infestation. This is a very thorough and necessary process that has to be carried out before the new owner can take possession, or the place would soon be overrun with bugs. Coming across an alert cockroach some time later would prompt a re-run of this essential process, which is supposed to be effective for twelve months but often isn't.

As a keen gardener I was fascinated by the difference in plants grown in a temperate zone such as most of the British Isles and those in a sub-tropical climate like Queensland, where the further *north* you go the *warmer* it becomes. Poinsettias bought at Christmas at home with stalks 8 to 10 inches high are midgets compared with those in Queensland, where they grow like weeds and are chopped down when they reach roof height. The lovely Amaryllis, which we nurture after flowering and keep in the hope of its coming again the next year, is taken up and thrown away. Ken told me that one year he disposed of 200 bulbs, the bulblets being left in the ground to flower again.

In residential areas a grass sward runs the length of the street. Residents are expected to keep this tidy, which they mostly do. People don't walk on it, preferring to take the car into town where there are no parking meters and you can park free for up to two hours. In the shops, assistants are genuinely pleased to serve you and are more friendly than their British counterparts. Customers come in all shapes and sizes, mainly fat (the women) while men tend to conform to two quite different models – either scrawny and wrinkled with skin dried and brown from the sun, wearing shorts that exposed hairy bow legs, or younger with protruding beer bellies. Here they dress for comfort, and it was amusing to stand in a queue at the Bank, looking down at a row of bare feet, then up to faces shadowed by the broad brown leather hat, brim turned up on one side, that Australian women have adopted.

The hats help to shield neck and eyes together with the inevitable "shades." Sun protection is taken very seriously, with prominent notices warning against exposing one's body to the sun. The catch-phrase *slip, slap, slop*, means "slip on a T-shirt, slap on a hat, slop on the sun-screen lotion." Such warnings are necessary. My nephew, exposed to the sun when a boy, has recently had 10 cancerous spots removed from his left arm alone. The recently discovered hole in the ozone layer that used to protect us from the worst effects of solar radiation has apparently much to answer for.

The overriding impression of Australians is of a very relaxed nation. Hurrying is anti-social, and things are planned with a view to reducing effort. In rural areas, the front doors of houses lack a letter-box. Residents use the American-style postbox, situated at the front of the property next to the pavement or road, that can be anything from an empty petrol-can swinging from a pole on its chain to something very sturdy and elegant with a little roof to deflect the rain. The postman arrives on his two-stroke motorbike, and with his engine still running, drops the post into each postbox in turn. Only if you live in an inaccessible area will you need a key to a central box outside the local post office from where you can pick up your mail at any time with the least inconvenience. The same philosophy is evident in newspaper deliveries, where the papers are wrapped in cling-film to be delivered/thrown by the newspaper boy on to your front lawn awaiting collection.

Rubbish collection is a well organised, one-man job. Households are provided with wheelie-bins, but with the important difference from ours that they are divided internally – the front half for actual rubbish, the rear for items that can be recycled. The proper working of the system depends on householders observing the rules, the most important one being to position the bin correctly by the roadside or pavement edge so that the driver can press the lever to operate the arm that takes the bin, knocks it and shakes the contents into the correct compartment and replaces it. It's a noisy operation but effective, though garden waste is taken only in small quantities and gardeners won't risk taking bags of rubbish in their cars in case some creature with a poisonous bite escapes. A trailer is preferred, the load being netted, since any spillage on the road would incur a fine.

Gardeners face an uphill struggle against drought conditions. Watering may only be done at certain times, as shown on the Water Bills that arrive regularly. In certain areas one can see enormous water-pipes alongside the road, evidence that the precious commodity is not always on hand but may travel hundreds of miles in a country this big to sustain life. Ken had sprinklers laid out across the garden for use on allotted days for short periods, all metered. The scale of the continent has required the creation of time-zones, which can lead to anomalies. Queensland is in a different time-zone from adjacent New South Wales, which made it difficult for my neice, a schoolteacher, whose children went to school across the border in another time-zone. We went by Queensland time on the radio, though we could often pick up transmissions from

NSW. In the town, one side of the street was NSW time and the other Queensland.

On a sightseeing expedition, roaming the mountainside, we crossed into NSW at the border, where the guards asked us a few questions and later let us back in with a friendly nod. From the designated look-out spots one has spectacular views of the Glasshouse Mountain and several extinct volcanoes. Here there are waterfalls and bush turkeys in the rain-forest, and even houses perched on rocky ledges with their backsides built into the solid rock and their balconied fronts cantilevered out over the drop, affording magnificent views.

The move to Currumbin Creek went very well, considering that we took a week to deal with the contents of 32 large packing cases and umpteen smaller ones. It was becoming a busman's holiday, made especially tiring from the after-effects of the *salmonella* poisoning I had contracted and which was to hang over me for two months. But it didn't stop me from enjoying mornings on the patio. Over coffee we would watch the birds sipping nectar from the *gravellia* bushes with gallardias and parakeets wheeling above while a bird like a magpie hogged the bird bath. Cheeky sparrows pecked crumbs from around our feet and gheckos scuttled about the patio. These tiny lizards are incredibly sensitive to vibration, making it difficult to approach them on foot. Once when I swept up one by mistake it instinctively shed its tail to escape, leaving the discarded appendage wriggling of its own volition for quite a time.

Ken was keen for me to see everything possible, which included trips to the beach at Hervey Bay, my favourite spot. From here one could see Frazer Island, though not the whales that rested there in September, this being August. It was fascinating to tread the white coral sand that squeaked underfoot at a certain temperature and to watch the antics of tiny crabs when the tide went out. No larger than your little fingernail, they would begin to trace intricate patterns on the wet sand like a pavement artist. They emerged with a scoop of sand which they threw from a front claw, then dive to repeat the process, each miniature heap landing just beyond the last. Continuing in straight lines, web-like from the centre, these patterns were all slightly different from their neighbour's and proceeded until their creator ran out of energy or was unwary enough to get taken by a patrolling gull.

Nearer to the tide-line were the soldier or platoon crabs that as their name implies progressed in a synchronised fashion, fifty or more moving as one in the same direction, as though directed by some unseen remote control. These too were small and relied upon their extreme sensitivity to vibration and a sharp look-out to stay beyond reach of predators, disappearing in a trice into the muddy environment at the first sign of danger. The balance between hunters and the hunted is a very delicate one indeed that humans disturb at their peril.

The beach was popular with fishermen who cast great distances with their rods and lines and caught so many fish that the authorities had provided them with stripping boards. These were flat, installed at waist height on poles for ease of gutting and beheading the catch. On the right day it was quite a spectacle to watch the pelicans catch a titbit in mid-air and whenever a man stood with his knife and pail at one of theses stations four or five hundred yards apart the birds gathered. Perhaps the most impressive sight of all was to watch a sea-eagle diving to catch a fishhead expertly in mid-air, only fluffing the manouevre if distracted by a competitor. Even here the battle for survival was apparent. Some fish have developed a defence against predators that can be dangerous to humans. I saw a stranded fish on the sand and was bending to pick it up when a nearby fisherman shouted a warning not to touch it. I hadn't realised it was a toad fish and poisonous to touch. The fisherman told me that these fish were now abundant as the balance of fish life had been upset by the removal of the predators that had kept it down.

The owner of the Oceanarium at one end of Hervey Bay elaborated on the problem. Over the years, fishing had been indiscriminate by commercial fishing fleets employing Radar and Sonar to direct huge nets that were dragged along the bottom of the Bay, catching everything and gradually emptying the water of its bounty. Before that one could watch sting-rays, turtles and many other varieties of marine life, now vanished along with the boats. The proprietor maintained a sort of hospital for injured or stranded fish which he returned to the open water whenever possible. He showed us around the great tanks where sharks twice the size of a man could be fed by hand. People pay money to don a wet suit and go into the water with them, and I watched anxiously as these fearsome creatures nudged the hand feeding them to speed up the process! At one tank which allegedly held a stone fish I couldn't see it until a morsel of food was dangled on a long pole. Then, in a movement too fast for the eye to catch, the food was snapped up and the fish was settling back into its perfectly camouflaged environment on the sandy bottom. Later I was kissed by a sea-lion and shown a huge crocodile kept in a small pen.

Ken did me proud during my stay. There was always something fresh to see and marvel at. Several times I was reminded of the films I'd seen of American life, especially when driving along the Gold Coast on the Pacific Highway. Here there were skyscrapers, flashing neon signs and hordes of Japanese tourists for whom many information signs were written in their language. Strangely some tourists resented this, claiming that they were there to see Australia as it really was.

To encounter their own language emblazoned everywhere detracted from that.

Australian wild-life was endlessly fascinating. Visiting a bird sanctuary at Currumbin Creek I was thrilled to be close to some flying foxes, one of which attached a hook from one of its leathery wings to my clothing and began to explore me, hanging upside down. They exert a very strong grip which the keeper had some difficulty in disengaging. At the other end of the size scale were the cassowary birds, whose 3ft high nests were dwarfed by the birds themselves – rather like a turkey in appearance but much bigger and, we were warned, quite aggressive. The sanctuary held several species of kangaroo but no snakes, which I had looked forward to seeing. But the billing outside was out of date. They had been withdrawn, we were told, suffering from stress due to people continually poking them.

We decided to have a meal at the café on site and enjoy the view from an outside table, though it was far from warm. While Ken was ordering food at the counter I watched some muddy-looking White Ibis trying to drink from a small pool of water at the base of a dripping tap. By laying their long bills sideways and moving along the puddle they could take in minute amounts of water. When the food and drink began to arrive on the table, the birds came up to dip their beaks into the drink. Then, when Ken called from the counter to help with the rest of the order and I attempted to leave my seat, the rest of the flock rushed up to gorge themselves on everything there, at the same time leaving their messy droppings on the table. We wished we'd gone inside, but hadn't expected anything like this, nor for the birds to look so dirty when those in David Attenborough's films appear as white as the driven snow.

On our tour of the sanctuary we were saddened to see a very distressed cuckaburra in a cage, apparently intent upon suicide.

It flew at a green-painted metal wall, beak first, dropped to the ground, then repeated the exercise, over and over again. It seemed unnecessarily cruel to keep it under these conditions. Elsewhere we had to stay in the car to feed kangaroos, ostrich and deer, until it was time to return to the house.

One trip we made to the mountains I shall never forget. Close to the rain-forest almost at the top of the Lamington Park Range the road narrowed to allow only one vehicle up or down. The curve of the mountain road prevented our seeing anything coming towards us. With the sheer cliff on one side and a sheer drop of hundreds of feet on the other, Ken's knuckles were white as he gripped the wheel and we both prayed that nothing would come towards us. Having to reverse under those conditions didn't bear thinking about. But luck was with us. We made it without incident to a clearing designated as a look-out post, and once we had drawn deep breaths we could begin to enjoy the most spectacular view, looking down through the clouds. It was cold and damp, but well worth the effort. Notices warn of the dangers of leaving the road or forest track, and while we were in the area three men did just that. After several days lost, a search party found them huddled into a cave, cold and hungry, no doubt regretting their foolhardiness. In a place where some trees are reputed to be 2,000 years old, the tree-frogs croak, mosquitos bite any exposed area of skin, and there are birds with strange calls like the crack of a whip. The rain-forest is an eerie place to be and calls for great respect. Luckily for us there was another way down from our high vantage point. A descent of the same narrow pass would have been even more terrifying than the climb up.

Australia had so many surprises there seems hardly room here to set them all down. For breakfast we'd pick grapefruit and bananas. The trees grew in most gardens so that at times there was a glut that made them difficult to sell. Some petrol stations offered free bananas with petrol, which varied in price according to whether you were in Queensland or NSW. Working out prices in English money was simple, as there were about two Australian dollars to the pound. I found clothing and furniture roughly the same price as in England, and food, especially meat, cheaper. Shopping expeditions were mainly to out of town locations like our Grosvenor Centre with huge parking areas for hundreds of cars, even bigger than Weston Favell. At the other extreme are the small and friendly local shops, more likely to be run by a Mr and Mrs Smith from England than the Patels from Bangladesh or Leicester.

One such shop had life-sized models of an elderly couple sitting outside dressed as OAPs. Sometimes one would be in a wheelchair, another day embracing each other, and in cold weather dressed for winter with blankets over their knees. We often used to call by to see what the old couple were up to that day. A fundamental difference in trading is in the trust that people have for each other. Boxes for money when the shop or facility is not manned are left about and used. Picnic areas for instance would be provided with a barbecue and a gas bottle to light it from, and a slot to put your money in. The council employs people to clean up afterwards. There is a proper respect for the other person's property, and at a large dam and reservoir we visited, kindling wood was bundled up for the public to use. Imagine what would happen to it in our country with its declining moral standards.

I'm sure I could go on, but one has to stop somewhere. I need only say that my Australian trip was everything and more I had hoped for. My one regret was that my weakness from *salmonella* poisoning prevented me from making a planned visit to New Zealand. On the other hand, Ken travelled back to the UK with me to propose to a lady friend, and that is another story…

CHAPTER TEN

Yes, I had butterflies in the stomach, but not from fear of the journey. Admittedly I'd suffered from altitude sickness six years earlier on the flight to Australia, and I was now 80, but my nervousness stemmed from worrying whether my son Geoffrey would be late collecting me from home. He does tend to leave things to the last minute, but on this occasion all was well, and at noon we were on our way. Surprisingly we reached Heathrow in only an hour and fifteen minutes, so with time to spare we decided to eat. Grandson Andrew was more than ready. He wanted to watch the aircraft coming and going, and the café provided a fine vantage point. I think I was as fascinated as he was, but all too soon I was queuing for my boarding card, weighing the luggage and answering the usual questions as to what prohibited things I might be taking out of the country. As I had requested an assisted passage I was asked to await the moving trolley for passengers. Instead a porter came with a wheelchair and asked me to get in. Dumbfounded I did so and waved goodbye to a laughing grandson. My face must have been a real picture!

Serving as I did on a committee for the disabled I thought this would be a good opportunity to savour some of the problems they encounter in transit. After a long stretch of walkway I was asked to wait for the transporter to take me across the tarmac to the plane. When it arrived, I was wheeled up the ramp and the chair secured to the floor for a five-minute ride. Stopping by the plane, the floor of the transporter began to rise until it was level with the passenger entrance to the cabin – all quite exciting. The porter slapped his hand on the door, the stewardess opened up, and I was wheeled to my seat before any other passengers were allowed in. I felt like a VIP. When all were seated the pilot introduced himself, there was the usual talk about safety, the plane began to taxi, and we took off under full power.

It was a British Airways flight, and I must say the food and service were very good, especially as I'd requested a vegetarian and diabetic diet. The TV screen, 6"-7" in diameter, is cleverly built-in to the back of the seat in front, and you're provided with controls on the arms of each seat and a set of radio headphones. The TV has a channel on which you can follow your route by means of a tiny aeroplane that moves across the screen and shows which country or ocean you are over, plus such detail as temperature, height, speed, etc. Alternatively I could have settled down to sleep beneath the blanket provided for all or part of the eight-hour journey.

As we approached Canada the hostess asked me to wait until most of the passengers had alighted, when I was helped on to a train-like transporter to collect my luggage from the carousel. It was now 8pm local time. I'd previously been told to give £1 to the porter who helped me to where my unknown relatives waited, which I duly did to the consternation of all. Apparently the usual gratuity is 5 bucks - £2-50! After much laughter at my expense we introduced ourselves and proceeded to where the car was waiting and set off through Toronto to the house where I would be staying. I was duly shown around, served a welcome meal and was glad to retire to a comfortable bed for a sound night's sleep.

Next day after breakfast and sorting out my luggage we went by car back to the centre of Toronto so that I could see

The Smell On The Landing

some of the 400 or so fibreglass models of moose, as widely known for a national emblem of Canada as the Maple-leaf. Painted in a variety of colour, fashion and style to suit the business they were promoting, these unmissable animal creations were the brainchild of the city's mayor. They lacked only their horns, stolen by the frisky local youth. As a means of attracting visitors to the city, the moose certainly earned their keep.Everywhere we went, people were photographing them. Those outside the office of the Registrar of Marriages were dolled up as bride and groom, attracting much attention for their novelty.

Our next visit was to a dome-shaped building called Roy Thompson Hall, named after the famous newspaper magnate. It was carpeted throughout in beige to match the colour of the walls – a most effective and pleasing décor. The occasion was a Senior Citizen day, held each year, when about 4,000 older people congregate to be entertained by other seniors. This was obviously a very special occasion, calling for one's Sunday best, and my, how smart they all looked, even those in wheelchairs. They'd come to be entertained by a cast of 1,000, and coaches were arriving from far afield carrying the performers and crowds of onlookers. All was highly organised, with nothing left to chance. Artistes were placed around the hall to entertain you while you sat or stood enjoying the refreshments. At 1.30pm precisely the show began, hosted by a 75-year-old who thanked the Royal Bank for their sponsorship and introduced the performers. I can't recall every act, each unique in its way, but remember being amazed at those brave enough to wear the scanty clothing of the old-style Tiller Girls. Some of those pairs of legs would have been the envy of much younger women.

The next day, Thursday, we went into town again and parked the car. In Toronto, car parks have several attendants, with a guard-room and barrier. Drivers have to hand in their keys, which are carefully recorded, and the attendants park the vehicles for maximum density. If, when you call back for the car and find it boxed in, an attendant will get the key of that vehicle and move it and any others to clear your way. You then pay for however long you've stayed, and the system works extremely well. My new-found relatives took us on a circular tour of the city which lasted about two and a half hours, though one can get off at any station en route and re-enter. We did some shopping and ate, when I discovered that Canadian sandwiches are doorsteps compared with what we are used to. Another attraction was the water-front marina, where we saw the tall ships and paddle-steamers, no longer a feature of British life. Here the temperature was noticeably lower than in town, from the wind blowing across icy water along the quay and cooling the air. After such an active day I slept well and comfortably, ready for the next.

Friday was really the main event. We set off for London, Ontario, for a family reunion at the Hotel Four Points. This gathering was convened as a result of a visit a year or two before from a genealogist who called on me at home on behalf of a firm of London solicitors. He explained that a member of our family had died intestate and that he needed to contact relatives. A house in Essex and its contents would go to the rightful owner if he or she could be found. I'd never heard of the folks he mentioned but was sufficiently intrigued to make enquiries.

I went to see one of my father's cousins living in Colchester who gave me names and addresses of those relatives he was in contact with, and I duly wrote them. They didn't have the necessary papers, but agreed to contact others further afield who might be able to help. Over the next few months letters began to arrive from Australia, New Zealand, Africa, England,

Ireland and Canada. The letters kept coming and soon I began to feel I needed a secretary, though the information the genealogist wanted was not forthcoming. It was all taking so long he lost interest in me, and no doubt the fee of 10% of the estate's value he would have come in for.

The letters showed enthusiasm for what I was doing. The Canadian branch said "Hooray! Let's have a reunion, even if we can't do anything about the legacy." So it happened that I crossed the Atlantic and was guest of honour in the Legion Hall, newly decorated, waiting to see how many of the few who had accepted invitations would actually arrive. We had requested that people bring food, and there was enough for the small number who were there at the appointed time. Then, little by little, the handful became thirty or forty, and eventually soared above the 100 mark. We were hugging and kissing each other in delight, and when the initial excitement was over it was noticed that the walls were covered in photographs, and many souvenirs lay around for browsing over. A very long chart of the family tree was displayed, to which several people made corrections or added names.

While the adults socialised and gossipped non-stop, games had been arranged for the children, who began to join in. Two of them danced a very passable Irish jig and another played the oboe until, around 9.30, the younger children's parents began rounding them up to take home while those that were left helped clear the hall. Everyone said what a great success it had been, meriting a farewell breakfast at the hotel which about 70 attended next morning. We exchanged addresses, embraced and went our ways once more. For me, it had been a most wonderful occasion.

Later we drove to Windsor, in the same province of Ontario, where I was thrilled to watch hawks wheeling overhead, impressive with their wide wingspan and perfect command of the air. When we arrived at the grave of an ancestor, whose headstone had fallen into disrepair, I was delighted by the chipmunks who seemed to be playing hide-and-seek each time we came too near. They are very like our squirrels, and in residential areas live even closer to householders. Here, like the streets and gardens, everything is neat and tidy. All dogs are on an extended lead and their droppings must be retrieved by the owner. Any that are found loose are taken to a pound, and the owner when found is charged for their return. People's front gardens reflect the sense of municipal responsibility apparent everywhere. Some tenants, my relatives among them, hire contractors to keep lawns fed and cut, enhancing the display of flowers for the annual competition of "Best Garden In Toronto." Nothing better illustrates their civic pride than the plaques they display on the house wall, recording the years in which they have entered. As in Australia the spirit of community, sadly lacking in much of our once-great country, is demonstrated by the respect for the other person's property. On a morning walk to "house-watch" I noticed that folk left chairs and tables out all night. It's many years since British people could do that with impunity.

My walk took me to a restaurant, where I fancied a nice cup of tea. I'd assumed that Canadians, so like we Brits in origin, would have shared our passion for a nice "cuppa." Not so. When asked my preference I was shown a cabinet of some twenty different teas, none of them suitable. I began to see why coffee has become the national drink. How true is the saying "when in Rome, do as Rome does." On the way back I was surprised to see a *black* squirrel, my first. Thinking I'd spotted a rarity, I mentioned it to my hosts, who then told me they were quite common, like the raccoons that live in the trees along the streets and only emerge at night to forage.

The Smell On The Landing

Next morning we arose at 5.30am, our destination Ottawa the capital city. Despite an early start to avoid the commuters who clog the roads, there were plenty of cars to be seen. At the railway station there were queues in the large booking hall, each facing the platform of destination. When the train comes in, an official removes the barrier and leads the queue on to the platform, where more officials are there to check that you are on the right platform and to find you the right carriage. The train reminded me of the *Chattannuga Choo Choo*, with its loud "yoo-hoo" each time it approached an unmanned crossing. Service aboard was exemplary. Every hour or so during the 4-hour journey a steward came by with food and drink.

We were booked in for an overnight stay at the *Chateau Laurer,* distinguished by its green roof, a product of verdigris accumulating on the copper over the years. Our first excursion was to the new War Memorial, which we duly admired, especially the beautifully designed and kept gardens it was set in. We had to pace ourselves to fit in everything we'd planned, so it was back to the hotel for a good meal, a freshen up and then to bed for a well-earned rest.

The following day commenced with the luxury of breakfast in our room, our destination the Canadian War Museum, where among other exhibits was Hitler's limousine, twice the size of other cars and befitting the God-like character he'd seen himself to be. In complete contrast, we went on to the Canadian Houses of Parliament and the Senate Rooms, where men were requested to remove their hats as a gesture of respect as they entered. Parliament was carpeted throughout in green, and the Senate in red – quite reminiscent of the distinction marked in our Parliament between the Commons and the Lords, the Lords of course having the more comfortable-looking seats! With its extensive use of marble, the overall impression was quite regal.

Leaving the buildings we heard a lot of whistles blowing, and in a moment it seemed we were surrounded by police, keeping us where we stood and clearing the streets of traffic. Before we could work out what was happening an advance guard of motor-cycles roared into view followed by a "stretch" of limousines that passed so quickly we couldn't see anybody inside them. In fact they contained the President of Mexico and his entourage. When the cavalcade had gone it began to rain and we made for the nearest store to buy umbrellas. Another taxi and we were back at the station for the return journey to Toronto where we were met by our host. It had been a tiring but very worthwhile day.

There was a welcome break for shopping after the rather hectic sightseeing – time to notice that on top of the marked price of goods in most shops you have to add 15% sales tax. A few shops display notices that the tax has been included in the price, but that doesn't really make them any cheaper. I actually bought very little, and as soon as we'd got our breath back we were en route for *Casa Loma,* Spanish for "the house on the hill," which turned out to be a beautiful modern castle. The Pallets, who owned it, had gone to extraordinary lengths to build it and install the most extravagant furniture and fittings. To take just one item, the elaborate doors separating the conservatory from the house cost 10,000 dollars each, it was said. Everything was on the same lavish scale, no expense spared. We walked up and down stairs, from turrets to cellars, and through the magnificent gardens until we could walk no more and were glad to go back to collapse on to our beds.

Canada is home to the Mennonites, a group of people who prefer not to live in a world of modern convenience and appliances. They dress in black and live as close as possible to their medieval ancestors. They were on our "must visit" list, so four of us set off by car to their village, St Jacobs. A craft fair had been organised that gave us a chance to admire and buy their work. Quilting, glass, metalwork, ceramics, teddy bears, woodwork, even shoes were for sale. It was interesting to see that labels on goods and announcements and notices are in both French and English. This seemed odd until you remembered the strong French connection in Canada generally and especially in Quebec, of which General de Gaulle the French President reminded the British pointedly in his heyday a few years back.

Around this time I was mindful of another cousin on my mother's side whom I'd not seen since 1949. She was on her way to see me from her home in New England USA. Her journey was to take 10 hours by car via Niagara Falls and I was much looking forward to seeing her on the morrow.

I recognised her immediately, and how the years slipped away as we sat in the garden watching the blue jays busily flying from tree to tree, and the little red and yellow birds that look like canaries. Canadian birds are much more like ours than the large, brash, brilliantly coloured species common to Australia. The black squirrels I had thought so rare were hunting for nuts close by while my companion smoked a reflective cigarette and we talked about the major events of our lives between then and now. Between her arrival and departure we seemed to talk non-stop, and very rewarding it was too.

The next big event was to attend a performance of the "Lion King" one evening, seated in Row D near the front. 85 dollars had seemed an exorbitant price to pay, but what a spectacle! Nothing had prepared me for the scene revealed when the curtain rose on a jungle clearing, with all the cast in their animal costumes and a huge elephant strolling down the aisle to the stage. I felt the tears begin to flow with the sheer emotion of the occasion, so life-like was it, and the show kept us enthralled until the last curtain call and much deserved ovation for all who had made it possible.

A practical observation now on the subject of plumbing. In the washroom above the basins was a long tube of water running the whole length, with spaced outlets. All you do is to put your hands into the flow and walk on to the drying facility. The toilets are different too. Waste is cleared by a swirling motion that empties the bowl, before the water comes flooding back again almost to overflowing. I found that one needed to be careful before sitting down…Other differences were noted in the electrical systems. Instead of turning off a light by pushing the switch *up*, you had to push it *down*. Small things, perhaps, but one has to ask *"why?"* Outside the theatre were rickshaws waiting to take people back to their hotels. Had it been a lovely warm evening we might have been tempted, but we decided to give it a miss.

There was still much to be seen, but with time running out and finding the round of sightseeing quite tiring, we conserved our energies with some leisurely shopping, from the stores large enough to warrant moving walkways, airport-style, to the "cheapjacks," where nothing is priced over 50p or one Canadian dollar. Then someone suggested we visit the Quay, which with its cooler local climate was a good choice. Even so, the temperature rose to 40C, which is as much as most people can stand. I was glad to use the umbrella I'd bought in Ottawa for shade. For an unfortunate minority it was just too much, and ambulances attended several sufferers from heat-stroke that day. I was certainly glad to return to the coolness of the air-conditioned house, though this relief was somewhat offset by the noise the thing made, which didn't allow me a proper night's sleep. One can't have everything…

Two more events would complete my busy schedule. There was an all-day visit to the Canadian Science Museum, which left plenty more to see, and in the café an encounter with self-service. It was all very well to provide lots of buttons to push, but not so good if you couldn't see before you did it what would come out. Perhaps I just didn't look in the right place for the selection of food available. I simply felt baffled by the technology, which made me feel as though I'd been left to find my way in a jungle without being told about trees, water or animals and what they did.

There were no such problems on our last major trip. We had breakfast early and were on the road to Niagara Falls by 7.30am for the two-hour journey. Early as we were, the place was already thronged with people on a perfect sunny day that set off the colours of the beautifully-tended gardens to perfection. First sight of the Falls was shrouded by mist and spray, so we were well prepared with raincoats for the walk along them, taking photographs. Then before it got any busier, we boarded the "Maid of the Mist," which I thought went dangerously near the deafening, tumbling water and was really thrilling. I could see that without protection everyone would have been drenched with the spray. When it was time for lunch we walked to the town, one of the prettiest I've ever seen, with plants in bloom everywhere, and finished the tour with a horse and buggy ride, learning much about the history of Niagara on the thirty-minute ride. Then it was back to the car and Toronto.

My relatives had wanted my visit to be memorable, and it most certainly was. They could not have done more, and our farewells were quite emotional. The flight back didn't go nearly as well as the outward journey. My request for an assisted passage was largely ignored, and I found myself struggling to pull cases off the carousel to load on to the trolley. But as I laboured with the trolley I knew that my daughter would soon come into sight, and there she was, holding a banner with the message SUPER GLAD scrawled on it. I was never more glad to see anyone in my life. I was back in the loving arms of my family, and it was sheer Heaven…

CHAPTER ELEVEN

As my narrative nears its close I realise that the chronological order I've tried to maintain has served its purpose. So this chapter and the next will be a collection of bits and pieces drawing together events and observations that for whatever reason didn't fit into the relevant period or which belong to this later stage anyway. I hope it will give the reader, especially my wonderful family, an insight into what has motivated me through quite a long – and certainly very full – life.

If my visit to Canada was a highlight of the Millenium Year 2000, the year was also important in other respects. February was marked by some happy days with sister Joyce, although one of our topics of conversation was the plight of my depressed neighbour, who was found drowned in the River Nene the following month. I was involved in the aftermath of this sad affair. There were other sorrows. People I had known or worked with passed on, and we had a nasty scare with Geoffrey's baby Adam, who suffered three heart attacks in two days. We feared the worst, but by proper medical care or the benign hand of Providence, the little lad survived and was trying to walk before the year was out. Frances moved to a larger house in April and was looking forward to seeing what would grow in the garden.

In May Ken came from Australia for a six-month visit, much of that time being spent with his wife in Stockton-on-Tees (yes, the same lady he was courting when he returned to England with me in 1996) In July the family and friends gave me a wonderful 80th birthday, and the next day surprised me with a helicopter flight at Sywell. We also went to Bletchley, home to the wartime code-cracking operation, but were unable to see the amazing *Enigma* machine that gave the key to the codes, as some bright spark had stolen it (since recovered undamaged, I'm glad to say) I brought myself into the new century with a few hours of tuition with my dear friend and Carers colleague Nuala Fitzgerald and hobbled about during Carers Week with a broken toe and somehow managed to drive (though my days behind the wheel were numbered, as you'll see)

Throughout that winter and into the following spring I brought up the subject of retirement at the monthly meetings of our local branch of the Carer's National Association. I pointed out that both the principal officers of the branch, Nuala and myself, were undergoing hospital treatment. Moreover we had both served our time, I as Committee Member from 1985 to 2001 and Chairperson from 1990 to 2001, Nuala as Committee Member, Treasurer and Secretary from 1989. Now I felt we should step down in favour of others who might wish to be considered, and called for nominations. None were forthcoming, so at the AGM the matter of Branch Closure was placed on the agenda. The whole situation was again explained to the meeting, the motion put to the vote, and the the result was "Closure."

The result came as a shock to many, but there was no alternative but to convene an Extraordinary Meeting to formalise it. I requested that those members who had served us in an official capacity from the establishment of the CNA in 1988 give a short talk about their personal experiences as carers. At the meeting we laid on refreshment to suit the occasion – strawberries and cream/ice cream, home-baked fairy cakes and biscuits, along with tea and coffee. The stories told by the veterans enthralled everyone, and in a marvellous party atmosphere it was agreed that some of our branch members might endeavour to meet, say, twice a year informally. The proposal to close the branch was then put to those present and a vote taken by show of hands. The outcome, which had to be accepted, was as before. The Northampton branch of the NCA would be no more, and from September 2001 the NCA would become known as Carers UK.

In a busy life there isn't always time to sit and reflect. Now, with fewer commitments, I could see that there had been a natural progression which began long before the caring for my parents. Caring is a state of mind, requiring love besides a strong sense of duty. Not everyone is suited to it, but circumstances can so easily pitchfork a person into a caring role, like it or not. Even a minor stroke can leave the victim temporarily unable to cope with certain everyday tasks and needing the help of a partner or professional. Nuala and I have so often given useful advice to those suddenly landed with a job for which they've had little or no training. It's a problem that grows with a population in which the expected life-span seems to creep up irresistibly. In a talk I gave about three years ago to NCA members I researched the startling fact that an estimated 2.9 million men and 3.9 million women are caring for either a relative, friend or neighbour in tasks varying from popping in to make a cup of tea or preparing a meal, to the most intimate and personal care.

At a practical level there is now financial help for those who qualify. It was four years after beginning to look after my parents that I first came to know about Attendance Allowance, mainly because the authorities failed to advertise the fact sufficiently. At NCA branch meetings we would outline to new carers the sources of help and information, from Social

Services, local councils, doctors surgeries, Post Offices and the Citizen's Advice Bureau. Once you have the information you can use it, but if you don't, you can often feel quite alone and cut off, as I did in the early days. We also circulated the addresses/telephone numbers of St John's Ambulance, the Red Cross, Salvation Army. Members of our committee served on Social Services and Health Authority projects to keep us up to date with developments.

Of course, there will always be exceptions. The Carers Recognition Act passed in 1996 at the instigation of the CNA aimed to ensure Social Services would listen to carers' problems and offer help as appropriate. But what can you do with young carers whose tender age puts them beyond the scope of any legislation? I well remember attending the launch at a Daventry Hotel of a Young Carers Project which sought to publicise and better the plight of children who found themselves thrust into a caring role. A young carer related to a hushed audience her experiences of caring for a family member from the age of twelve. I could imagine how she tried to cope with the conflicting demands of school attendance, homework, doing the shopping and preparing meals. Some children placed in that situation by illness or a dysfunctional family turn up at school red-eyed from lack of sleep, unable to concentrate properly on lessons, sometimes having to miss school altogether because of the prior family commitment and never being able to confess to someone who might help because of the intimate nature of the caring or the fear of ending up in care themselves. I have served on the committee of Young Carers, and can see progress in winning over the confidence of these children who can now get help and move towards the fuller life of work and play that every child is entitled to. *Tell someone*, and help will follow. That message is slowly being acted upon.

Caring takes many forms, and my voluntary work saw me elected to the Executive Committee of Age Concern. In 1995, the fiftieth anniversary of the ending of the Second World War, it was decided to compile a book of wartime memories. I was asked among others to contribute and give a talk about my Army days at the next AGM. When the book was published under the title *Fifty Years On*, there was my photograph on the front cover in Army uniform, and next to it one of me at the age of 75. I must say I was a little shocked at the difference! The local *Herald and Post* helped promote the book with an article and (another) photograph on August 24th that year. Later the WEA (Eastern District) were collecting stories from the public on events over the last 100 years, and Bob Chapman the organiser accepted my story of the ATS on the Racecourse during the war at Talavera Camp. In partnership with Age Concern, the WEA Federation published *A Northampton Century* which carried on its cover a picture of Northampton Market in the time of horse-drawn carriages.

When I was in the Army during the War a favourite saying among the other ranks was "never volunteer for anything." Perhaps I should have heeded that advice in later life, but my nature seems to have driven me to get *involved* in things, sometimes to my detriment. Mostly the jobs I took on coincided with my own interest, as when I began attending meetings of the Northampton Fuschia Club. They needed a secretary, and when nobody wanted to take it on I volunteered. This position was very rewarding, as I made several friends among the members and we travelled to different nurseries and grand houses in the Midlands and South. I would have to take the children with me on the coach as I did on our visit to Chatsworth House to wander round the extensive and beautiful gardens. There I'd arranged that we should all assemble at the coach at a certain time, but I had the embarrassing experience of having to confess that I'd lost my daughter. Georgina was about four at the time, and had somehow given me the slip. A search was mounted and she was soon found, and subsequently I had to write up what we had seen that day for the Newsletter. Needless to say, I omitted the detail of the children's travel-sickness (so like their mother!) and Georgina's little escapade.

An early interest in Spiritualism – more of this later – led me to question the religious beliefs I had been brought up with. It appeared to me that conventional religion, with its images of worshipping a Supreme Being who was "out there somewhere" and only accessible by prayer, left a great many unanswered questions. When I came across a pamphlet of the Theosophical Society which apparently offered a way of life on Christian principles without the dogma I began attending meetings and soon became Secretary to the Midland Federation of the Society. Quite a lot of travelling was involved in getting to meetings, but I didn't mind as I enjoyed driving. By the law of averages, each motorist's risk of an accident – and there are no exceptions – increases with mileage driven. I must have been due, for hardly had I picked up a fellow member from Bletchley when – bang! – another car hit me. The young man driving it was very bolshie and blamed it all on me. With all that has to be done after even a minor incident I was very late arriving at Letchworth Lodge. The looks I got from the assembled members, who could do nothing until my arrival with all the information we needed to begin, were not at all friendly. But when we explained the circumstances the atmosphere lightened. Subsequently the bolshie young driver offered an apology, which I accepted. He was very worried at the time, he said, and had no licence, so that exonerated me.

In the thirty years or so since that first meeting I've come to understand more of the philosophy behind it all. We are all part of the same comprehensive, universal system, in which every thought, word and deed has its effect on others, domino-like. So the first thing to do is to weed out negative and hostile thoughts in oneself, since they stand in the way of understanding what is required of us as individuals. This weeding out is a long, painful process. I found it difficult not to feel resentment, and frequently gave vent to exasperation when something failed to happen in the way I wanted it to. Theosophists, like Spiritualists, believe that everyone has an aura about them that some mediums claim to see in colour – red for frustration or anger, blue for illness, and so on. I lack that vision, but have good reason to accept that others have it. What wouldn't one give to be seen with an aura of gold at all times!

I've come to believe in the concept of eternal re-creation. Scientists now tell us what the sages have believed for centuries. A recent programme on TV showed how the spark that began life on this planet could have emanated from a passing meteor or have been contained within the giant clusters of matter that go to form new stars. This was not a fantasy of the programme-makers but reflected the informed views of recognised scientists. I believe that when my time comes the Great Adjudicator, by whatever name, will assess my suitability to progress to the next dimension. In the same way as Nature's evolution seeks perfection, so the spiritual part of us that survives physical death must be re-born again and again in the search for the ultimate. My beliefs have helped me face the thought of death with equanimity.

In July of 2001 I wrote to a visiting Spiritualist medium about a recent attendance at Northampton Spiritualist Church. When routinely checking the local *Chronicle & Echo* on the last Saturday of the month to see which medium would take the meeting I saw the name Geoffrey F Hayward, someone I hadn't met before. As the "vibes" were good, I decided to attend. The question was, what to wear.

It happened to be a very hot summer's day, calling for a blouse. Then an inner voice whispered "put on the pink sleeveless pullover." Astonished, I said aloud "no way." With the temperature at 80F it would have been too much. But past experience had shown that disregarding the inner voice usually turned out badly, so on went the pink pullover on top of the blouse.

The service started as usual with a hymn and a prayer before the clairvoyant reading. I'm feeling quite comfortable in my pink woollie while the medium is introducing himself, and suddenly I'm looking at his outstretched arm and realising it's pointing straight at me. "I want to come to the lady in the pink top."

To my amazement he began telling me about my mother, who was with him, he said. He described her to a "T", even to her expressions of speech, and told me she wanted to thank me for my caring role during her last few years. She had met several relatives and friends in the spirit world, some whose names I could recall, others that I couldn't place. Apparently she knew of my health problems such as *angina* and the high blood pressure and emphasised that I should "keep taking the tablets." While I struggled to take all this in, the medium had paused, trying to establish an important date he was getting and which finally came out as June 16th, my father's birthday.

The service continued with other readings until Geoffrey could not place a man whose name was George. Well, there should have been a good show of hands for the name, but this man was specifically a printer, who loved his job and had appeared to the medium standing next to his machine. Suddenly the penny dropped. My late husband's given name was George, though he was known to all and sundry as Jack, ever since he was called up for the Army. He certainly loved his work, so I had to speak out. Geoffrey went on to describe his mild nature and talked of those he had met in the spirit world, with a big "thank-you" to me for my care in his lifetime.

After the meeting Geoffrey handed me a leaflet, and following this I wrote to thank him as there was a chance he would want to include my remembrance of such a vivid experience in his proposed book. I have enjoyed much benefit and peace of mind through meditation, which allows one to "recharge the batteries" if I can use that rather hackneyed phrase. Not long after my father died, he appeared to me in a way that recalled my childish and unwitting vandalism, when with the best of intentions I pruned the needle-sharp spikes on a favourite *Aloe* plant he was cultivating. The spikes had gone into my fingers, as related in an earlier chapter, but while I recovered, the plant did not. In this manifestation father took me to the gardens of Nazir in Egypt where he had found peace and solace during his service in WW1. He explained at length that it no longer mattered that the plant had died. Now he could spend as much time as he wished in the gardens full of specimen cacti. I began to follow him along a stony path, but something prevented me from going further and his image faded. I felt reassured that at last forgiveness had been offered.

I reflected on his death at St Crispin's Hospital, now closed to patients like my father. In 1986 it was very busy and quite uplifting to visit, surrounded as it was by extensive woods, lawns and open spaces filled with wildlife. At about 9 on that January morning I had a telephone call from the hospital to tell me he was failing. Sadly he was dead when I arrived. I kissed his forehead and said "better luck next time round father." When I touched his body I realised it was much warmer than when he was alive, when his skin always felt chilled. I wonder if medical science can explain this, since I can't.

We chose to have the chaplain of the beautiful St Crispin's Chapel, built in the hospital grounds, conduct the burial service, and the hymn *Abide With Me* recalled childhood days when he enjoyed playing the harmonium at home. Then it was on to the crematorium, where his coffin with the Masonic Emblem placed upon it was committed to the furnace. His ashes were scattered around the Crematorium gardens and life carried on, busy as ever, with a loving thought now and then towards him in our memory.

I've mentioned that St Crispin's Hospital, once known as Berrywood Asylum, has since closed for the admission of patients with father's problems. Worse was in store for the beautiful chapel, which has been put up for sale so that the site can be developed for residential housing. The chapel has been designated for community use, and one hopes that the associations and the wonderful interior will be preserved, whichever group ends up as its custodian.

Last year (2002) was the 25th anniversary of St David's Day Centre opening, when I applied for and got the job of Care Assistant. I and Mr Morris the manager worked hard at washing all the plates, cups and saucers, checking the chairs as suitable for the elderly and a multitude of other tasks to be ready for the day of opening. From our first client, a blind gentleman, the attendance grew over the weeks to some twenty or thirty souls, and the staff swelled to look after their needs. We were a friendly group and the work was rewarding. I was very sad to leave when my parents' needs became the priority but kept in touch with Mr Frost, second-in-command, who took over when Mr Morris left for another position. So I was delighted when a letter came inviting me along with all staff past and present to the 25th Anniversary.

I arrived alone about 7.30pm to find celebrations in full swing and Day Centre clients, some in wheelchairs, busily devouring an excellent buffet meal. I couldn't put a name to any of them, even the smartly-dressed man who spoke as though he knew me. It was none other than my old boss, Mr Morris. We soon drew up chairs to talk of those long-gone clients who had stood out in our memory at the time, and for a while I was back in time, seeing it all again. Then the music began, deafeningly, the brash music of today. I felt most uncomfortable, and not wanting to make excuses or complain about the noise of the band, I slipped quietly away. It was a sharp reminder that we are all of our time, and I had become an intolerant, very elderly lady...

The Smell On The Landing

CHAPTER TWELVE

Leafing through one's diaries can be a sobering experience. The obvious drawback is that it can encourage living in the past rather than looking to the future. Yet it is a fact that beyond a certain age, the accumulated memories far outweigh the somewhat limited prospects for the future. I've had great satisfaction recalling the past and am blessed with a family who will ensure that whatever the future holds I shall never be unloved or alone. The biblical metaphor of reaping what one has sown keeps coming back when I consider that I'm still in touch with people I met half a century and more ago. In 1998, for instance, I met up with my old friend Gladys Holloway to celebrate her 80th birthday. I'd arranged to take along another old comrade from my ATS days, Florence (Florrie) who lived in Grays, Essex, en route to where Gladys lived in Chadwell Heath. We Three Musketeers all became NCOs during the War, and first met at Talavera Camp on Northampton Racecourse in 1940. Gladys earned promotion as Sergeant, Florrie as CSM (Company Sergeant Major) and I became a Staff Sergeant (CQMS).

Florrie and I searched for a gift suitable to celebrate an 80th birthday and spotted some orchids in a pot. Very elegant and heavy with bloom, we congratulated ourselves on our choice and continued our journey to Chadwell Heath, where we presented it to an admiring Gladys. As the plant seemed quite dry, water was called for, and to everyone's surprise, failed to penetrate. Only then was it realised that these were not real orchids we'd fussed over and discussed the care of but imposters – imitation flowers cunningly made to look like the real thing. What a come-down! The discovery caused an embarrassed ripple of laughter among the assembled guests, until they began to see the funny side and put it all down to the age factor. I doubt whether we shall all assemble again, given the distances between us and the fact that I can no longer drive, which makes this particular memory the more poignant.

In that same year I decided to do something about my bedroom – give it a makeover in today's lingo. I toured the shops with son Geoffrey for a nice bedroom suite in white, a bedside lamp and matching shade for the ceiling light. A new bed and carpet would also have been nice, but the money…Shortly after, out shopping with Hazel, I bumped into Sheila, one of my tenants you'll remember from Boughton Green Rd. When she heard about my little refurbishment she jokingly suggested I should have an opening day. In the same vein I laughed and said she should have the honour, if I did. She took me at my word, and in no time I was sending out invitations, avoiding sleeping in the room meantime. We did the thing properly, sealing the door with black plastic bags decorated with white pom-poms and there was a fancy wooden box with a plush lining to hold the small knife that Sheila would use to slit the seal on command. On the day, Sheila and husband Alan, Michael Merriman and family members met in my lounge to reminisce and recall some events from our time together at Boughton Green Rd, which Sheila remembered as a very happy time in her life. Then we all traipsed upstairs to watch as Sheila, knife held aloft, uttered the solemn words "I declare this room open to view." The knife sliced through the plastic, we all clapped, and eased ourselves through the open door to do homage. It was a mad thing to do, and everyone simply loved it.

Talking of Boughton Green Rd takes me back even further, to 1951-2. At the rear, a narrow, rough service lane gave access to

The Smell On The Landing

the back gardens. The lane was used by vehicles to deliver coal and other supplies, and strangely a horse-drawn cart to service the house drains. As there was no through-way and no room to turn horse and cart together, the driver would release the horse, which was content to be fed sugar, carrots and the like offered by the neighbours and their children. One day the neighbours failed to appear on time and the horse, accustomed to his treats, decided to go looking for them. My garden gate happened to be open, so this huge creature somehow got himself under the lattice arch and was trampling the lawn and borders when the driver, having turned the cart, came in search of his horse. He tried everything to get it out of my garden, but it baulked at the rose-arch. No way was it going under *that* again.

Opposite our back fence was the gate to the garden of a house in the next road, newly occupied by a young woman with two little boys. Alerted by the shouts of the driver to persuade his wayward horse out of my garden, she and her children and mine watched the drama unfold. Finally the horse was tempted by some tasty morsel to fosake my flowerbeds, brave the arch and allow himself to be harnessed once more to the familiar shafts. They went off, and the neighbour introduced herself as Beryl. We got on well, her eldest son Peter becoming a playmate to my Josephine. Her youngest, Timothy, was still in a pram.

Our friendship developed, and one day Beryl invited me to share a chalet she and husband Michael had booked for their family holiday at Snettisham in Norfolk. I was not very well at the time and they thought the sea air would be good for me. It was an exciting prospect, for which I'd cooked the huge ham we'd bought and stored it in the cellar meat-safe (no 'fridges for the ordinary household in those days) Next day we were on our way in Michael's car when I suddenly felt uneasy. Nearing Peterborough it came to me. The precious ham was still in my cellar!

I had to confess. They could hardly believe it. Michael stopped the car. There was nothing for it but to go back. Money was so tight we couldn't have afforded to replace that ham. So, with an ill grace, he took my house keys, let us out of the car and turned back, leaving myself and Beryl walking the streets with the children until he returned. The atmosphere was distinctly chilly, and I felt so ashamed to have forgotten the one thing I had promised to remember that I just wanted to hide away somewhere.

By the end of the journey I had been reinstated and forgiven. The chalet – or more accurately a wooden hut – was in a row of similar ones set on a ridge in a rather featureless area. We had a lake behind us and the sea in front. There was little to do except take walks in the bracing air and look after ourselves and the children, but it was a complete break from our normal routine and we enjoyed it. Timothy was twelve months old, enjoying his first bath in the galvanised tub provided and splashing around, when we noticed bubbles coming from his mouth. We realised he must have put the soap in his mouth, but when we searched and couldn't find it we began to panic. Supposing he'd swallowed it. Could it poison him? Get stuck inside?

He looked fine, though the bubbles continued to stream down his chest and tummy. Michael took the car to find a doctor while Timothy, unaware of our concern, was having great fun with the bubbles. In due course, Michael came back. He couldn't find a doctor. Since the baby was still gurgling happily, we decided that whatever the consequences we could do no more. We took him out, dried him and put away the bath. On straightening the mat, what should we find but a small piece of soap beneath it. Timothy must have bitten into it, didn't care for the taste, and dropped it on the floor, where our movements worked it under the mat. What a relief!

The Smell On The Landing

With the change of air I should have slept well there, but being a light sleeper I could hear the sea getting rough towards high tide. Getting out of bed to find the sea frighteningly close I realised that it would only have to creep a little higher before we were awash in seawater, our escape cut off by the lake behind us. Only when the high-water mark had passed and the waves began to subside did I return to bed. When the great floods hit the North Norfolk coast in January 1953 and swept away everything in their path with tragic loss of life I realised that my fears had been all too well founded.

Soon after this holiday, Beryl was diagnosed with cancer and commenced treatment with Radio Therapy. I nursed her through the ordeal in a downstairs room in my house, where I could prepare the special diet required by the treatment. At Christmas many of her friends and relatives thought it would be her last and overdid things with presents to the children, but when the treatment finished there was a great improvement. Her monthly hospital check-ups showed no sign of the illness, and soon a visit once a year was deemed sufficient. I still treasure the warm letter of thanks she sent me for my care in her time of need.

The family eventually moved to Moulton, where I would visit them pushing my pram through the lovely country lanes. When their boys had grown into teenagers they moved again, the boys duly got married and Beryl busied herself with the Church and charity work. For more than thirty years we kept in touch, almost like sisters, until I received the dreadful news that the cancer we all thought she'd overcome became activated, and this time nothing could save her. Most of my family managed to attend the funeral, and my only consolation at losing such a dear friend was that the early treatment had preserved our friendship for a long, fruitful time. Whenever possible I keep in touch with Michael and the boys.

Some people seem accident-prone, and I count myself one. Around 1983 I booked bed-and-breakfast accommodation in Bournemouth, along with a beach hut well-stocked with crockery and utensils, kettle and a Calor-gas stove and of course deck-chairs. Zena and her young daughter Laura accompanied Jack and myself, plus Ronka the dog. Ronka's thick coat, more suitable for Antarctica, made him most uncomfortable in the extreme heat. He was in his element in snow, which he'd gambol in until the snowballs clinging to his fur made it awkward for him to walk. He suffered so much on this holiday that we had to keep cooling him under the water-taps provided on the promenade. Guess who was the one holding him there in the blazing sun? I should have known that with thinning hair and no hat I had little protection from sunburn, but in those days few people knew about the hole in the ozone layer that let dangerous radiation from the sun penetrate the atmosphere, with its attendant risks. We returned home and I forgot all about it until 10 years later, when I found a growth on my scalp. I picked it off and it came again, each time getting larger, so I went to the doctor, who diagnosed a skin cancer and referred me to a clinic where I had it surgically removed. Six or seven weeks later, all was healed, but nothing would bring back my lost hair...

The Millenium Year, as I was saying, was memorable in lots of ways, not all of them pleasant. When I travelled alone by car to visit sister Joyce in Sussex, I could feel the anxiety of my children for my safety on the roads at nearly 80 years old. But there is nothing quite like the freedom of driving wherever you please, except when impeded by the vehicle ahead whose driver clearly isn't very capable, when I want to stop and give them a lecture. I'd had a few horns tooted at me too, so when I read an advertisement in the local paper that offered to improve one's driving I enrolled for this Advanced driving course.

The Smell On The Landing

The instructor first of all inspected the car to ensure it was clean inside and out with nothing to distract attention like dingly-dangly dice swinging from the mirror. Mirrors inside and out had to be correctly positioned and clean and the seat-belt adjusted for safety and comfort. When all was done he told me we would go on a test-drive. It lasted for about 15 minutes, after which he pointed out my faults. I'd made some mistakes on gear-changes and my commentary, but considering I'd never been used to speaking my thoughts on what was going on around me as I drove, I wasn't too worried about that. At any rate I was accepted on the course and began attending once a week, watching videos and listening to lectures about the mistakes drivers make and how to avoid getting into dangerous situations. Came the day for my trial-run exam with a qualified examiner, who then took me to view the skid pad so that I would know what to expect on the day.

Out of the blue I was struck down by an unknown virus and carted off to hospital, not knowing what was going on. Josephine who accompanied me told me later that I spent 14 hours on a hospital trolley, waiting to be seen by a doctor. The verdict, when it came, was that my insulin had deteriorated and should be thrown away, and meanwhile I was too unwell to drive. So the car stood for weeks in the garage, and then the insurance on it was due.

I lay awake for nights trying to come to terms with the situation. To renew the insurance, as a diabetic with cataracts and 80 next birthday would cost £1,000, and I still owed half the cost of the car. When I found out about the cataracts it explained the difficulty I had with watching the television and threading needles, which always seemed to have two eyes. Quite recently too I'd had a scare when trying to park the car alongside some railings to make room for an ambulance sounding its klaxon. When the traffic started to flow again I found that the bonnet was stuck, and in backing to free it managed to pull the front of the car off! That little episode cost me £500, and here I was, losing sleep wondering how I could afford to renew the insurance when really it was obvious that I ought to give it up.

Common sense prevailed, but it was no easy decision. Without the car I became more dependent on others and had to give up the voluntary work I found so rewarding, as virtually all the meetings were in places inaccessible by public transport. It was small consolation to be able to smile when passing a speed camera in a bus or taxi, but the cards I received from former colleagues on my retirement were a welcome acknowledgement of my contribution over the years.

The following year (2001) after my neighbour Frank Clifford had passed away, his property was bought by a developer who wanted to return his cottage to the two originally built on the site. The developer wished to put a lead flashing on top of the boundary wall between us, so needed to know who actually owned the wall. Contacting my solicitor for the property deeds (the wall did belong with my property) took me back to Boughton Green Rd again in 1963, before Georgina was born. Geoffrey was the baby of the five children, and I regularly took him in his pram to be weighed at the Baptist Church rooms in High St Kingsthorpe, a few hundred yards away. Opposite was a site on which five three-bedroomed houses were to be built. Watching them rise from their foundations week by week I remember thinking how nice it would be to live there.

One Sunday afternoon, out on a family walk, we passed through Kingsthorpe High St and noticed that number 40A had been opened as a show house and was for sale at £4,500. I went inside to view, which only strengthened my desire to own, though it was out of the question then. I was not the only one to be impressed. My father, visiting from London, took the same route, and on his return remarked. "I wouldn't mind living in one of those houses in High St."

Years later, in 1979, he had his wish when the family arranged to move him and my mother to Northampton. By the sheerest chance, the show-house I had so admired was up for sale (at a much higher price of course) and my offer for it was accepted. Father's health had deteriorated in the meantime with Altzheimer's disease, but the layout of the house was so similar to the one they had left in London he hardly noticed the difference. It was only when he went outside that he became disorientated and had to be accompanied.

Another event in 2001 is worthy of mention. I'd heard that the Royal Star and Garter Home in Richmond, Surrey, was looking for contributions from those who had served during WW2. I wrote an account of my own service in the ATS to highlight the part played by women during the war, which I had long felt had been given scant mention. I sent the piece to Simon Weston, who was coordinating the project known as the Odyssey Timeship, along with my cheque for £10 towards the expenses. The idea was to compile a computer disc from all sources, to be kept at the Imperial War Museum until the year 2101, when hopefully our successors would be able to access the information from it and learn from first-hand accounts how it was then.

I was delighted to hear from him later to say that my memoir had been accepted, and to receive an invitation along with other contributors to attend a ceremony at the Imperial War Museum in London introduced by the Duke of Kent. It was quite an occasion as all those memories came rushing back. If only I could be there when the disc is played in 2101. With all the efforts of modern science to prolong life, that is likely to be more a matter for the spirit to arrange than the body!

Another year, another birthday – my 82nd. As usual, I stand on a chair while my family sing Happy Birthday. I've blown out the candles on the cake, complimented the daughter responsible for the magnificent spread, admired again the mass of flowers and count myself lucky to be surrounded by all this love. I get to wondering what the rest of the year will bring and whether I shall ever master (should that be "mistress"?) the modern technology my children take for granted. I refer, of course to my very newest toy...

Cousin Charles was good enough to leave me £1,000 in his will, and that's what really started it. For years I'd been promising myself and family to take this major step into today's world, and now I had no excuse, with Frances turning up just after the Jubilee celebrations and listening to me bemoaning the loss of my lovely car. She whisked me off to the shops before I could protest, and stoically followed me from shop to shop until – there it was – a corner table that had the right design and didn't take up too much room. Now I needed something to go on it, and there was this beautiful new model looking like something from the future. We left the store with a trolley full of purchases, and when I got home found that I needed help with the flat-pack items. Frances said how she loved spending other people's money and organised husband Duncan to come along later, when they spent the evening setting up everything in the chosen corner of the front room.

When all was complete, I sat back and wailed *WHAT HAVE I DONE?* The thing needed to be fed with a new telephone line before it would work, and I hadn't the least idea how to use it. "Don't worry, mother," I was assured. "Give it three months and you won't be saying *Oh dear* any more."

The first thing I learned from experimenting was that computers don't think in the same way as humans. I'm told they're based on logic, but whenever I apply logic to look in the instruction book I can never find what I need to know under the right heading, and sometimes not at all. So I decide to enrol on a computer course for beginners, which concentrates on explaining how a computer works, but all the time I'm wondering when they'll get to the bit about how to stop my text disappearing when I try to use the spell-check, why my *mouse* persists in hiding just when it should be doing things for me, why my e-mails don't fly to their destination when I press "send," why…I'm sure the course can't answer all the questions I have, so it's back to this tome of a book called *Windows For Dummies*, which is most instructive provided you know *exactly* what to look for. Your first guess is usually wrong, and I've spent many more hours trying to sort out problems than actually producing text that can be understood and printed out. *Where's my faithful old typewriter?*

I return to my knitting. Frances has given me a challenge. I have to knit a *uterus* to cover a doll 12" tall, made as a foetus to fold up. It's for one of her Nursing friends to instruct new mothers on what happens at birth, but where are the instructions? It looks as though it'll be up to me, so I cast 74 stitches on to the size 8 needles to begin at the *vagina* end, having measured the doll's head for size, otherwise it will need a caesarian to get it out. I make some holes for a draw thread at the cervix so that it will open and close when demonstrating. Then I continue knitting until I have a bulbous, full-term baby with *placenta* and umbilical cord which was already attached to the foetus doll. I decrease to completion with more holes for a drawstring to allow the demonstrator to push the baby out through the birth canal. I try it, and lo and behold it works! I'm so delighted I smack baby's bottom and make a realistic-sounding squeal on its behalf. If only that computer would co-operate as well…

This year of 2002 we shall be missing my only granddaughter, Laura, backpacking and working her way across Australia. When I think of her I also remember Holly, Hazel's daughter whom she lost after 18 weeks of pregnancy. I always count her in the tally of 13 grandchildren. The eleven young men who now greet me began to arrive in 1972, when I was working as an Auxiliary Nurse at Harborough Rd Hospital. A telephone message came through to me at the Isolation ward to give me the news. Was I pleased to hear that I'd become a grandmother? Frankly, No! While I was relieved to know that mother and daughter were doing well, I had enough to think about with my immediate family without taking in this new responsibility. I'd borne six children in 18 years, and my youngest, Georgina, was only seven. I felt I was still learning how to be a good mother. And taking on the role of *grandmother* at the age of 52 made me feel prematurely old. How was one supposed to deal with it, apart from the expected present-giving at Christmas and birthday?

Over the years I've learned how to get by – whether satisfactorily or not I can't say. When we all meet now I'm confronted by this football team of youngsters dressed in ragged jeans and gabbling away to each other in a strange tongue. How could the generation gap throw up such a different world? At least, that's how it seems until I realise that beneath the American-inspired casual clothes that in my day nobody would have been seen dead in, these are caring young people, watching out for me. I see it in the glances they throw me from time to time, though displays of affection with the older ones are confined to a hug in response to my kiss on the cheek to mark their departure. The three younger ones run to kiss their Nan-Nan, as I'm known to them all, with sighs of relief, since it means returning home to have mummy back to themselves again. In the void left by their going I can't help comparing the lot of their mothers with mine. They missed the chore of washing by hand 100 Terry towelling nappies every week for years, the careful liquidising of baby food – now available tinned or jarred, in infinite variety. They could go out to work when the children reached school age, or even take advantage of the crêche facilities that some organisations provide. Few families today could support a mortgage on a single income, though some would say that family ties are less strong as a result, and we've all heard of latch-key children.

The three eldest grandchildren deserve a special mention. They are almost like brothers to son Geoffrey, all play football for a team and are polite, clever and greatly loved by their grandmother. Alone among all these boys is Laura who, perhaps inevitably, grew up preferring to play boy's games, to the extent of enrolling in a girl's football team in her teens. I'm sure her experiences back-packing around Australia will have given her a better idea of what to make of her life. Oddly enough, while she was there, Ken arrived on a visit to us here in November. With Christmas to look forward to, it wasn't such a bad year at all…

So here I am, with another birthday passed, looking back. It's November, and desperately-need rain is replacing the apparently endless sunshine of this year of record-breaking weather. Again, I'm aware of how much in the past links up with today. Take my pram for example. Many years ago I was rummaging in a Council tip when I espied a white doll's pram frame, minus its carriage. It gave me an idea, so I paid the 50p asked and loaded it into the back of my car. At home I found a large cardboard box, popped it into a plastic bag of the type that fits supermarket trolleys so as to waterproof it, dropped it into the pram and tied it all together with an old leather belt which was threaded through the handles of my money-bag so that nobody could run off with it. Now I was prepared for the next shopping expedition.

You might be wondering why I couldn't just get a "sholley" like everyone else. Well, I've tried and found that it doesn't work for me. The holding bag was so deep that anything soft at the bottom got squashed. Then there's the problem of having arms too short to reach a purchase at the bottom, to say nothing of the business of trying to find a purse quickly in the vast, black depths. My home-made carrier was ideal. The wheels were of a decent size for quick progress, I could load it with soft things at one end, heavy things at the other, and it was much more comfortable to *push* rather than drag. Listening to its "clickety-clack" over the paving stones was a happy reminder of my very first pram. I was two years old again, with a whole exciting new world opening out before me just waiting to be explored.

One day Josephine came to visit, and after an embarrassed silence came to the point. In a roundabout way she suggested that I needed a shopping contrivance that had a seat. I had to accept that my legs had been very painful when going uphill, and although medication helped, it wasn't the right answer. Now my daughter was suggesting I give up the shopping pram that was recognised everywhere I went and attracted such comments as "what will you do when a wheel comes off?" The thought of abandoning my precious helper filled me with horror. "Josephine, I'm not ready for that yet," I told her severely.

She wouldn't let it rest. "You need a trolley or something with a seat on it," she persisted. "You must agree with that."

I hardly knew what to say. The pram *was* rather dilapidated. We'd grown old together, and I had no wish to change the situation. Drawing a deep breath, Josephine said "Mother, have you thought of putting your name down for a home? You may need it in a few years time, and it helps if your name is already on the register."

That was the last straw. "I'm not ready for that either," I said, "and it's time you went." I propelled her to the front door. "Thank you for calling."

I thought that would be the last of it, but not at all. A few days later she was back with a walker that incorporated a seat and a shopping bag. "This is what you need," she assured me. "Just try it and see." While I was doing so she got hold of my faithful companion and loaded it unceremoniously into the boot of her car. "Say goodbye to this." She closed the boot-lid and drove off to the tip, leaving me to brood on the end of an era and face up to my age, which was the last thing I needed to be doing.

On my first shopping excursion I found I could not buy quite as much because the new contraption lacks storage space. There's a small basket under the seat, and a large holding bag on the back. But it's deep and black inside, and my arms haven't grown any longer. Also the wheels get locked, just like a supermarket trolley with all its disadvantages. But Josephine bought it for me out of concern for my welfare, and I do appreciate her doing it. The wheels don't make that "clickety-clack" that I shall always associate with that far-off childhood and the arrival of my sister who has been so supportive throughout my life. Who else but me could possibly feel this too?

My diary at age 83 has more hospital appointments than social ones, and I'm reliant on other people more than I ever imagined I would be. I count my blessings in having all my children living within a few miles of here. Hardly a day goes by without a visit or phone call from one or the other. They help keep me from fretting over such annoyances as waiting two years for an appointment to operate on my cataracts. A few weeks ago I was all set to have it done when the hospital told me they had to cancel it because they had "reached their quota." Is it any wonder that some people are prepared to use their savings to pay for private operations? If I lived somewhere else it would have been done by now, but I try to be philosophical.

I'm also fortunate in having loyal friends, among whom Vernon has remained an important part of my life. His oppressive treatment of me in the early days has mellowed, perhaps due in part to the close shave he had with death in 1986 with a severe heart attack at work. On the way to hospital the paramedics had to resuscitate him three times, and their commitment may have been the deciding factor in his survival. Some habits of his remain unchanged. Unable now to work, he's reverted to sleeping during daylight hours and being out at dark. He visits me five times a week, when we talk or listen to classical music or both. The relationship has moved on from the earlier crazy, sex-mad affair, when we could not get enough of each other and took every opportunity to go to bed and satisfy each other's passionate needs, made all the more exciting by the fear of being caught.

Nowadays I share him with a lady friend who keeps dogs and lives a couple of doors away from him locally. From what he tells me their friendship is a curious one that at times seems as though it will develop and somehow never does. I look forward very much to his visits, which break the monotony of living alone. The gypsy who read my fortune when I was a teenager told me there would be two men in my life (how many other people had she said that to, I wonder?) She went on to tell me that one would have a name beginning with G and the other N (Vernon's other Christian name) Many would dismiss this as sheer coincidence, but some things defy explanation, and I have to accept that.

I think this would be a suitable note to end on, though doubtless when the book has gone to the printer I'll wish I'd put in such and such. I've really enjoyed the experience of looking back and trying to put events into a proper perspective. Now all that remains is to compile a short appendix with the family history and hope that the book finds favour with those who know me, or at least gives them something to mull over in the future...

Appendix

Editor's Note:

For convenience and ease of access, this Appendix gathers together genealogical data and profiles of SHAW family members and certain antecedents, along with other material that would not fit easily into the main text which is largely chronological.

FUNERAL EULOGY FOR ADA ADELINE CLEMINSON
(d. Aug. 25th 1993)

Aderline had a very traumatic childhood – one of ten children whose mother, Ada, was a sick woman who could not look after her. From the age of five, Aderline was sent to other relatives for varying periods. There were happy times, and others when she was placed in an atmosphere of hostility. During visits home she was teased mercilessly by her older brothers. Eventually she found tranquillity with her maternal grandparents, where she was known as "grandma's little helper," until her grandmother became ill and died.

At the age of twelve, she returned to her parent's home, only to nurse her own mother until she died soon after and the weight of the family chores fell upon Aderline's young shoulders. Her father, John Soar, was first violinist to Sir Henry Wood and played with the orchestra in Paisley, Glasgow, Edinburgh and Stratford in London, where at seventeen she met her future husband Leonard Cleminson at the Wesleyan Methodist Church. At the outbreak of the First World War he was called up and served five years in the Army. They were married shortly after his return in 1919, when Aderline found herself living with a virtual stranger. Their children Gladys, Joyce and Kenneth were born between 1920 and 1924 and grew up in the difficult years of the Depression.

During the Second World War Aderline joined the Home Guard to learn about firing rifles and Sten guns. She also became an Air Raid Warden, patrolling the streets and rescuing people from their bombed houses. Her three children had all left home in the space of a week – Gladys to the Army, Joyce evacuated with her employer and Kenneth to pursue his medical studies.

Aderline and Leonard did much for their community and for years worked voluntarily for the local hospital, from which they received a Certificate of Governorship for Life. Although this was revoked on the introduction of the National Health Service, she continued knitting and raising money to comfort patients through the Aid Committee. She was also a blood donor who continued beyond the laid-down maximum age of sixty-five until she reached eighty because nobody at the hospital queried her age.

In 1979 the Social Services in Hornchurch where she lived became alarmed when she began falling over due to Ménière's disease. It was arranged for her and her husband to move to Northampton, where a property was found close to the home of their eldest daughter Gladys, who looked after them both until they required professional care. Leonard died at the age of ninety-three, in 1986. Aderline spent the last three years of her life in King's Heath Elderly People's Home, until as the result of a fall she was admitted to St Edmund's Hospital where she died shortly after her 100th Birthday. Many of her immediate family, comprising three children, thirteen grandchildren and fifteen great-grandchildren were present at her Centenary on 4th August 1993.

I've reached a land of corn and wine and all its riches freely mine.
Here shines undimmed one blissful day for all my night has passed away.

Oh Beulah land, sweet Beulah Land, as on thy highest mount I stand,
I look away across the sea, where mansions are prepared for me.

And view the shining glory shore
My Heaven, my home for evermore.

Profile of her mother by Gladys Shaw

Mother was a curious mixture. It was only in later years that I began to understand how she could have treated me so severely in my childhood, when everybody outside the household saw her as a compassionate neighbour who would put herself out to help someone who needed it. I needed her to love me, and she didn't – at least not in the way I wanted her to. Before her incapacity made her dependent on others she told me about her earlier life. One particular occasion stands out.

She sat on a wooden dining-chair, elbows on the scrubbed-top kitchen table, hands cradling a cup of steaming tea. "Pass your coop oop," she invited me in the broad Scots accent she'd never lost.

I watched while she poured the tea from the old pot, noting the lines about her neck and arms. A knock at the door galvanised her small frame. "I'll not be a minute," she called over her shoulder as she rose. "It's only the insurance man."

Watching her, I mused that I'd inherited her quick movements and tiny physique – just five feet one and a half inches. She wore old-fashioned shoes with a bar across the instep and two-and-a-half-inch heels, and her dress, while scrupulously clean, had seen better days. On returning to the table she carefully arranged dress and pinafore before sitting down to resume the narrative that an old photograph had sparked. "How my brothers teased me at mealtimes," she recalled, "and worse. They'd even steal the food off my plate. I was a slow eater, you see, and they couldn't wait."

She sighed and leaned back in her chair, pushing stray grey hairs away from her pallid face towards the bun gathered at the nape of her neck. Her voice softened. "But not Tom. He was always so gentle."

Tom was apparently the champion she needed in a house full of boisterous brothers, and it was his photograph, always prominently displayed in the house, that had begun her recall. Handsome, and a talented violinist like his father, he had died tragically early from cancer in his thirties. Mother paused to use her handkerchief. "We were always moving to wherever my father could find work, so I was forever changing schools. Then one day I was sent to stay with an uncle and had to share a bed with an older girl cousin who didn't want me and had a cruel tongue. In those days I had thick, curly hair that people admired. It bounced about when I ran and jumped, but then I caught head lice. It must have been too bad to comb out, so they chopped off my hair within an inch of my scalp and burnt it on the fire."

This event had left so deep an impression on her that years later when I was nursing her she wouldn't let me or anyone else touch her hair. Other things would have affected her too and helped mould her into the woman she became. I'm sure that being unwanted made it impossible for her to reach out to her children or show them them an affection she'd never received herself.

Despite the poverty of our early childhood, mother had high standards. She would not allow us to mix with what she called the riff-raff of London's East End. This was unfortunate for me because my best friend Rose lived there, and our friendship caused lots of friction. Yet she had no racial prejudice. Friends of any colour or creed were accepted, so long as they didn't bring May blossom into the house, for instance. Though she denied being superstitious, she would not have any picture of an owl in the house, nor goldfish bowls. In her early life a burglar had been discovered hiding behind the piano in a corner of the front room, so she would never lay the breakfast table overnight. Knives could be used as weapons.

The Smell On The Landing

For similar reasons she wouldn't sit with her back to an open door, which one could understand. But where did the idea come from that you should never cut a baby's finger-nails? They had to be *bitten,* to avoid the child becoming a thief in later life. I never did discover the origin of this one.

One of the saddest aspects of our family life, which we didn't realise until later, was that mother could not return her husband's feelings. Yes, she looked after him well and let him do more or less as he wished, but all without warmth. He adored her, and she couldn't reciprocate. He seemed to be unaware, for when Ken tried to discuss it with him in later life, father wouldn't hear of it. When he died she offered me her wedding-ring, saying she didn't wish to wear it any longer. Perhaps that says it all.

Throughout her life with us we gave her sprigs of lily-of-the-valley in season which were her favourite flowers, but for her funeral wreath had to make do with imitation sprays, which we retrieved after the crematorium service for Joyce and I to display in our own homes as remembrance. Oddly, when subsequently attending the Spiritualist Church, the medium came to me with a message that she saw me surrounded with lily-of-the-valley blooms which came with love from the Other Side. I had no doubt at all who the sender was…

The following is a true copy of a letter (original lost) from Sapper L.J.Cleminson, serving in Egypt, to his father, dated March 23rd 1917, Alexandria

A true copy of a letter from

Sapper L.J. Cleminson

89536 13th Base Park Coy

Royal Engineers

Exped Forces in Egypt

Alexandria

Egypt

March 23rd 1917

To His Father

My Dear Dad

My holidays are now past and over, and I am back once again in Alexandria, so while the events of the past few days are fresh in my memory,I will try and give you a few details and descriptions of them, and I sincerely hope: that they will prove interesting to you, and all.

On Monday March the 19th;- I finished my duties at midday and got ready. I applied at the Company's office for my pass to Cairo- I then left the camp at 3 o'clock and proceeded by train to Cairo station in the centre of Alexandria, and boarded the 4 o'clock train to Cairo. The scenes as I went along were very interesting as the train goes through parts where the Egyptians are still living, as in the ancient days, in mud and reed huts, and they seem scared when the train rushes past. Their attire is very scanty indeed, and they are also filthy dirty. The distance from Alexandria to Cairo is roughly 210 miles, and nearly all the way the country is one mass of fields, corn and vegetation of all kinds,and not a sandy waste ground as one would imagine. On the way we past 4 of the largest and most important towns in Egypt, and eventually after 3 hours journey arrived in Cairo. On my arrival I made my way to the "Anzac Hostel" and after booking a bed for 3 nights and having some refreshments, I had a walk through the main streets,then returned to the "Anzac Hostel" had my supper and retired at 10.30p.m.

Tuesday March 20th I arose at 7 a.m. and had a good breakfast, then visited the Kas-rel-Nil Military Barracks, and after that I went by tram to the citadel. The citadel is a Muslem Church, or rather a Cathedral, and is the second largest building of its kind in the world and it appears a very imposing sight from the town as it stands on the Maccadonian Hills, It is a very costly building, being built entirely of Alabaster, and the carvings are wonderful. On my arrival at the entrance I was stopped by the keeper who informed me that if I went inside I should either have to take of my boots, or put slippers over them, as the carpet was sacred and belonged to "ALLAH" (The Mohammedan God) who would be displeased if the laws of the faith were broken,so I put slippers over my boots, and went inside when I was astonished at the beautiful sight, the interior of the place presented;it was lit by a huge chandelier of glass, holding over 2000 electric lights which shone on the Alabaster walls and pillars, and made me gaze with wonder at the spectacle. The carpet was about 2 to 3 inches thick, and was deep red, and the roof (which formed a huge dome) was nearly all crimson and gold. The pulpit was built of Cedar wood, and was inlaid with gold,silver ivory, bronze etc; and its value is enormous. The place was built by Mohammed Ali Pasha, taking 30 years to build, and when it was completed the ruling Sultan of the time ordered him to be blinded, so that he would not be able to see to build another place like it. When He died his body was placed in a tomb built inside the Citadel. The entrance to his tomb is made mostly of Gold and Silver with massive doors, and it is considered a very sacred chamber indeed. From the top of the building I could see the pyramids, and also the dead city of Sacahra, and also those of Giza (mentioned in the Bible). I then visited the Mosque of the Sultan Hussian. It is a very ancient place,The doors of which are about 12ft.across and 30ft high. They are inlaid Mosaic work of gold silver bronze,and ivory, and are worth thousands of pounds.then I visited the Blue Mosque. It is the only Mosque in Egypt containing blue glass from Mecca, which is very sacred at both of the places. Before I could gain admission I had to put on slippers because of the sacred carpet I then visited Jacobs Well. supposed to be the place where Joseph was hidden by his brothers. it is 300ft deep. I went about 200ft. down. then gave it up as it was dangerous to climb. I also saw the place where they found Moses in the Bullrushes. I then returned to town by tram, and had a good dinner, and a good rest.

After that I went to Gezerha (Geyser) Zoological Gardens which are very similar to
the Zoo at Regents Park, but contain animals, birds and reptiles that cannot be kept in
England owing to the climate. There was a beautiful grotto in the gardens called
"The Citadel Grotto", and is a very picturesque piece of work, and it is covered with
all kinds of foliage. I then returned about 5.p.m. and had tea at the Y.M.C.A. Head
Quarters in Esbekiah Gardens in the centre of the town. After tea I visited the
Russell Soldiers Home and had a very interesting talk with a lady in charge ho came
from Woodbridge Bridge. After that I went to the Gardens again, and saw the pictures
in the open air, and returned to bed about ten very tired indeed.
Wednesday March 21st; I rose at 7 a.m. and had breakfast, then went by tram to the
Hezirha (Geyser)Pyramids, then by camel to the foot of the Sphinx, which is a
wonderful piece of work,and then went to the foot of the great Pyramids, which are a
marvellous piece of ancient Egyptian building. They are built on huge blocks of stone
and granite which weigh on average 17 tons each, and are placed in a position so
exact that you could not get a cigarette paper between them. It is about 350 ft high
and was built 3,733 years B.C. and is still in very good condition it was originally
built by King Toofoo, for a tomb for the King and Queen, and their bodies were found
a few years ago in good condition and taken to the British Museum in Londonm but the
granite coffins are still inside the large pyramid. I went inside the large pyramid
and saw the chambers of the King and Queen which are right in the centre of the
pyramid, and to get to them I had to climb a steep slope of polished marble, which is
so slippery that I had to take my boots off, so that I could walk on it. It took
roughly about 30 years to build the pyramids. After seeing all that was possible to
be seen , I returned to town and had a well earned dinner and rest. In the afternoon
I visited the Cairo Museum. It is a very fine building on the bank of the River Nile,
I saw there the bodies of several of the ancient Kings and Queens of Egypt. Of course
they are in mummified state. but are very well preserved. They also have the jewellery
that was buried with them. I was very interested in the Mummy of King Pharoah, who
caused all the trouble and plagues with the Israelites. His hair is still in good

page four

condition, and is very fair, but his features are very hard and cruel. I then had some
tea, and went by electric train to Heliopolis (New Cairo) I have bought some views
of the place and will send a few at a time.It is a very beautiful place, and all
the buildings are pure white.I returned to Cairo about 8 o'clock, and had a walk
through the town-had supper and went to bed absolutely tired out at 10.30.p.m.
Thursday March 22nd Rose at 6.30-had a good breakfast and caught the 7.55 train
to Barrage (Barrarsh). It is a magnificent Garden-city about 20 miles from Cairo.
The river divides into 3 parts in these gardens, but to hold the water back from
the main river they have built a huge dam right across the three rivers. It was built
by an English Engineer, and took ten years to build,and by opening either of the
3 dams, they could flood the country almost down to Alexandria, and the river on
the upper side of the Dam is 90 ft.higher than the other side,so you will get an
idea of the immense size of the Dam,and also the pressure that it has to resist.
The entire length of the 3 Dams is about 1 miles. The gardens are a sight worth
seeing, and are one mass of colours;The plants are very peculiar and, and very rare
indeed. You can imagine how lovely the air is with the perfume from all the
flowers. Well, at midday, it was too hot to walk about, so I went back to Cairo
by train,and had dinner. I then went by tram to Old Cairo, and that was very
interesting indeed as some of the streets and buildings are the same as they were
when the Egyptians of Biblical History were alive,I had a walk round the Egytians
Bazaars, and bought the enclosed souvenir for you,after which I returned to the
Y.M.C.A.in town, and then caught the train backto Alexandria, and arrived safely
backat 10.p.m. and was not sorry when I got back to camp and into bed.
Now Dad, you are almost as wise as I am myself, will give fuller details when I
see you all, trusting you are all well,and Kind regards to all enquirers ,

                    Your loving Son

                        LEN 89536   Sapper Cleminson
                                       Royal Engineers
                                       Expeditionary Forces
                                          in Egypt.

A copy of this letter was sent to the Imperial War Museum and placed into
a time capsule to be opened in 100 years timeOdyssey Timeship organised
by the Star and Garter Home, Richmond Surrey

GEORGE HENRY (JACK) SHAW

Scattering of the ashes on Father's day 15th June 1997
at Aldwincle village; a family remembrance led by his
wife Gladys.

When I am dead, my dearest,
Sing no sad songs for me;
Plant thou no roses at my head,
Nor shady cypress tree:
Be the green grass above me
With showers and dewdrops wet;
And if thou wilt, remember,
And if thou wilt, forget……………*Christina G Rossetti*

Today is Father's Day, which I feel is very appropriate. We are
gathered here as a family to pay homage to George Henry Shaw,
near to Fern Cottage where he was born in the year 1918 on 17th
June. This being the nearest weekend to his birthday, we give
thanksgiving for his life. There was nothing he liked better than to
visit the place of his birth, when his parents were living here before
their eviction from Fern Cottage by the syndicate who bought the
land and tied cottages from Lord Lilford. His father William Henry
was a gamekeeper on this land, and was promised by his employer
that he would be able to live in Fern Cottage until his death, but this
promise was not honoured owing to the death of Lord Lilford when
all was sold, this being a great shock to them all.

We as a young family would travel by train from Northampton
station on the now closed Peterborough line to Thrapston, then
walk to this lane to visit his parents. This visit was always an
emotional one, and it remained so to him in memory recall during
his life. Often in his last years he would ask me about happenings
in Aldwincle, which often I knew nothing about so could not
satisfy his enquiry.

In his last hours his mind was back here often, so this is why his family and loved ones are gathered now to bring his ashes "back home" to be scattered in these fields from whence they came, where as a young boy he roamed in play, went to school and church and became a member of the church choir and campanologist. He gained his indentures in Printing after a seven-year apprenticeship at Vase Press in Thrapston. Two weeks after taking his first full pay packet he was called up as a Militia Man in 1938 and joined the 5th battalion of the Northamptonshire Regiment, then on to the War Zone of 1939 and its dreadful happenings.

George at heart was a pacifist and some of his duties as a serving soldier haunted his sleeping hours for many years with nightmares that brought back scenes of horror he had witnessed. As he got older this scene gradually faded and was replaced with tranquillity. This land we are observing around us became a haven of rest for his tortured mind. It seemed fitting to bring his mortal remains "back home", but our presence and purpose is in Love...Love of this man who is one of many titles to us all. He is brother, father, father-in-law, granddad and uncle and in each title there is an expression of love towards him on different levels. Should you have any occasion to feel anger or disappointment with him, I ask you now to quell those thoughts if possible and try to forgive, remebering that to err is human, to forgive is divine.

A few moments for inner thoughts and prayer until I speak again...

I would like to make a wheel of love...standing in a circle, imagine you are a spoke leading towards the hub of the wheel, the hub being his casket...the outer rim unites us. We shall project our own personal thoughts and love towards the casket. Thoughts are living things, especially thoughts of love which are golden and can be picked up by him, enabling him to move forward into the light of God's consciousness, so that he can travel into his next existence with our love and blessings. During your next meditation give thanks for the life he has spent with us.

From body to body our spirit moves on…it seeks a new form when the old one has gone. We will not mourn, for you are more free than we.

Please send your loving thoughts in meditation now…

Fast asleep, fast asleep at last, though the pain was strong, though the struggle long. It is past…it is past. Go forward towards tomorrow's light…

Death is nothing at all. I have only slipped into the next room. Call me by my old familiar name, speak to me in the easy way you always used. I am I, and you are you. Whatever we were to each other we are still. Wear no false air of solemnity or sorrow, laugh as we always laughed at the little jokes we enjoyed together. Smile, think of me, pray for me and let my name be the household name that it always was, let it be spoken without any difference of meaning. Life means all that it ever meant, there is total continuity. I should not be out of mind because I am out of sight. I am but waiting for you, just around the corner. All is well…

Dust to dust, earth to earth, ashes to ashes we scatter…

Amen

A formal Service of Remembrance for the life of GEORGE HENRY SHAW was held on 14th June 1998 at St Peter's church, Aldwincle, attended by the family. The address was given by his wife Gladys Shaw.

THE OPENING BAT

A tribute to her husband by Gladys Shaw

From the pavilion he strode, young and handsome
Confident the bowlers had no chance
With bat in hand to acknowledge the cheers
He stood at the crease and made his stance
Ready to face those googlies that came thick and fast
His timing foot would tap the ground.

The ball has left the bowler's hand
Keen of eye and sleight of movement
The willow could not fault his demand
The umpire in his white coat would signal
The ball was "out of the ground".
"Well played", the club members would shout
The leather ball would rise and fall
Sending the visitors running about
They knew it would be hard to get him out.

Wives and mothers sipping tea, with giggles of glee,
"We should win now, shouldn't we?"
Hail fellow cricketer "Well played Jack",
With a slap on the back and a joke to crack
Knowing they could rely on his play, on a special Cup day.
It was a gentleman's game – he knew that,
Then into the pavilion to remove gloves, pads and hat.

Each week for the local press, about four
Reporters came round to collect the score.
In the Sports section his name was there
So often it almost became a bore!
Those who had contact with this giant of sport
Would sometimes remember these reports

As time went on, he opened no more
Sadly accepting this loss of play
He'd await the "News" and "Match of the Day".
His innings in life were played by the law.
The rules of the game always came to the fore.

George Henry Shaw, who was known as "Jack"
Has gone to a land of greener grass
Where others he knew had gone before,
Some of whom had died in the War.

Now it is Jack's turn to pass
Before the Umpire dressed in white.
To hear him say "Well played, my son",
Will be his glory and delight.

Gladys Shaw   *19th December 1996*

MEMORIES OF DAD

By his daughter, Frances Billingham

As we sit in this church and most of us weep
We remember him lulling us gently to sleep.
In cold draughty rooms where we laid our heads
Dad put hot water bottles in all our beds.
And while we slept safely (and some would snore)
Cleaned shoes would appear by the old cellar door.

On bright summer days, while watching the cricket
We'd gobble Mum's tea with our eyes on the wicket
Where Dad toiled at run-making, batting so well
Our carefree young hearts with great pride would swell

He'd bring the wages home each week
But for us kids, one thing we'd seek.
On Thursdays – pay-day! We would wait
For the familiar sound of that front gate

Then all of us rush to the dining-room door
For the Mars bars, Crunchies, Maltesers and more
Which he'd give with a smile, protesting "hang on.
Strike a light, kids, I've not been in long!"

Technology grew while printing waned
And so a Reader our dad became.
He'd read the paper – mistakes to discover
Then read it at home, from cover to cover!

Other memories stand out, like Christmas morn,
The silver tree, tinsel, decorations adorn;
Warm room, coal fires dad rose early to light
So the house seemed festive, alive and bright.
The stockings so full, all those presents we had!
Thanks to the quiet hard work of our dad.

His sixpence on Saturdays quickly spent
On liquorice, sherbet-fountains – all of it went!
We'd sit by the fire watching football and racing
And laugh at the horses' pompous names
While throwing sweet papers into the flames

What would we have done without dad being there?
In front of the fire with Ronky Dog,
Who devoured cheese sandwiches, pork pies and cake,
Then took long walks to get rid of the fat,
With dad – out one Christmas in red party hat!

I can hear his voice, as we'd come in
"Hello, m'duck, can you go down the front?
I've no tobacco in me tin
And bring me some Rizlas – the green ones will do
And while you're out, get old Ronka a chew."

Sadly dad's twilight years were hard
His quality of life was marred
By many strokes. But now his seeds have grown
To flourish, marry, and produce their own
And make him proud of all the crop he'd sown.

So, dad, we send you safely off to bed
Like the last editions you once read
We thank you, each and all, for our beginnings
And say goodbye, at this your final innings.

Frances

The Smell On The Landing

MEMORIES OF EARLY LIFE AT NO. 32

I remember the day I came home after my sister Zena was born. I was about 18months old and had been staying at Aunty Beryl's in Moulton for about a month to give mum time to get sorted out and rest. I guess I found it very strange to be home again, as Aunty Beryl's house was very quiet compared with ours. Throughout my childhood there was always something going on in our house. Relatives, friends of mum, school friends of my older siblings coming and going all the time; mad, but a warm and loving home. Sometimes the only place to have to yourself was the foot of the attic stairs. This space was not a heavily used thoroughfare, and you could read or while away the time with your own thoughts until summoned to eat or bath or wose still – bedtime!

My next memory is when I was about three and before I started school. *Watch With Mother* used to be broadcast every weekday lunchtime, and I can still remember watching it with my sister while outside a pale, weak and hazy winter sun shone serenely through the window of the back room.

Starting school was a revelation to me, the opportunity to learn and have answers to the questions in my head. Sadly it took a great readjustment, as my sister was too young to join me, and I can still see her sobbing in the classroom doorway as mum took her home. I felt our relationship was never the same until we were adults.

School was something I whole-heartedly enjoyed. Later at secondary school I relished tests and exams, especially History. We had a brilliant teacher who made us laugh so much that we remembered everything, and I still have a passion for all things ancient because of this man. It became a real competition between teacher and pupil constantly to get 100%. It makes me smile now to recall the time I only achieved 99%. He wrote alongside the one wrong answer – *Gotcher!*

From an early age we were all assigned jobs in the house. With six children to look after mum needed help as she had no relatives near to assist with a large family. These hated jobs were the bane of Saturday mornings. We had to strip and remake feather mattress beds, hoover the house, polish the brass and clean out the grate. I can remember how embarrassing it was to tell friends who called that I couldn't come out until later. No exceptions were made.

I had a few mishaps. Having survived a potential drowning at Billing Aquadrome, I coughed for weeks after. There was also a brief dash to the hospital A & E when Hazel inadvertently put a garden fork through my left foot; my remaining early years were largely uneventful. Then there stretched before me the tumultuous journey through adolescence.

This I call my religious phase. Mum had left it mostly up to us kids to sort out our own belief system. I read a lot and tried a number of churches and institutions, coming to rest for a while at Abington Avenue United Reform Church. I think this decision was mostly due to the lively and adventurous Youth Club, to say nothing of the young men attending. I grew up and moved on, having a lasting memory of many good Saturday nights at the Badminton Club, and weekends in Derbyshire or Wales.

I was out a great deal at this time. Once homework was completed and the jobs done, I was off. Something was always planned and I tended to walk everywhere as funds were limited. We provided our own entertainment and forged our own destinies. I got a Saturday job and paid for my first holiday £40 for two weeks in the Isle of Mull at fifteen. I had a great time, but returned to find that dad had had a severe stroke at only 47. It affected me greatly to see him unable to walk down the garden path unaided. It showed me that life was unpredictable, and opportunities should be taken as and when they presented themselves. I have always lived in the fast lane, and this taste of stark reality did nothing to slow me down. We each paid for our own driving lessons at 17 and 18, and after 'A' levels I left school to go to Oxford to begin my Nursing career, which is another story…

Frances

PATERNAL LINE – *Pannifer*

Nathanial Pannifer was an editor at the *London Morning Post* in 1860. The paper merged with the *Daily Telegraph* in 1937. His daughter **Laura Jane**, (the author's grandmother) was a sickly woman whose weak lungs incapacitated her from October to May most years and led to her death from pneumonia in 1915 when aboard ship. Her eldest son **Leonard James**, whose letter from Egypt in 1917 to his father **James Cleminson** is reproduced here, had such a remarkable affinity with Egypt that he "felt as though I had come home"as he said later. Although he had not been abroad before he apparently knew where certain landmarks were without consulting a map and would point out the way to his comrades. When quizzed by them he would reply "I feel as though I have lived here before." His understanding of certain Arabic phrases stood them in good stead when the local populace demonstrated against the unpopular British presence.

Leonard's younger brother **Albert Edward** (b.1895, England, d.1917 during WW1) was buried in England. Both his sisters **Florence Lilian** and **Dorothy,** born respectively 1899 and 1901, died in Wanstead, east London; Dorothy in 1972. The date of Florence's death is unrecorded.

Of the three Cleminson children, whose details are given elsewhere, **Gladys** the eldest initiated this book and became involved with the family history in 1984 when a firm of Genealogists contacted her seeking details of a deceased cousin, **William John Mullan**, who had died intestate. Gladys commenced enquiries that uncovered relatives in Canada, New Zealand and Australia and led to her visit to Canada in the summer of 2000, where she stayed with the **Galloways**. **Joyce**

PATERNAL LINE – *Pannifer* (abbreviated)

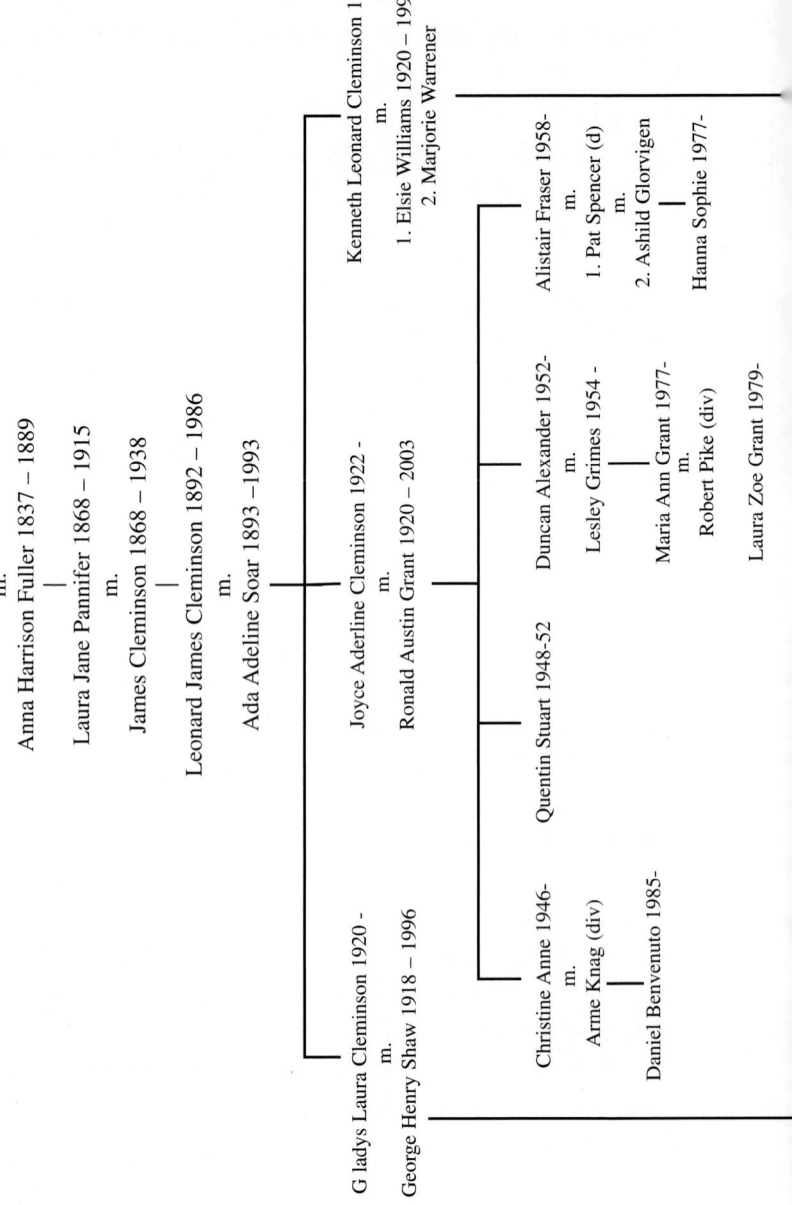

Nathaniel Pannifer 1830 – 1877
m.
Anna Harrison Fuller 1837 – 1889
|
Laura Jane Pannifer 1868 – 1915
m.
James Cleminson 1868 – 1938
|
Leonard James Cleminson 1892 – 1986
m.
Ada Adeline Soar 1893 –1993

Kenneth Leonard Cleminson 1924
m.
1. Elsie Williams 1920 – 1993
2. Marjorie Warrener

Joyce Aderline Cleminson 1922 -
m.
Ronald Austin Grant 1920 – 2003

G ladys Laura Cleminson 1920 -
m.
George Henry Shaw 1918 – 1996

Alistair Fraser 1958-
m.
1. Pat Spencer (d)
m.
2. Ashild Glorvigen

Hanna Sophie 1977-

Duncan Alexander 1952-
m.
Lesley Grimes 1954 -

Maria Ann Grant 1977-
m.
Robert Pike (div)

Laura Zoe Grant 1979-

Quentin Stuart 1948-52

Christine Anne 1946-
m.
Arme Knag (div)

Daniel Benvenuto 1985-

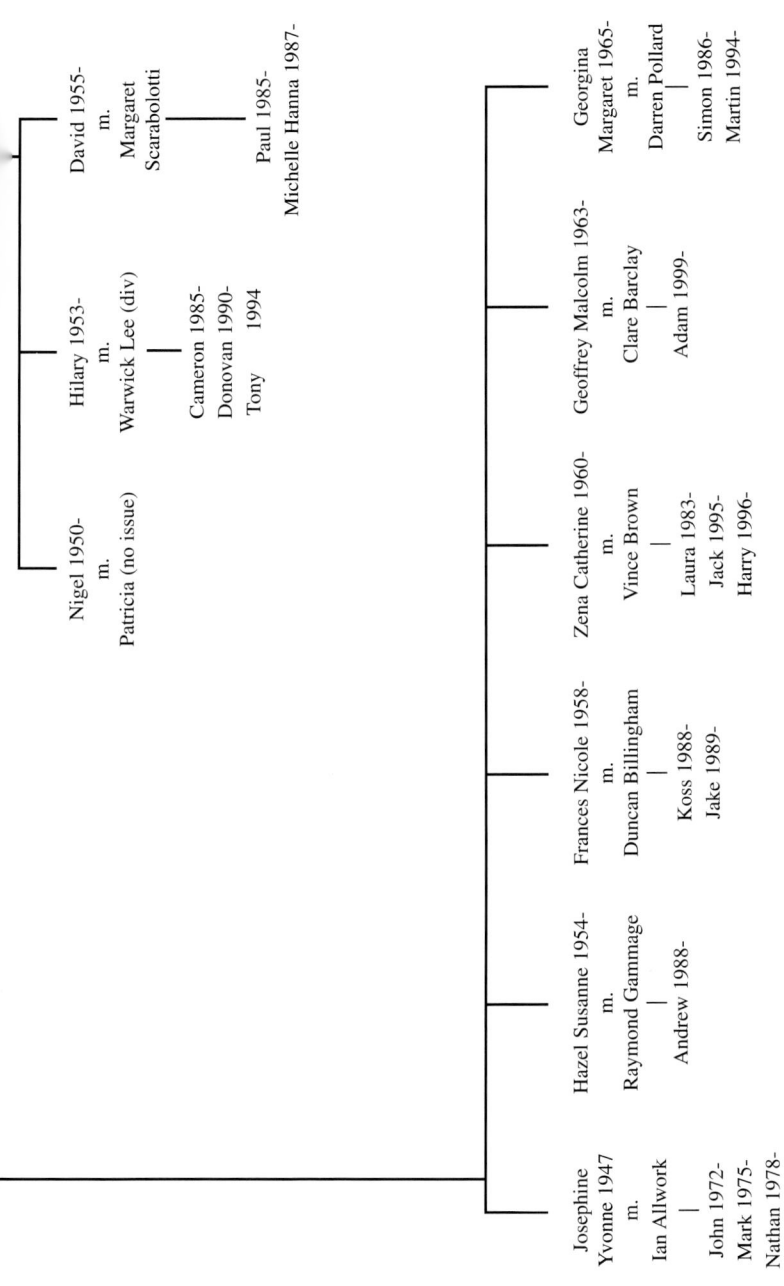

Nigel 1950-
m.
Patricia (no issue)

Hilary 1953-
m.
Warwick Lee (div)

Cameron 1985-
Donovan 1990-
Tony   1994

David 1955-
m.
Margaret
Scarabolotti

Paul 1985-
Michelle Hanna 1987-

Josephine
Yvonne 1947
m.
Ian Allwork
|
John 1972-
Mark 1975-
Nathan 1978-

Hazel Susanne 1954-
m.
Raymond Gammage

Andrew 1988-

Frances Nicole 1958-
m.
Duncan Billingham
|
Koss 1988-
Jake 1989-

Zena Catherine 1960-
m.
Vince Brown
|
Laura 1983-
Jack 1995-
Harry 1996-

Geoffrey Malcolm 1963-
m.
Clare Barclay
|
Adam 1999-

Georgina
Margaret 1965-
m.
Darren Pollard
|
Simon 1986-
Martin 1994-

Cleminson her sister researched the family at length, and the genealogical detail here has been distilled from her work and that of the Galloways.

The third Cleminson, **Kenneth** (now in retirement) embarked on a sucessful medical career and twice became a Fellow of the Royal College of Surgeons. He emigrated to Australia in 1957 where he was commanded to attend HRH Queen Elizabeth the Second on her tour of the country. For his work with the Flying Doctor Service he was made a blood brother of the Aboriginals in recognition of his dedication to the tribes.

MATERNAL LINE – *Soar*

Descent is from a French Huguenot family who fled France in 1685 during one of the periodic purges of Protestants by Catholics. They had adopted the Calvinist version of the Reformed religion and settled in England where they searched for an English name like their own. The name of the river Soar was chosen as being closest.

John Soar was first violinist to Sir Henry Wood and frequently accompanied the famous singer Dame Clara Butt. He worked closely with Sir Edward Elgar and played many of the composer's new works for him to hear before publication. His mother **Sarah Richardson** was related to the Emmeline Pankhurst of Suffragette fame. **Ada Grainger,** whom John Soar married, was related to the composer Percy Grainger.

MATERNAL LINE – *Soar* – (abbreviated)

Joseph Soar (1791 - ?)
m.
Anna Fisher
|
Isaiah Soar
m.
Sarah Richardson
|
John Soar (1861-1953)
m.
Ada Grainger (1861-1917)
|
Aderline Soar (1893-1993)
m.
Leonard James Cleminson (1892-1986)
|
Issue(3)

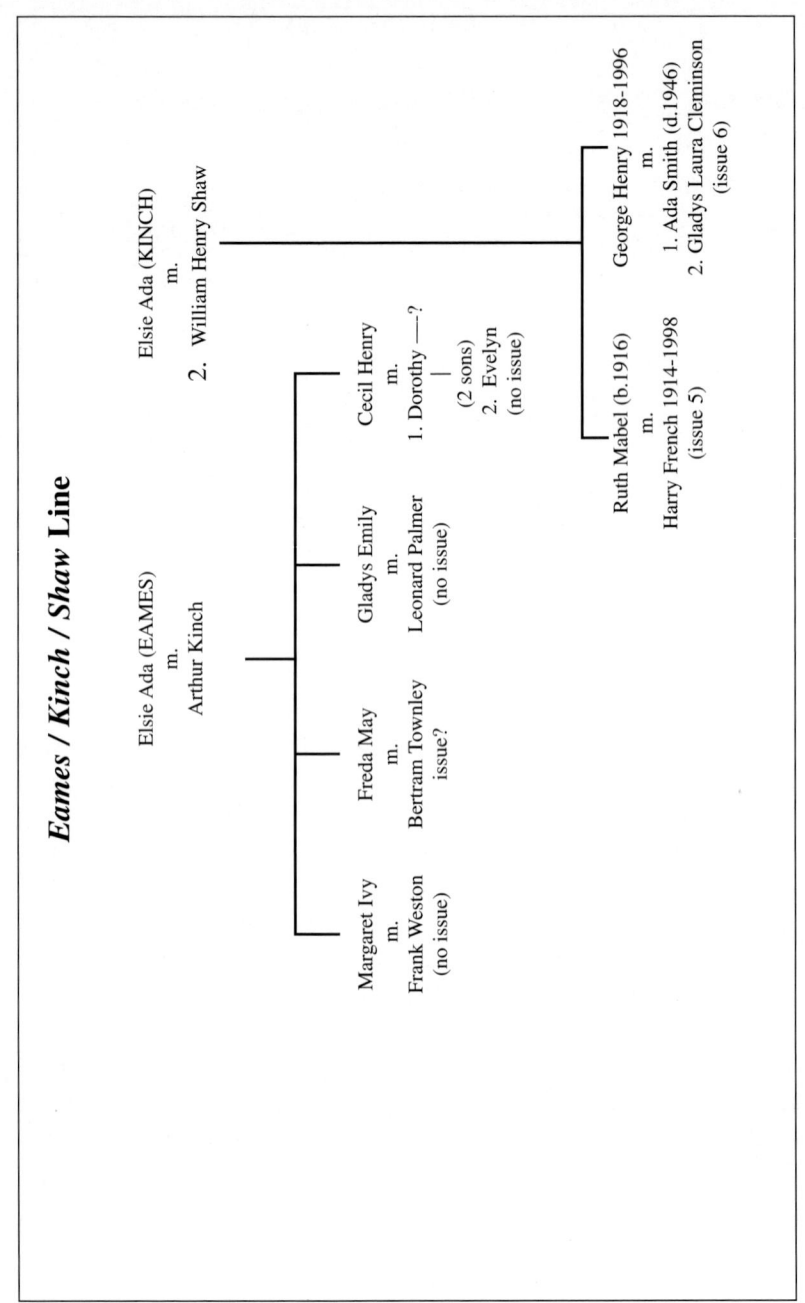

Eames / Kinch / Shaw Line

Elsie Ada (KINCH)
m.
2. William Henry Shaw

Elsie Ada (EAMES)
m.
Arthur Kinch

Margaret Ivy
m.
Frank Weston
(no issue)

Freda May
m.
Bertram Townley
issue?

Gladys Emily
m.
Leonard Palmer
(no issue)

Cecil Henry
m.
1. Dorothy —?
|
(2 sons)
2. Evelyn
(no issue)

Ruth Mabel (b.1916)
m.
Harry French 1914-1998
(issue 5)

George Henry 1918-1996
m.
1. Ada Smith (d.1946)
2. Gladys Laura Cleminson
(issue 6)

BIOGRAPHICAL NOTES

*The somewhat sketchy information below represents all that is known of the **Eames/Kinch/Shaw** Line*

Elsie Ada Kinch (nee Eames) Born Nov 11th 1880. Widowed with four children when her husband died with cancer of the bowel. An aunt, **Emily Martin**, adopted her son **Cecil**, who went to live with her in Coventry. With no financial support Elsie was obliged to send her three girls **Freda**, **Margaret** (always known by her second name **Ivy**) and **Gladys** to a home, whereupon she left her native town of Bexley Heath to be trained as a Nurse.

Her brother **David** married **Ruth**, who was said to be a very hard woman, tall and willowy with a shock of wiry hair that caused the villagers, who feared her, to call her a witch. She and David lived unhappily in a bungalow in Brixworth where he died in the 1930s.

When **Elsie** qualified she was posted to Aldwincle as District Nurse, cycling in all weathers to deliver babies in neighbouring villages, attend mothers for pre-and post-natal care, dress wounds etc. One day she was called to attend **William Henry Shaw,** gamekeeper to Lord Lilford, who lived in a tied cottage on the estate (Fern Cottage, Cross Lane) William had encountered a poacher who shot him in the face. During the course of the twelve months she treated him, he and Elsie became close and married on June 4th 1915. Elsie's three girls joined them at Fern Cottage and on April 29th 1916 a daughter, **Ruth**, was born, followed by **George Henry** on June 17th 1918.

With help from the girls, Elsie was able to nurse until her official retirement in 1937, though she continued to help the villagers of Aldwincle in sickness and trouble and was well-known by itinerant tramps who would regularly call for a meal when passing through.

Freda and **Margaret Ivy** came to Primrose Hill, Northampton, to work as domestics in one or other of the big houses there. Ivy became pregnant and had an abortion which left her unable to have children when she married. Meantime **Freda** became **Mrs Bert Townley** and went to live in a smallholding in Earl's Barton. When her husband died she moved in with Ivy and husband **Frank Weston** at Wilmcote near Stratford-upon-Avon. It was not a happy arrangement as the two women were suspicious of each other, and it came to an end when Ivy died in hospital of a wasting disease. The two sisters had become dutiful godparents to **Josephine Yvonne Shaw**. Widower Frank left Wilmcote to move in with a lady friend who came into his fortune on his death.

Gladys Emily remained in Aldwincle to marry **Leonard Palmer**, who worked in the pig-iron foundry in Kingsthorpe Hollow. For a time they lived in the top flat at 32 Boughton Green Rd, occupied by the Shaws, prior to moving to 91 Cambridge St. When Gladys died, Leonard re-married and emigrated to Australia.

Cecil Henry Kinch, although adopted, always knew who his mother was. He married, first, **Dorothy**, by whom he had two sons, **Michael** and **Gerald**, of whom Michael saw naval service as a lieutenant aboard the Ark Royal aircraft-carrier. When Dorothy died Cecil married her sister **Evelyn** (known as **Cissy**) They moved into a Residential Home in Barnards Green, Malvern, where Cecil died.

William Henry Shaw hailed from Nottinghamshire. On taking the gamekeeper's job in Aldwincle, he was assured by Lord Lilford that he could stay in his tied cottage until his death. Unfortunately Lord Lilford pre-deceased him, and the syndicate who bought the estate knew nothing of this (verbal) promise. Accordingly he and **Elsie** were evicted and found refuge with other members of the Shaw family at 32 Boughton Green Rd, Kingsthorpe. William became unwell and died in St Edmunds Hospital of testicular cancer in 1954. Elsie then moved in with **Gladys Emily** who soon became bed-ridden and died, also in St Edmunds Hospital (1963) Both are interred in Kingsthorpe Cemetery.